COVER PHOTOS

Upper left, **Vulturine guineafowl** *(Acryllium vulturinum)*
Upper center, **Mountain quail** *(Oreortyx pictus)*
Upper right, **Arabian Red-legged partridge** *(Alectoris melanocephala)*
Center, **Roulroul partridge** (Rollulus roulroul)
Lower left, **Ocellated turkey gobbler** (Agriocharis ocellata)
Lower center, **Mearns quail** (Cytonyx montezuma)
Lower right, **Temminck's Tragopan pheasant** *(Tragopan temmincki)*

Upland Game Birds

Their Breeding and Care

"Practical information for the beginning and experienced game bird breeder on how to raise upland game birds including quail, partridge, pheasant, junglefowl, guineafowl, and wild turkey, with helps on game bird breeding and a section on health and diseases"

By

Leland B. Hayes, Ph.D.

"For we know in part …but when that which is perfect is come, that which is in part shall be done away."

—— I Corinthians 13:9-10

This book is available to dealers and Bird Clubs in wholesale quantities.   Write or call for information.

Dr. Leland B. Hayes
P.O. Box 1682
Valley Center, CA 92082
(619) 749-6829

Area Code (760) After October 1, 1997

Preface

There has been a great need for a comprehensive work on how to manage and breed upland ornamental type game birds by a person with an extensive and authoritative background in game bird research, breeding and pathology. This book and its author, Dr. Leland B. Hayes, fill this need. We've known the Hayes' for many years, and without question Dr. Hayes is one of the most skilled and knowledgeable game bird breeders in the world, and is therefore eminently qualified to produce this outstanding book. He has been raising and marketing all kinds of game birds (more than 350 species), since a young man, and during the past 45 years or more has read and researched just about everything that has ever been written in this field by other leading and successful breeders, University poultry and game bird departments, government agencies, feed and medications laboratories and manufacturers, and along with his own expertise and knowledge about game birds, Leland has drawn on these resources to produce what we believe is a most authoritative work.

Dr. Leland Hayes is the most well- grounded and experienced breeder we can think of for this important task. Some of his credentials include: Bachelors, Masters and Doctorate Degrees, Member of the Avicultural Hall of Fame, President and Director for many years of the American Game Bird Breeders' Cooperative Federation. He is an author of other books and magazine articles on game bird management and propagation, and recipient of other awards and honors in the game bird breeding field. Probably no other person has as much total knowledge about raising all the different kinds of commercial and ornamental type game birds as he does.

How can a good book be made better? Dr. Hayes has done it in this second edition. Some of the new chapters that have been added include the latest information on wild turkeys, junglefowl, and guineafowl. Besides the new and updated material, this new edition has many pages of color plates and new black and white photographs.

This book covers the subjects of managing, breeding, and selection of species of upland game birds thoroughly. This book is filled with information that is not only good, solid, practical information for everyday use, but is also useful and valuable as documented references. It is written in understandable English easy for the experienced as well as the inexperienced breeder to understand. It has complete descriptions, breeding and management of 14 species of quail, 15 species of partridges, 15 species of pheasants, (including four species of junglefowl), five species and subspecies of wild turkeys (including the Occellated turkey), and five species of guineafowl.

Part One through Part Six, deals with the raising of quail, partridge, pheasants, junglefowl, wild turkeys and guineafowl, with excellent information on feeding, managing breeding, hatching eggs, and raising chicks to maturity.

Part Seven, is a very handy section on disease. It includes treatment of the most common ailments that affect upland game birds. It can be used as a handy reference in the diagnosis and treatment of sick game birds.

Part Eight, an Appendix with reference material and information on Artificial Insemination.

This is a *"how to"* book on raising game birds if there ever was one. It is documented from the extensive research that went into its preparation which gives credible information for the reader. It contains a complete alphabetized index that gives the reader easy reference.

We endorse and highly recommend this book to everyone interested in all types of game birds.

George A. Allen, Jr., Publisher
Game Bird Breeders' Gazette
Salt Lake City, Utah

Contents

PART 1 — RAISING UPLAND GAME BIRDS

PART 2 — SOME FAVORITE QUAILS

PART 3 — SOME FAVORITE PARTRIDGES

PART 4 — SOME FAVORITE PHEASANTS

PART 5 — SOME FAVORITE WILD TURKEYS

PART 6 — SOME FAVORITE GUINEAFOWL

PART 7 — KEEPING OUR BIRDS HEALTHY

PART 8— APPENDIXES

Color Plates

PLATE A (Photo by Lincoln Allen)

Mountain quail male *(Oreotyrx pictus)*.

PLATE B (Photos by George Allen, III)

Upper left, **Mountain quail** *(Oreotyrx pictus)*

Upper right, **Male Mearns quail** (Cyrtonyx montezumae)

Middle left, **Bamboo partridge** *(Bambusicola thoracica)*

Bottom right, **Philby's Rock partridge** *(Alectoris philbyi)*

PLATE C (Photo by Lincoln Allen)

(Photographed by Richard Robjent)

Upper, **Columbia Crested Bobwhite** *(Colinus cristatus)*

Lower, **Ferruginous Wood partridge** (Caloperdix oculea)

PLATE D (Photos by Lincoln Allen)

Upper, **Palawan Peacock pheasant male** *(Polyplectron Emphanum)*

Lower, **Roulroul partridge** *(Rollulus roulroul)*

PLATE E (Photos by Lincoln Allen)

Upper, **Yellow Golden pheasants** *(Chrysolophus pictus luteus)*

Lower, **Golden pheasants** *(Chrysolophus pictus)*

PLATE F (Photos by Lincoln Allen)

Upper left, **Blyth's Tragopan pheasant male** *(Tragopan blythi)*

Upper right, **Satyr Tragopan pheasant male** *(Tragopan satyra)*

Middle left, **Western Tragopan pheasant male** *(Tragopan melanocephalus)*

Middle right, **Temminck's Tragopan pheasant male** *(Tragopan temmincki)*

Lower left and right, **Cabot's Tragopan pheasants** *(Tragopan caboti)*

PLATE G (Photos by Lincoln Allen)

Upper, **Grey or Sonnerat's junglefowl** *(Gallus sonnerati)*

Lower, **Red junglefowl** *(Gallus gallus murghi)*

PLATE H (Photos by Lincoln Allen)

Upper, **Vulturine guineafowl** *(Acryllium vulturinum)*

Lower, **Reeve's pheasant male** (Symaticus Reevesi)

List of Photographs and Figures

(Bold type indicates black and white photographs)

Acknowledgments

So many have made a contribution to this book. Those that wrote or telephoned their encouragement made a real contribution especially when the work got tiring and tedious. We would like to name the many that helped but it would be impossible to list everyone.

We thank the Universities that provided their research papers: The University of California; The Pennsylvania State University; Clemson University; Texas A&M University System; and Mississippi State University.

Gratitude is expressed to G.E.S. Robbins and the World Pheasant Association for their kind permission to use their photographs.

Special thanks to the George Allen Family for their continued encouragement and support during this project. I am grateful for their kind permission to use the drawings, articles and photographs from back issues of their magazine, *The Game Bird Breeders' Gazette*.

Leland B. Hayes, Ph. D.

February, 1996

Introduction

THE GALLIFORMES

Galliformes is a very fascinating and popular family of birds. They are found all over the world and most are ground dwelling. They have become a very popular back yard species where room for aviaries is limited as some are quite small. Other members of this family are quite large and striking.

The *galliformes* include New and Old World quail, partridge, francolins, pheasants, and grouse. Now there is still some contradiction as to the proper classification of this family and different authorities give different scientific names to the same species. This is rather confusing to the novice, but should be of minor concern if one's main purpose is the propagation of the species. However, even the novice must be aware of proper classification if he is to keep the strain pure in the wild form in his breeding program.

One lovely thing about the upland game birds, they are very colorful for the most part. While some may be called drab in coloration, the male birds sport outstanding coloration with patterns that only Mother Nature could design. Besides being attractive, their undying popularity is due in part to the fact that some species can lay many eggs. I have had quail that laid from 60 to 100 eggs in a season. The Coturnix or Pharaoh quail are known for their many eggs produced by the females beginning at six weeks of age. This is not a hard rule as some upland game birds lay as few as two eggs per clutch.

While the chicks are fragile after first hatching, they loose much of their delicateness after the first two weeks. There is nothing more exciting to see than the tiny newly hatched chicks of the Button quail or the giant awkward newly hatched chick of a wild turkey.

The following is a well-accepted system of classification:

Order *Galliformes*

Superfamily *Megapodea*
    Family *Megapodidae* — megapodes or mound-builders (12 spp.)
Superfamily *Cracoidea*
    Family *Cracidae*— chachalacas, guans, and currassows (44 spp.)
Superfamily *Phasianoidea*
    Family *Phasianidae*— Pheasantlike birds (206 spp.)
        Subfamily *Meleagridinae*—*turkeys (2spp.)
        Subfamily *Tetraoninae* — grouse and ptarmigans (16 spp.)
        Subfamily *Odontophorinae* — *New World quails (33 spp.)
        Subfamily *Phasianinae* —*Old World pheasants (151 spp.)
    Tribe *Perdicini* — *Old World partridges, francolins, and *quails (106 spp.)
    Tribe *Phasianini* — *pheasants,* jungle fowl, and peafowl (49 spp.)
        Subfamily *Numidinae* — *guinea fowl (7 spp.)

*These families and subfamilies contain the species that are discussed in this book.

One could call the above species *"upland game birds"* which would include even those that are not kept in captivity. Although this is a broad term, it is specific enough for the reader to understand the general species discussed when the term is used.

Many New World and Old World species have been successfully propagated in captivity. They are rather delicate in that they are susceptible to most diseases and have to be kept in rather clean surroundings. However, when mature and acclimatized, they seem to have some resistance to disease. A few specimens have lived ten and upward years in captivity. In most climates, quail must be kept in wire-bottomed pens as they cannot stand to be in close contact with excrement and other ground-dwelling germs including parasites. This is not true in the very dry desert-like climates.

WHY AVICULTURE?

A most important trend that has developed in aviculture within the last few years has been the renewed interest in the propagation of upland game birds. Perhaps this has come about because of the rapid rate of destruction of the natural habitat of the world. Several species of birds are added to the endangered species list each year.

Many of us believe that the most logical approach to the preservation of these species is to get a strong gene-pool of the species reproducing themselves in captivity. This will leave at least two options available for later use: 1) re-populate back into the wilds when conditions improve and 2) maintain a captive population. The problem with any approach is where will the funding be found? Here, the private aviculturist has a wonderful opportunity to make a real contribution to the cause. If strong bloodlines are maintained, the species has a chance to survive. The keeping and breeding of upland game birds by the private breeder, if done with the correct intent, can be a boon to the threatened species. While the average breeder will not be able to keep birds on a very large scale, in most instances success has come to the small scale operation even if the setup is in the back yard. When full attention is given to the one task, the results are usually much better. For the private breeder to have a part in this venture it is necessary that the authorities be willing to issue special permits and cooperate in getting breeding stock to work with.

Where does the commercial game bird breeder fit into the scheme? He has a well-earned place! It is because of the research and monies that the commercial breeder has poured into problems of propagation and disease through the last few years that aviculture is in step with other industries. Where would we be without this research? Financially, it could not have been supported nor would it have been supported by the private breeder. Economics prohibits most private breeders from the very expensive proposition of research. Our thanks to the commercial breeders that have opened doors of husbandry for upland game birds.

WHY THIS BOOK?

You should understand that we have hardly discovered all of the answers. With nearly 45 years of breeding experience we are constantly learning from our birds. This is one of the many exciting things about working with the various species of upland game birds, they teach us more than we can teach them. Usually, the failure to learn these lessons results in the deaths of our little *"teachers"* and we will not make the same mistake again. So really, **we learn from our failures**. Aviculturists, then, in a real sense **never have failures** if lessons are learned from them. Thus, we come to the purpose of the writing of this book.

Passing along our mistakes, so that you will not make them, **showing you our failures** so that you can learn from them, **telling you how we** do it is the primary reason for writing this book.

This is a *SHOW and TELL HOW TO* book! Giving answers to questions, and getting you to question our answers will help aviculture in general. The only way that we can **keep** our knowledge is to **give** it to you through this book. So, here it is with our best wishes.

Your comments are most welcome. Please let us know what you think about this *"second edition"* and give us your opinion as to how the next edition can be improved to meet your specific needs.

Part 1

RAISING UPLAND GAME BIRDS

GETTING STARTED RIGHT

Raising ornamental upland game birds has been going on for thousands of years. Early recorded history reveals that men have *"kept"* birds from the very beginning. Raising game birds is an art. Included in successful game bird propagation is a natural talent and a desire to succeed. There are thousands of bird species alive in the world today that have not been successfully kept in captivity for any reasonable amount of time. Among these species are many classed as ornamental upland game birds. We will include in this work only the species that are currently or have been previously kept in captivity.

Of course, the value of a species is not judged entirely on its scarcity either in the wilds or in captivity. There is the aesthetic beauty to consider along with the personality of the species. When it comes down to the bottom line, the value of a particular species is determined in the mind of the breeder as **he or she is the one that must make the final judgement.**

We know many people who think the common Bobwhite is the greatest bird in all the world even though its monetary value is only a few dollars. Another person would have only the very expensive birds though they are not nearly as *"pretty"* as some of the common ones. Some more common species are actually very beautiful. Some of our favorites are the more common desert quail of the West. The poet said it years ago much better than anyone since, *"to each his own."*

Even though some of the ornamental game birds may be rather expensive in today's market, there are some that are very reasonably priced. Many of the species that we will discuss have been propagated with only a degree of success, so the breeder who gets them will know that he indeed has a challenge, but not an impossible one.

Cost is a very important consideration. Another is how easy it is to propagate the particular species. This may determine if the species is suitable or not. It is a sad thing when a novice aviculturist gets over his head in dealing with a difficult species. The truth of the matter is, there is no help available many times or if help does arrive, it is too late. You should start with a species that is not difficult, then graduate to the more difficult species. As many times as this is said, there are still many people that do not heed the advice. I get a chuckle out of the fact that every once in a while I hear of a breeder that starts with the most difficult species and has outstanding *"success"* with his birds. I do not feel put down at all. I still stick to my advice. For every successful breeder there are dozens or more who are not successful. Just this week I talked with a breeder in another state who described his operation in great detail. He was doing everything that should be done and was having tremendous success. When questioned about his length of experience with birds, I was shocked to discover that it was very short. Yet he knew all of the *"basics"* and was very successful. After I hung the phone up, I came to the conclusion that this gentleman was indeed fortunate as he is a **fast learner!**

The real test of success does not come in just one breeding season. Sometimes, a breeder is very successful for a year or two and then things *"bomb out"* for him. When this happens, it is sad indeed. The distraught breeder gets new birds and starts over, or he gives up and quits. The breeder who realizes that there are no failures in aviculture, if lessons are learned, is the one that makes a lasting contribution to aviculture. The question to be answered by the novice or experienced aviculturist is, *"which species should I raise?"* There is no answer that would please everyone as it is a very personal matter. I always advise that the species be one that meets the individual's goals, whatever they may be. It would be impossible for me to make that decision for anyone who is looking for an upland species to propagate. I have a very hard time determining which is my favorite species. Sometimes when you have a day or two of time let's talk about that subject.

I will never forget the answer that the late Everett Judge of California always gave to justify his keeping a common sea gull on his farm. He had to get special permits to keep the bird, which was no easy task. It was noisy, pugnacious, messy and a dozen other bad things. Mr. Judge would always put his critics in their place by answering, *"I **like** it."* I can think of no better reason for raising any species of game bird.

Check the Law

The very first thing a prospective upland game bird breeder should do is **check the law** in the state domiciled regardless of the number of birds he or she plans to raise. Most states have laws governing the keeping of native (and some foreign) game birds in captivity. The regulations in each state are different, so be sure and check before ordering eggs, chicks, or stock. I know of some game bird breeders that got into serious trouble and were fined for failing to meet the requirements of the law.

All aviculturists should operate within the law. For the sake of the whole fancy, we should not only obey the law ourselves, but encourage others to do the same. When only a few violations occur then broad regulations are imposed on us all.

Some Basic Equipment

To produce game birds there are some items that will be needed such as feeders, waterers, nest boxes, dust boxes, breeding coops, brooders, heating elements, growing pens and some miscellaneous items. Some of the equipment can be homemade.

The breeder will need some sort of breeder unit to satisfy the needs of the breeder-birds. Consider these facts as you plan for your breeder units:

● **Size** — breeder pens for pairs can be as small as one foot square. Keeping birds in this small space brings on the threat of feather picking, cannibalism, and spread of disease. We prefer more space for our quail breeders and as a result can expect more egg production. Since most strains of Bobwhite, Coturnix, and Chukar partridge have much of the wildness bred out of them, they do quite well in the smaller cages. I have found that the Ringneck pheasant stock never seems to calm down. However, when you get your breeding stock be sure that you are getting a "gentle" strain if this is what you want. If the market requires "wild natured" birds for release, then consideration should be made concerning the size of the breeder pens.

- **Wire** — all wire should be small enough to prevent the birds from getting their heads caught in the openings. The floor wire should be smooth ¼ inch hardware cloth for quail size birds. Larger wire floors should be used for keeping pheasant size birds off of the ground.

- **Roofs** — there should be a waterproof roof on pens that are kept outside to protect the feed and water from the rain. In hot climates, the birds need shelter from the hot sun also. The dark area under the roof gives security by providing a place for the birds to hide. When we raised Ringneck pheasants in large outside pens, a shelter was placed in one end. They refused to roost in it even on nights that got below zero. At first we were concerned, but then relaxed over the situation and never lost a bird.

- **Nest and dust boxes** — for quail, a good size for the nest box is 6 X 6 inches and about five inches high. The nest box can be open-topped or closed-topped with an entrance. Fill the box with straw. Years ago we used coffee cans for nests quite successfully which proves that the birds are not particular. For pheasants, junglefowl, guineas and turkeys, we have used bales of wheat straw and even garbage cans placed in strategic places. Wooden boxes can easily be made and most of the time the birds will use them with the exception of a few hens that seem to drop their eggs when they get the urge. Dust boxes for small wire bottomed cages can be made from wood or metal. If they are made from metal, be sure they do not have any sharp edges that could cut the feet of the birds when they climb into the box. I like dust boxes to be large enough to hold at least five birds. Place them away from the feed and water to cut down dust contamination.

Indoor V.S. Outdoor Production

The breeder will have to make the decision as to which method he wants to use. His decision will be based upon one or all of the following criteria. 1) The cost that is involved in a particular method of propagation. The cost of pens and other special equipment should be considered. Carefully consider the long range costs, as many times better birds can be produced by spending a little more "up front." 2) It would not do to try to brood very young chicks outdoors in a very hot or cold climate. Some sort of compromise will have to be made if this is necessary.

Perhaps, the best method would be a combination of both indoor and outdoor propagation. For example, start and brood the chicks inside until they feather out fairly well, then place them outside in a controlled way. Let them get out of the night air and still enjoy the warm sunshine on clear days. Actually, this method will produce much healthier and better feathered birds.

Litter Information

The type of litter used in floor brooding is very important. Birds raised on the ground pose a different set of manure problems than those raised on wire (Smith, 1984). They are in constant contact with the manure and subject to all of the hazards associated with it. Many different types of materials are used for litter. Many years ago when we lived in Montana we used a material that was purchased from the local feed store called "bothilumeum." It was mined from the ground and cleaned up before packaging. It was absorbent and very inexpensive and worked like a charm. I have not seen any in a number of years and fear that inflation has made the price so high it is no longer economical to use the material for litter.

Pine shavings are probably the best litter for general use as they are readily available and inexpensive, while having a high absorbency. Hardwood shavings are not as good as they tend to promote fungal growth which causes brooder pneumonia (Aspergillosis). Clean sand does not absorb moisture well (it holds it between the grains) and it is hard on feet of birds as it tends to pack. Also, sand is eaten by the chicks and this can cause problems. Materials such as cane fiber and shredded newspapers are generally too expensive and often hard to get. A good litter will be as free of dust as possible.

I would recommend that the old litter be removed after each batch of chicks. Some breeders simply place a new layer over the old and it works well for them. Of course, if the litter is wet, it is imperative that it be removed so as not to have any excessive dampness in the material. I would never reuse old litter. There is too great a risk of spreading disease from one group to another. The thought in using old litter is the chicks have a chance to build an immunity and thus are "vaccinated" naturally by developing an immunity to the disease present. At any rate, remove all litter at least once a year and completely disinfect the house and furnishings.

The better litter will absorb twice its weight in water. The following chart (Smith, 1984) shows the moisture holding ability of some common litter materials (Pounds of water/pounds of litter):

LITTER MATERIAL	MOISTURE ABSORBED
Pine Straw	2.07
Peanut Hulls	2.03
Pine Shavings	1.90
Pine Bark/Chips	1.60
Corn Cobs	1.23
Pine Sawdust	1.02

Male Golden pheasant

FEEDING ORNAMENTAL GAME BIRDS

For years, the two primary reasons for failure to propagate rare upland game birds were **disease** and **nutrition** problems. The development of modern drugs has helped greatly in controlling disease. Vaccination procedures, antibiotics, sulfa-drugs, and other *"miracle drugs"* have revolutionized bird keeping. A very important part of *"caring"* for our birds is the provision of the proper nutritional requirements. Each species requires a different diet that complicates feeding rations. In general, ornamental game birds have similar diet requirements and can all be fed the same. There are many exceptions to this and these are noted under the discussions of the various species.

Providing Adequate Nutrition

Proteins, carbohydrates, fats, minerals, and vitamins are the five types of feedstuffs in a game bird's diet. Proteins are essential to all animal life for maintenance and growth. They are a major part of most tissues in a bird's body. These tissues include muscles, connective tissue, skin, feathers, and beak. Birds cannot make proteins from chemicals, so they rely on plants and other animals as sources. Proteins repair old tissues and make new tissues. They are in constant demand, and the only source is dietary protein that must be available at a constant level. Proteins are some of the largest chemical compounds in the body. Each protein is made of smaller subunits called amino acids. There are about twenty-two major amino acids and many more minor amino acids. Some amino acids cannot be converted by the bird from other amino acids, so they are called essential amino acids. These amino acids must be present in adequate amounts in the diet. There are ten essential amino acids in birds. The remainders are called nonessential amino acids because they can be synthesized from other amino acids.

It is important that an adequate amount of each essential amino acid be in the diet. The protein level may meet recommended levels, but high production cannot be maintained unless all essential amino acid requirements are met. The two most critical amino acids are lysin and methionine. If a diet is deficient in any amino acid, it will usually be either lysin or methionine (Smith, 1983).

Protein Requirements

BOBWHITE	COTURNIX	PHEASANTS
0-4 wks 26%	0-3 wks 25%	0-4 wks 30%
4-9 wks 24%	3-6 wks 23%	4-9 wks 24%
9-18 wks 18%	6 wks – 18%	9-18 wks 18%
Breeders 19%	Breeders 18%	Breeders' 19%

Many of the leading game bird breeders feel that a great problem is the lack of adequate nourishment from a good balanced diet for our birds. Each of our birds require a special well-balanced diet that we must do our best to give them if they are to be in good physical condition and lay strong fertile eggs.

There are many excellent game bird feeds on the market. The key to the feed is the protein content. The weather, size of pen, type and age of bird, and time of year will determine **how much** to feed and **what protein** content we should use. Commercial feed mills have spent millions of dollars in developing proper rations that meet the nutritional needs of game birds.

We would recommend that professionally prepared feed be used rather than grains fed alone which may not have all of the necessary nutrients. Sometimes the game bird breeder will be tempted to **cut corners** in order to make ends meet. While we have no problem with this philosophy, we definitely would not cut the quality of feed. I can think of other things such as housing to cut rather than the feed quality.

Some "extras"

There are some "extras" that the game bird breeder can do which will help keep the birds in good physical condition.

One of our habits is to feed our birds grain by hand every day. This gives us a good chance to look them over for problems, and it also gets us involved with them in a more personal way. The extra corn during periods of stress such as cold weather gives them the needed body heat to get through cold winter months in an outside pen. Actually, they would eat only grain if I would let them, but I prefer they have balanced game bird feed. Grain is not fed in large quantities (if any grain is fed, be sure to provide grit).

Feeding grain by hand daily **gives me a chance to study the habits** of the birds. When they come to the hand for feed, I can observe them easily from a different perspective. Tame birds show off better to visitors. Our birds come over to the wire fence to get their treats. I tell our visitors that they love me and want to be near me. Of course, soon the truth comes out that the birds really love the feed that I am about to give them.

"Nutritional extras" that keep our birds healthy and happy include various vegetables from our garden. The birds just love them and look forward to getting them daily. (Another thing that most quail and partridges like are apples). Chopped carrots from the garden are readily eaten by some species. Give the birds as much "green foods" (fresh vegetables) as they will eat. Not only does this give them the extra nourishment, but just as important, keeps them occupied during the day.

BIRD CORNBREAD is another way breeders can insure their birds get proper nutrition. Bernard Teunissen gives us his recipe. He uses four-sided cookie sheets instead of baking pans, as this makes a dryer product which is less open to spoilage. The bread can be cut up and fed in pans or crumbled directly on the feed in the feeders. Both ways provide an extra treat for adults and chicks alike.

The recipe: Mix three cups small bird seed (such as millet); 2 cups each of whole wheat flour, soya meal, cornmeal; 1 cup Vionate (vitamins); and 1 cup baking powder (yes, 1 cup! I tried it without, and it was like a rock); and four teaspoons of salt. You mix all these dry ingredients and then make a *"well"* and add five cups eggs (shells included); 1 cup milk; and ½ cup wheat germ oil. Then bake at 425° F. in two cookie sheets, 12 by 16 inches, for about 25 minutes or until firm to the touch. You'll need to oil the pans.

The bird seed is put in basically to give the bread body, otherwise the bread will be tough. When feeding the formula to non-breeding birds it is best to replace the wheat germ oil with plain cooking oil since the bread need not be as rich and oily (*Gazette* Editors, 1978).

Another nutritional need is **vitamins and minerals**. When birds are kept on wire, they cannot get trace minerals or vitamins from the soil. To help, we add commercially prepared vitamins to the diet. Some breeders sprinkle a powdered vitamin product (Vionate) over the feed in the troughs. Vionate can be put on treats. You may prefer to put vitamins in the water every other day as during hot weather the enriched water spoils rather rapidly.

When deciding on a vitamin product, you should be sure that it is formulated for "birds" and not for other livestock. Livestock's vitamins will do no harm but they lack some of the essential elements that birds need. The breeder should vary the diet as much as possible to be sure that needed trace minerals are available for the birds. A good idea is to buy **mineral mixes** made for the pigeon fancy. The powdered mineral is mixed with locally purchased grit and is kept before the birds at all times. We use little wooden pans placed in each pen. Metal pans seem to quickly corrode.

Do not overfeed your birds. Overfeeding and lack of exercise can cause many of our birds harm. If you have the time, the best plan is to regulate the feed intake carefully. This means that time will have to be taken to feed the birds a small amount in the morning and in the evening. Since most upland game birds are high energy burners, they need feed every few hours during the day. The amount of feed intake and the feeding schedule should be determined by the species of birds we are raising. Remember, some types of birds have high energy requirements and need feed more often than others. Also, the age of the birds will determine how much feed they need.

DEALING WITH BAD TRAITS

Almost without exception, every species of game birds kept in captivity has a bad trait or two that must be dealt with. The best solution to these problems is to face them *"head on."* The experienced game bird breeder will be very aware of the following bad traits. Any new breeder will be well acquainted with them after a season of experience. It is impossible to change these traits. The wise breeder will learn to adjust to them rather than expect the birds to adjust to the conditions the breeder dictates.

Cannibalism

The most serious fault of upland game birds is **cannibalism**. We have found this habit to be common among most quail in captivity and totally absent in some partridge species. Picking the nose between the eyes, and of course, toe picking can kill young chicks.

Several things can be done to prevent toe picking. Once started, this habit is hard to break and the offender must be debeaked or isolated. If we can determine the cause of the problem, it can be prevented. Some strains of rare birds are extra bad about this while others are not bad at all. Even different hatches of the same strain can develop into *"pickers."* The truth is that we do not know the cause of this habit. It could be one thing once, and another the next, so any general conclusions could be misleading.

We put stemmy alfalfa hay in the bottoms of the pens which seems to discourage toe picking. The hay stems break up the outline of the toes and thus no picking. The bird droppings fall through the hay and wire and most of the time the birds live happily ever after. Red lights and a dark box seem to help also. Every so often we hang up some lettuce and let the birds pick at it. Several years ago some of our immature Masked bobwhites started toe picking. This was a horrible experience for us as well as for the poor toeless birds. We did everything we could think of to get their feet healed. Some had no toes left, others had one or two left. The wounds would not heal so we began to experiment. A first step was to medicate the wounds and then wrap the entire foot in surgical gauze. This was then taped up with masking tape. To our amazement, we discovered that it was not the neighbors doing the offence but each bird **pecking his own feet** that kept the wounds open. We concluded the pain caused them to do this. After many weeks, the problem was overcome but we had some birds with no toes which were better than dead birds. This fault did not stop their breeding ability.

In chicks, watch also for feather picking. The soft quills which are filled with blood are especially appetizing to the chick that picks one of his fellows. Small feathers on the back and wings are most easily accessible. Long tailed pheasants have blood feathers in their growing tails that are susceptible to picking. Feather picking often occurs around the vent and tail area. Once blood has been drawn from a bird, its companions go to work picking blood and meat from the victim. Unless the picked bird is removed and treated, it will be picked to death. Feather picking, once started is very difficult to prevent (Wilson, 1972). We have found this to be a real problem with pheasants when kept in groups. To help solve this problem, we have used a product that is a red, foul tasting paste which is said to prevent feather picking. It seemed to help. I am not sure how to control this problem when conditions are not perfect. Isolating the individual *"picker"* is one solution but impossible when large numbers of birds are kept.

One of the most valuable pieces of equipment that we own is a debeaker. We really don't debeak the birds. We just touch the end of the beak to the hot blade. The little beak soon grows back and will have to be seared again within 10 to 14 days. We do not think this is very painful to the bird. If it is, surely it is better than the pain and suffering they would have to endure if cannibalized. This debeaker machine has paid for itself in just one year, and we have had it over 40 years. That figures out to be only a few dollars per year over the life of the machine. Anyone that raises ornamental upland game birds should make this investment for about the price of one pair of birds. Out debeaker is by far one of the best investments ever made as a bird breeder. If you are interested in getting a Debeaker, let me know and I will be glad to send you a catalog from the manufacturer.

One must conclude that the so called *"causative"* factors related to picking are controversial and complex. Cannibalism may occur under the most favorable conditions and not under less favorable conditions. Of all the problems that the game bird breeder faces, the problem of cannibalism takes more energy and resources to cope with than any other problem. One must be constantly on guard against this. A regrettable fact about cannibalism is that it can occur so suddenly that the harm is done before any preventive actions can be taken. We make it a point to look at our chicks about every two hours or so to see if they are all eating, drinking, and not picking. When the breeder discovers what works for him or her, continue to do the same things. If it works for you it is good and should be continued regardless of what species you are working with.

A pair of beautiful Reeve's pheasant.

Cannibalism is common among some pheasants species.

Some good recommendations for cannibalism prevention are (Woodard, 1977):

Cannibalism Prevention

✔ Provide adequate space for the birds.

✔ Remove sick, or weak birds immediately.

✔ Remove obstacles that may cause injury.

✔ Avoid introductions of new birds.

✔ Restrict human traffic near bird facilities.

✔ Provide adequate feeder space and waterers.

✔ Avoid sudden changes in texture of feed.

✔ Avoid sudden changes in conditions.

✔ Provide adequate shelter, ground cover, etc.

✔ Use proper methods for control of cannibalism.

Disease Susceptibility

Another bad trait that must be mentioned is susceptibility to **many diseases** that do not infect other birds. In fact, they *"catch"* more diseases than common domestic poultry. This is one reason some are "rare" and difficult to raise. The game birds that are native to the colder climates sometimes never build up a resistance to the deaseases that occur in the warmer climates. This is the reason that "wild caught" birds have such a difficult time adjusting to captivity.

To overcome this disease susceptibility, extra care must be taken to insure that the area around the birds stays as clean as possible and the birds themselves are not allowed contact with any excrement. Some breeders spray some sort of viral disinfectant on the grounds where their birds are housed. This has worked well with Arctic ducks at the Game Bird Preseveration Center in Salt Lake City. Visitors to your farm should not be allowed around the rare birds especially if they have birds of their own as they may bear disease virus on their shoes and clothing. We always keep our rare birds off limits on a back side of the farm where no visitors are allowed.

The best way to combat disease with these birds is to raise them on wire to maturity and then put them in ground pens if the climate is dry. Wet and cold ground is an unfavorable condition for these birds and cannot be tolerated by some species. Many upland game birds never can tolerate the disease factor in ground pens. It seems that they die no matter what is done if exposed to the bacteria and virus found in the ground.

The prospective species should be researched thoroughly before they are placed on the ground. Find out what and how other breeders do it. A good source of information is the *Gazette Index* from which articles can be ordered from past issues of the magazine.

Egg Eating

Some upland game birds are *"egg eaters."* Nothing is more discouraging than to have rare birds that will lay eggs and eat them. There have been many home remedies with claims of great success. Ed Krakowsky of Pennsylvania gives us the following information about egg eating. He writes: *"During the summer I ran into the problem of egg eating. I remembered how a friend was telling me about how he used a new chemical on his cherries that made birds sick. They never returned to his orchard again. It was harmless to birds and man. So, unable to get this chemical, I bought Ipecac Syrup from my druggist for $1.00. I coated some old eggs and gave them to the quail. I watched them eat the eggs and then regurgitated. It was funny, but they never ate eggs again. I have used it on Button quail, and it always works completely with no side effects. It might work on feather picking also."*

Wild Flight

Some members of the family of upland game birds have the disgusting trait of flying up and hitting the top of the pens. We have seen Masked bobwhites literally knock themselves silly on the top of the pen while frantically flying up. Mearns quail are bad about this, but not nearly as bad as members of the Coturnix family. Pheasants often will break their necks when hitting the wire in wild flight. We have had all kinds of disasters from this distasteful bad trait. The answer is to keep their wings clipped. (Always clip both wings as this gives them balance and they can probably keep themselves upright in a tall pen). Each species should be watched to see if they have this bad habit. Mountain quail never exhibit this trait. Seesee partridges will circle round and round the top of the flight pen but never fly into the wire. Other upland game birds show individual peculiarities when it comes to behavior in captivity. It is fascinating to discover these behavior patterns.

Nervous Disposition

Often, upland game birds will have a nervous disposition that will require special care. There is a natural fear that game birds have about anything that gets above them. Perhaps this is the natural fear of the predator hawk. To help the chicks adjust to all the activity above them, I train them to enjoy it. Every day or so I cut a boiled egg in half and grate it over the feeder through the top wire of the box. The falling crumbles of egg soon become a great event for the chicks. They will rush and grab up the grated egg. It is quite comical to see a chick run around the box with some egg in his beak with two or three others in hot pursuit. Of course the runner is telling everyone how bad it is to be chased about. Soon the chicks will learn what to expect and will run out from under the light bulb hover to get the treat when they see a head peer down at them. I have found that quail and some other game birds raised under these conditions are much tamer and make better breeders the following year. This is true of any upland game bird that has been hand raised. We have never had a problem of imprinting and believe that the birds should be as tame as possible. I believe that having tame birds really adds enjoyment to game bird breeding.

Tame birds can definitely form a relationship with their keepers which helps their well-being. Few game birds will be *"pets"* although we have had some individual birds with personalities that were a far cry from the majority of their *"wild"* brothers and sisters. When one of these "jewels" comes along, they are treasured above the rest. Tame birds many times become good breeders faster than wild birds.

Slow to Mature

The more impatient breeder often complains that upland game birds are too slow to mature. To be sure, some require a two-year wait until maturity and others require longer. With the well-balanced rations fed to ornamentals and under ideal captive conditions birds mature much faster than when they are in the wild. It often is not necessary to wait for the normal maturity. Our Mountain quail laid at one year of age, when in the wild they wait until their second year to lay. This is true with some pheasant and partridge species. If you are impatient, try a member of the Coturnix quail family which mature and lay eggs at six to eight weeks of age.

Difficulty in Finding Mates

The final trait that I mention is really not the fault of the ornamental upland game bird species. It is often very **difficult to find mates** for odd birds. The difficulty of finding *"replacements"* has done much harm to the captive population. When it takes much more to pay for the air freight to ship a bird than it is worth, this gets discouraging. Not only is the cost high, but often there are no replacements available at any price and the breeding season is lost.

One way to overcome this problem is to always get at least three pairs of birds of the same species to work with. Five pairs are even better. If one or two are lost then there is still the chance of getting some fertile eggs. It is our practice to get our new pairs from different blood lines so inbreeding will not take place. One of the greatest injustices against captive birds of any species is inbreeding. Probably, more harm comes from this practice than any other by unenlightened aviculturists.

Other traits, both good and bad, will be discovered through experience. As these traits are discovered, we must adopt methods to deal with them. Do not be discouraged if you are not successful on your first attempt to propagate a favorite species of upland game bird. It takes, sometimes, many tries before one has success. Unlike the breaking of a pony, the breeder will never be able to *"break"* his birds to his liking.

HATCHING EGG MANAGEMENT

Every game bird breeder has the goal of clean egg production which always pays off in good or better hatches. Although eggs can be cleaned or washed, there is no substitute for clean eggs. Some experts recommend that dirty eggs not be set, even if cleaned, as bacteria will likely have penetrated the shell and membranes. Others have found that if eggs (poultry) are properly washed the hatchibility is greatly enhanced. The breeder should make every effort to avoid floor contamination of eggs by providing plenty of nest sites and having ample dry, clean litter in the corners and laying areas of pens. When the egg is highly contaminated with manure, the risk of increasing the incidence of rot and spoilage is greatly multiplied.

Producing hatching eggs

Dr. J .R. Cain from Texas A&M says that there are three goals that would make any game bird producer happy.

Goal #1. Increase the number of fertile eggs per hen per year. This would mean fewer hens to produce eggs. Attainment of this goal requires increases in both egg production and male fertility.

Goal #2. Increase in growth and feather rates. This requires a look at genetics and nutrition.

Goal #3. A bird which looks and performs like one from the wild.

To attain these goals the breeder must control and use the mechanics of genetics and environment. If careful selective breeding is continued over several years, the breeder can develop the ideal bird for his particular goal. The application of a genetic selection process has been overlooked by the game bird breeder at large. Most breeders just pick out birds that they think look good for next year's breeders without any understanding or purpose of what their breeding goals are. For example, if three lines of birds were selected for specific characteristics, the three goals mentioned earlier would be attained in about five years.

LINE A. Selected for increased egg production. This characteristic would be the chief concern in selecting the breeders for each succeeding year.

LINE B. Selected for feather quality and wild appearance. If birds are produced for "show", then this obvious characteristic would be chosen.

LINE C. Selected for fast growth rate, body size, and good fertility. By crossing the lines, good quality birds could be produced to meet the criteria of the breeder.

Speaking of selection to improve the birds, I read of an experiment by Nesbeth and his co-workers at the University of Florida. These men began with 400 female and 200 male Bobwhites and selected for body size and hatchability for two generations. With only these two selections the body weight was increased over 12%. Needless to say, after several generations this could be increased. Every breeder should have some knowledge of genetics even if they do not deal in mutations and their variables. A plan for stock improvement should be developed.

Using artificial lighting

The practice of using artificial lights on game birds is not exactly a new one. Its advantages probably couldn't be fully achieved in all parts of the country due to the cold winters where the problem of winter brooding would off-set the advantages of having early birds. However, most everyone would like to have early chicks for whatever reason. Using artificial lighting will accomplish this goal if applied correctly to the breeder birds.

The following information can be adapted to most any species of upland game bird although the species is the Ringneck pheasant. Someone should do some research with the rare birds to see if the egg laying ability could be enhanced. *"We started experimenting with the possibilities when the demand for full flight birds came in for the early retriever trials. To do this, we would need eggs about six weeks earlier than normal. So we brought the hens into lay on the 21st of February.*

Then the market for meat birds for freezing increased so we thought if we could get eggs still earlier, we could raise these birds out and get them off to market and have our pen space for the later flying birds, thereby increasing our production and not increasing our overhead too greatly.

Last season we started the hens early enough to get eggs on the 29th of December, thus, we had prime birds for market in June. We also had another flock begin to lay February 21, which took care of the early retriever trial birds.

Then the group picked out for the natural laying season produced their first eggs April 2. These took care of the late retriever trials and the Thanksgiving and Christmas market birds.

The following is what we have had the best results with. The cocks you select for breeders and the number, depending on the amount of the hens to be used, should be placed in fairly close confinement, say, about three cocks in a pen 12 x 12 with a sixty watt light bulb and reflector. As the cocks become more pugnacious, you should separate them. The hens are put with the cocks (we use six hens to one cock) when the cocks start to show brilliant coloring in the wattles approximately one month later. A good feeding program all the way through is imperative. Try to give the birds fifteen hours of light per day. We have found that if the lights come on early in the morning about 3:00 A. M. and then let the birds go to roost at dusk, the hens will lay earlier in the day, making egg gathering more convenient. It will take about four to six weeks, depending on the weather conditions, before the first eggs are laid.

The mortality held average with the spring hatched chicks, although we had to raise the temperature of the brooders and give them access to the brooders for a longer period. As all pheasant breeders know, there doesn't seem to be any steadfast rule to hold to. Whatever works best for you is the thing to do. However, the experience had by other farms can sometimes be adjusted to suit your requirement to an advantage" (Carlson, 1953).

The above shows that extended photoperiod works. Allen Woodard answers questions about this interesting subject:

QUESTIONS AND ANSWERS

WHAT IS THE OPTIMUM AGE TO STIMULATE GAME BIRDS?
Research indicates that pheasants, chukars and bobwhites, etc., respond best when they are at least 30 weeks of age provided they have been preconditioned under a short daily photoperiod of 8 hours per day for a period of 6 to 8 weeks. Males respond more slowly than females and must be given stimulatory light two weeks in advance of the hens in order that both reach sexual maturity at the same time.

HOW MUCH DAILY LIGHT IS NEEDED FOR OPTIMUM STIMULATION?
A continuous period of daily light of 13 to 16 hours is generally adequate, and amounts in excess of 16 hours are a waste of energy. Presently, little information is available on the use of intermittent lighting programs for egg production in game birds. Once the birds are in lay the daily photoperiod should never be decreased for any reason.

IS THE QUALITY OF LIGHT IMPORTANT?

Previous research has shown that birds are sexually stimulated by the longer wave lengths of the visible light spectrum e.g. yellow, orange and red bands. Most incandescent and the daylight or warm fluorescent lamps produce the desired color emissions needed for starting and maintaining optimum lay. Be careful to get the light source close enough to the birds to receive the correct intensity.

IS THE INTENSITY OF LIGHT IMPORTANT?

Light intensity can be measured in either foot candle (fc) or lux. One lux equals .0929 foot candle. The optimum light intensity for laying game bird breeders has never been determined nor has the minimum level been established. Good production has been reported for pheasants and partridges given 10 foot candle, measured at bird level. It is quite possible that game birds will require a higher light intensity (at least 5 to 10 fc) to induce lay for the first cycle of egg production but a lower light intensity (2 or 3 fc) after they have experienced at least one cycle of lay.

Photoperiod Chart

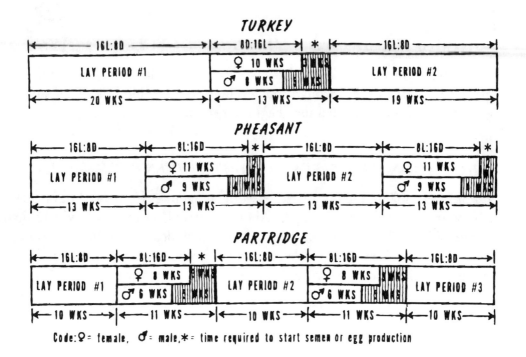

Code: ♀ = female, ♂ = male, * = time required to start semen or egg production

MUST THE PERIOD OF DARKNESS GIVEN DURING THE "REST" PERIOD BE ABSOLUTE, AND HOW LONG SHOULD IT BE GIVEN?

For optimum response, the room must be reasonably light tight, i.e. no light seepage around the doors, windows or ventilation system. The dark period must never be disrupted by a flash of light or the use of overhead lights for any reason. Recent investigations have shown that refractoriness in partridges can be terminated on a light intensity of less than .1 fc (1 lux) irrespective of the day length. The usual practice is to reduce the amount of light to 8 hours per day, preferably given during the natural daylight hours, for a period of eight and ten weeks for chukars and pheasants, respectively.

HOW OFTEN SHOULD GAME BIRDS BE CYCLED TO LAY?

Limited information shows that favorable rates of lay can be maintained in pheasants and chukars through four cycles of egg production. Thereafter, egg yield, fertility and hatchability begin to decline.

HOW SOON WILL BIRDS LAY AFTER GIVEN STIMU-LIGHT?

For both chukars and pheasants, onset of lay requires from 18-21 days after the birds are given stimulatory light. About ten days later the flock will attain 50% rate of lay. The duration of the production will depend on the species and system of management. Favorable production can be expected from Chukars and Pheasants for about twelve and sixteen weeks, respectively.

Cleaning Hatching Eggs

Dirty eggs can often be saved by dry cleaning or spraying and washing. Hatching eggs can be dry cleaned with fine sand paper. Only a very small percentage of eggs should be cleaned at all. While the more rare species will certainly get more attention than the common ones, it may be better for the whole hatch if dirty eggs are discarded. You could use a small incubator to hatch the soiled eggs separately from the clean hatching eggs.

Studies at Texas A&M University have proven that if done properly egg washing actually improves hatchability of some hatching eggs. There are several commercial egg washing solutions available. The local feed store can help locate these cleaning solutions. The manufacturers directions should be followed especially if the game bird breeder is working with valuable eggs.

It appears that hatching eggs should be cleaned and sanitized within three hours following laying. For egg washing to be successful several conditions must be met. These conditions are variable, but they can be used as guides for the general principles which if followed will give optimum hatching:

Hatching Eggs Guidelines for Cleaning

1) Wash the eggs immediately after being laid.
2) Use water fit to drink and low in iron.
3) Heat the water to 100° F.
4) Always keep the wash water 10° F. or more warmer than the washed eggs .
5) Use a recommended sanitizing agent.
6) Continually add clean water and sanitizing agent to the washing system.
7) Clean equipment frequently.
8) Pack the eggs on clean flats and use clean cases (Krueger, 1977).

It is essential that the egg embryo not begin to develop before being placed in the incubator. Gladish says that there are three main responsibilities in getting good eggs. The male bird, the female bird, and the handling of the eggs by man (Gladish, 1956). To keep the embryo dormant during holding most studies concludes that hatching eggs should be stored in a cool place with temperature about 55° F. Humidity should be around 75% to get the optimum storage life from the egg. The best average holding period is about seven days. After this period, hatchability is reduced each day by up to 2% which can mean quite a few chicks lost. Woodard and Morzenti (1975) have found that the shelf life of fertile eggs from the pheasant and quail is very limited and they should not be held over seven days before setting. The chukar egg showed much higher hatchability after seven days than the pheasant or coturnix, but not as high as the chicken.

Incubating Hatching Eggs

For the more rare ornamental game bird hatching eggs, many breeders prefer the bantam hen. They have a good case for her *"natural"* ability as she will, on the whole, do a better job than an incubator. However, there are some drawbacks to the use of *"ol' Bitty"*. She not only can be a carrier of infectious diseases and parasites, but she can be a pain to cope with because of a grumpy disposition.

Generally speaking, we would recommend that an incubator be used. There are many good ones on the market. Most are very effective in getting the job done provided they are run according to the manufacturer's instructions. We prefer the *"forced air"* type as they seem to do a better job for us. Our favorite incubators for many years have been the Marsh Roll-X manufactured now by Lyon Electric Company. You can call or write to me and I will send you a free catalog. We have several of these incubators and have excellent success with them. Lyon Electric is in the process of developing some state-of-the-art incubators which are just amazing. The accuracy and ease of operation will amaze even the most skeptical. One of the most exciting innovations is the ability of one of their incubators to be hooked up to a home computer and the temperature and humidity can be monitored for periods through a printout which gives the variations and time of occurrence. This will do an enormous amount of good for those who like to track every possible variation in the incubation of their eggs.

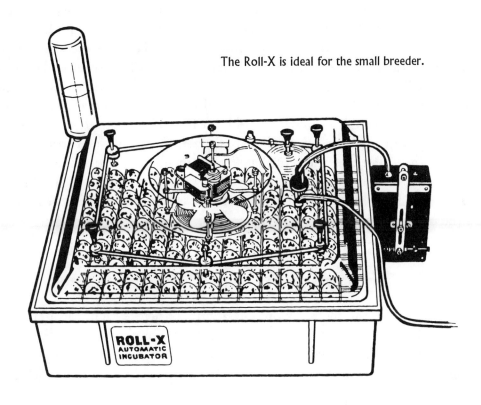

The Roll-X is ideal for the small breeder.

Many breeders like the *"still air"* type and get good results from them also. There are several models made that are especially designed for game birds. These are preferable to the ones made for other species of birds, but all will work when operated correctly. For years we used a homemade still air incubator with much success. We still use it when we run short of incubator room.

There is no substitute for a modern reliable incubator when it comes to hatching the few rare eggs that we are fortunate enough to produce. Temperature, humidity, oxygen, and turning are the four basics of incubation. We run our incubators at approximately 99.75° F. and the humidity is kept at the required reading for the particular species of birds. If the humidity is too high, chicks will be too large to hatch out properly. We discovered these large chicks were the result of too much humidity regardless of the species. This may not be true for your situation if your altitude and relative humidity is different from ours. Keep at least one air vent open for oxygen. Research done by us, and at the Game Bird Research Center in Salt Lake City by the George Allens, seem to indicate that any one of these basic factors can vary and still result in good hatches. Perhaps the humidity in the incubation process is the most important. Fortunately, it can be controlled with a little effort. Still, the goal should be to keep conditions in the incubator as close to nature as possible to get the best hatches.

Thermometers and Hygrometers

Incubator thermometers should be accurate. Before each season, be sure to check all of your thermometers with an accurate standard. To do this, place your thermometers in a container of hot water and check to see if all of the readings are the same.

A hygrometer is a thermometer fitted with a wick kept wet. The cooling effect of the forced air in the incubator is measured on the hygrometer in degrees and is converted into percent of humidity. Some breeders get confused about the method of wet bulb conversion. However, when studied, this is a simple and accurate procedure. The *wetbulb thermometer* method of reading humidity is a common standard for most incubators. For easy conversion, consult the chart to find the relative humidity percent. For example, a wetbulb reading of 83.3° F. and the dry bulb at 100° F., actually means the humidity is 50%. An easy way to know what the humidity is in your incubator is to use a "conversion chart" such as the one given below.

WET BULB READING FOR INCUBATION TEMPERATURES

Relative Humidity			Temperature, F°	
	99°	100°	101°	102°
			Wet Bulb Readings	
45%	80.5°	81.3°	82.2°	83.0°
50%	82.5°	83.3°	84.2°	85.0°
55%	84.6°	85.3°	86.2°	87.0°
60%	86.5°	87.3°	88.2°	89.0°
65%	88.0°	89.0°	90.0°	91.0°
70%	89.7°	90.7°	91.7°	93.7°

To use the chart, find the dry bulb temperature that you normally use, then compare that column with the relative humidity column.

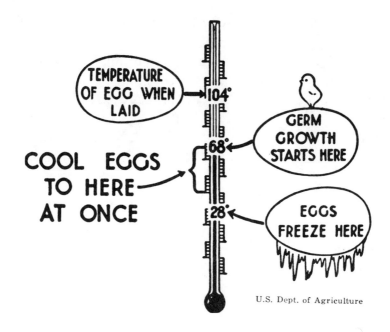

TEMPERATURE OF EGG WHEN LAID →104°

GERM GROWTH STARTS HERE

68°

COOL EGGS TO HERE AT ONCE →

EGGS FREEZE HERE

28°

U.S. Dept. of Agriculture

Length of incubation

The following DAYS OF INCUBATION CHART for the various upland game birds may not be precise due to differences in incubators, altitude, local humidity, and freshness of the hatching eggs. The guide can be used as a general rule only. Try your incubator out on common eggs before setting the valuable ones. Be sure and consult the incubator instructions! It would be helpful to have an idea of the length of incubation required by the various game birds.

QUAIL

14-15 Days	African Harlequin
16 Days	Chinese Painted
17-18 Days	Coturnix
18-19 Days	Rain
21-22 Days	California Valley, Benson, Gambel
23-24 Days	Barred, Bobwhites, Mearns, Mountain, Blue Scale

PARTRIDGE

18-20 Days	Bamboo, Roulroul, Ferruginous, Redlegged
21 Days	Seesee
23 Days	Chukar
24 Days	Hill, Hungarian
25 Days	Barbary, Madagascar
27-28 Days	Himalayan Snowcock

PHEASANTS

23-24 Days	Amherst, Golden, Ringneck, Jungle fowl
24-25 Days	Reeves
26-27 Days	Silver

GUINEAFOWL

28 Days	Pearl, Vulturine, Crested

28 Days . . . . Wild, Ocellated

Egg Candling and Examination Procedures

Any game bird breeder can use to his advantage a good method of learning how efficient his hatching operation really is. To know this important information will produce many more chicks.

To get the basic data in determining hatching effectiveness, you will need a good **egg candler**. For years we used a homemade one that we devised from a light bulb and some wood to make a box-like contraption.

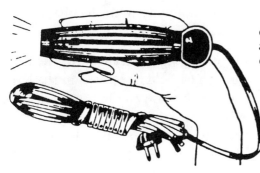

Every bird breeder needs a way to candle eggs. Using this version is very simple and safe as you need not touch the eggs and there is no damaging heat from the light.

Recently we were given one of the *"cool light"* versions that is hand held and it works like a charm. Now we can pass the light over each egg and pull out the infertiles. It is not necessary to pick up the good eggs using this method. (I cannot count the number of eggs we have dropped over the years . . . no more!).

Eggs that do not hatch should be **examined** and **classified** into two categories: 1) pipped and 2) not pipped. Each finding should be recorded for study. Before breaking the unhatched eggs for examination, test them to see if they are still alive if they are late hatching. A good way to test the egg is to use the "WATER TEST." Put warm water, about 105° F., in a bowl deep enough so the eggs will float freely without touching the bottom of the bowl. Place the eggs carefully in this water. The change in temperature will cause the fully formed chicks to kick which will cause the eggs to "rock" in the water. If you see the egg "rocking," you know it is still alive and it should be put back in the incubator. If there is no movement, you can be quite sure the chick is dead. Use this method only on chicks that are due or late and have not pipped. It will be observed that some of the eggs will float differently in the water. Some will sink to the bottom; these are the infertiles that have not developed an air cell. Some are partially submerged; these are eggs that have probably died early in the developmental process. Some will float very high in the water; these eggs have dehydrated due to early death or too little humidity in the incubator. Do not be concerned if you cannot find why every chick died.

When you are sure there is no life in the egg, it can be opened for examination. Make a small hole in the air cell (should be located in the large end of the egg), and peep in to see if there is life. If not, you can break open the egg to discover the approximate time the chick died. This may give you some clue as to the cause of the problem. Note the size of the air cell. Also, note the condition of the membrane separating the chick from the air cell. When the chick if fully developed, the membrane will be clear and you can see the chick clearly and even see the down on its body. If the membrane is cloudy, you can guess that the chick died early in the developmental process. Some of the items that should be noted about each hatch are:

- Eggs per day per hen,
- Percent of eggs that are not suitable for setting (due to malformation),

- Data from candling program including the number of true fertiles,
- Fertiles which have failed to develop,
- Early dead embryos and finally,
- Late dead embryos.

After examining the hatch and recording the data on some type of chart, there can be a "curve" of mortality developed that will tell the period in which most of the loss occurred. This information gives some ideas for corrective measures that can be taken based upon the recorded data. Do this for each hatch and adjust your hatchery procedure to correct some of the problems discovered. You may get 5% to 10% better hatches.

Causes of Mortality

A great concern among many game bird breeders is the loss of chicks, while the eggs are in the incubation process. Many, many theories have been advanced in the past, but due to modern scientific research some answers are available to the breeder which will help him overcome the problem. Egg incubation is a complicated process and can be called a true *"miracle."*

I guess this is as good a time as any to be hard hearted. The game bird breeder must develop a hard and cold ability to cull his birds that do not meet his standards. In the long run you will find this is best not only for you but for your birds. It is natural for us all to especially love the "underdog" but you will save later heartbreak if you go ahead and cull early on. I cannot tell you how many birds I have culled through the years. It was hard. The end of the season when my pens were filled with perfect specimens I was glad that I was just a little bit mean. You certainly have the right to disagree with me on this point. If you choose to do it another way, I have no quarrel with you at all.

INCUBATION TROUBLE SHOOTING CHART

PROBLEMS	POSSIBLE CAUSES
True infertility	**1)** Males sterile. **2)** Males not mating because of disease. **3)** Nutritional state. **4)** Infestation of external parasites. **5)** Peck order or preferential mating.
Fertile–no development	Problems during holding or shipping; held too long, subjected to extremely low temperatures for several days or too high temperatures during egg washing.
Blood ring w/o embryo	**1)** Eggs held too long or held at improper temperature. Temperature of 70° F. or above or fluctuating temperatures will increase the incidence. **2)** Rough handling of hatching eggs. **3)** Disease in the breeder flock including those affecting egg quality. Infections that can be eggborne. (salmonella group). **4)** Eggs from a highly inbred line. **5)** Aged or abnormal sperm. **6)** Parthenogenesis, chromosomal abnormalities.

Heavy embryo mortality (Near end of incubation)	**1)** Improper incubation temperature. **2)** Power failure. **3)** Eggs not turned during incubation. **4)** Suffocation. **5)** Disease or nutritional deficiencies in breeding stock. **6)** Inbreeding.
Mortality from first candling to transfer	**1)** Nutritional deficiencies. **2)** Egg infections. **3)** Too high or too low incubation temperature. **4)** Some lethal genes.
Mortality in the hatcher; many pips stuck to shell	**1)** Eggs transferred too late. **2)** Hatcher humidity too low or hatcher opened during hatch.
Excessive residual albumen	**1)** Incubator humidity too high. **2)** Improper turning. **3)** Lack of oxygen.
Chicks pipped and dead	**1)** Disease. **2)** Some lethal genes. **3)** Lack of turning during first two weeks.
Chicks hatch too early; are thin and noisy	**1)** Temperature too high during incubation.
Chicks hatch late	**1)** Eggs held too long. **2)** Inbreeding; temperature too low.

The above table summarizes the most likely causes of concentration of mortality in different periods and of specific symptoms (Abbott, 1983).

Lyon Electric of Chula Vista, California has several models and styles of incubators especially designed for the upland game bird breeder. Pictured is the PROFI-I incubator which has seven tilting trays. Each tray can be set for a different species.

The Incubator and the Egg

Gilbert H. Gladish gives the following excellent information: *"If at all possible, your best place to locate your incubator is in a room below 80° F., and not under 60° F. temperature.*

In order to hatch an egg it must be a good fertile egg. This egg must come from a well mated flock which has been fed properly.

The care of the egg from the time it was laid until it goes into the incubator is very important. In cold or hot weather, the eggs should be gathered more than once a day. After the eggs have been gathered, they should be placed in storage in a room or egg cooler of from 50° to 60° F. and must be moist. The reason for this is to keep the density of the egg from the time it was laid and to keep the germ or embryo of the egg in the best possible hatching stage. If the eggs are to remain in storage longer than two days, the eggs should be turned once a day. We have found the age of the eggs will do more harm and the egg should be in the incubator for eight hours before they are turned.

In traying eggs, it is best to place the eggs in the tray at a 45° angle with the small or pointed end down. If you do not have positioners or holders for your eggs, it is permissable to place the eggs flat in the tray. The reason for placing the eggs in the tray as pointed out, is to insure each egg of obtaining the correct 90° turn when the eggs have been turned to a 45° angle in the opposite direction. Also, it is to help the chick form in the egg with its beak toward the air cell.

Turn your eggs at least three times a day at eight hour intervals. If eggs are turned more often, it is suggested you use an uneven number of times. This way, if there is a longer time between turnings during the night, each side of the egg will receive the same treatment. It takes eight hours for the germ or embryo to travel from one side of the egg to the other. This is the reason for turning at eight hour intervals. In case the egg is permitted to remain in one position for a longer period of time, there is the danger of the embryo becoming attached to one side of the egg. This will result in either a deformed chick or the chick being unable to emerge from the shell.

In some instruction books, you are told to cool the egg for a certain period of time. This is especially true with duck and goose eggs. The point here is, you are not necessarily cooling the egg, but you are allowing the egg to absorb additional oxygen, more than it could inside the incubator. If you are able to maintain proper moisture and temperature and at the same time, permit oxygen to reach the egg in sufficient amount, it is not necessary to cool the eggs (Gladish, 1955)".

Incubation Progress

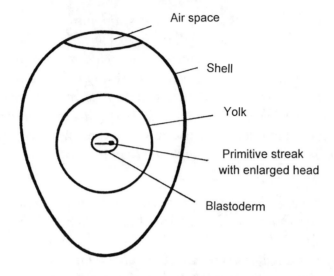

Air space

Shell

Yolk

Primitive streak
with enlarged head

Blastoderm

CORRECT POSITION OF 18 HOUR EMBRYO

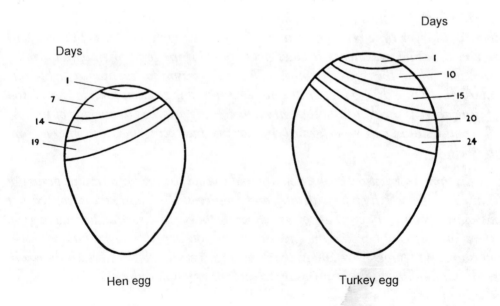

Days

1
7
14
19

Hen egg

Days

1
10
15
20
24

Turkey egg

BROODING GAME
BIRD CHICKS

The keeping of young chicks at the right temperature is called **brooding** and is well known to anyone who has ever seen a barnyard broody with her young chicks. Surprisingly, in most areas the job of keeping the chicks at the correct temperature is harder then one would imagine. Most would think it hard to keep the chicks warm enough, but the opposite is true in most of the cases. Many times each year I get calls from distraught breeders that cannot keep their young chicks alive. Upon questioning, I discover that they have "cooked" the chicks and dehydrated them and of course, they die. **Overheating** rather than not enough heat is prominent in the South and warmer climates during the summer months. You can be sure that if the chicks are cold they will tell you about it. Their consistent chirping will indicate that something radical is wrong with their world. By the way, chicks have a language all their own which the observant bird breeder can use to the advantage of the chicks. The smart breeder will take time to listen carefully to the sounds of his chicks to determine what the different calls mean in "chick talk". When real trouble comes he may be able to advert a disaster by knowing what the chicks are trying to say to their keeper.

There are three basic methods of brooding chicks whether they are pheasant, quail, chukars or any other species of upland game birds.

1) Spot heat brooding which simply is giving the chicks a localized heat source in which they can come and go according to their own body temperature regulator. This is probably the most commonly used method. Many would agree that it is the safest as the chicks can regulate themselves. I have used this method most of the time. The main consideration, other than being able to sleep at night and not worry about the temperature of the chicks, is the cost factor. Since a small area is heated the cost is lower. One can use one or several of the efficient heat lamps to throw an area of heat in one corner for the chicks to use. Another advantage of this system, if several heat lamps are used they can be turned on and off to keep a rather constant temperature. The use of thermostats is very easy with this method.

2) The second method of brooding chicks is called **whole house heating**. The whole house is warmed to the correct temperature and the chicks have no choice in the matter. In colder climates this may be a problem as the area heated is on the floor and the heat naturally rises.

3) The last method is a variation of the first two and is called **partial house heating**. This simply is a system that heats only a partial area of the house and gives the chicks the option of going to the desired temperature. The area heated is just big enough to hold all of the chicks at one time and is made larger as the chicks grow. This makes the method more economical then the second method.

Brooder Arrangement

The first priority of spot heat brooder arrangements is to **meet the needs of the chicks**. This means that the **heat source** should be available to all of the chicks. Also, the **feeders and waterers** should be available and spaced so that each chick will have ample opportunity to eat and drink at will. A good plan is to alternate the feed and water around the heat source so that the needs of each chick are met.

All methods of brooding require adequate **ventilation** for the chicks to grow healthy. The house brooding method especially requires good ventilation.

A common brooder temperature is shown in the following chart:

AGE in DAYS	BROODER TEMPERATURE
1-7 Days	90-95°
8-14	85-90°
15-21	80-85°
22-28	75-80°
29-35	70-75°
36 Plus	70°

The above chart will vary under certain conditions of course. It is always a good idea to let the chicks themselves tell you which temperature they prefer. You can know this by watching their actions while sleeping. If they bed down in a close group next to the heat source then perhaps they are too cool. If they scatter out and are not in any apparent group then they are about right. Excessive chirping can indicate they are too cold. Panting with wings drooped indicates too much heat.

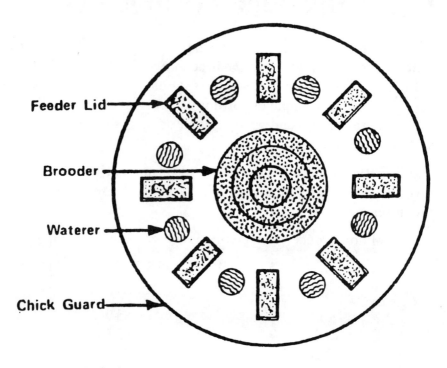

Feeder Lid

Brooder

Waterer

Chick Guard

Above is a good method of making sure the chicks can have access to feed and water as they learn to eat and drink. The chick guard is only 18 inches high and can be expanded as the chicks grow.

Brooding schedule guide by age

The following guide gives information for Bobwhite quail. It can be easily adapted for any species of upland game bird. The guide applies regardless of the type of brooding you are doing.

Age of birds — 24 hours before removal from hatcher

Turn on all brooders, set at 100° F., and check temperature of each brooder at edge of hover (or heat source) and 3 inches above litter or wire. Leave brooders on so they will settle down.

Place fresh water in jars around each side and just outside hover so that water will be warmed by brooders. If wide troughs are used, place marbles or clean stones in trough to prevent drowning.

2 hours before removal from hatcher

Place egg flats, paper towels, or corrugated cardboard near waterers. Place starter feed on these. Remember, do not use slick paper or slick cardboard for feed trays; birds will become straddle legged on slick surfaces.

As you take chicks from hatcher to go to brooding area:

Cull weak and crippled birds. Debeak lightly for cannibalism prevention.

1-7 days

Check brooders daily and nightly to observe chicks and see if they are comfortable. Birds at this age cannot stand wide variation of temperatures.

Keep waterers filled and cleaned.

Remove paper or flats containing feed each evening to prevent collection of droppings from creating a problem. Place fresh feed on fresh paper daily.

Finely chopped greens or lettuce may be placed on feed trays also. Do not use greens that are stringy. Providing green feed is helpful but not necessary.

On the third day move brooder guard out so it is 4-5 feet larger in diameter than hover.

Weather permitting, brooder guard may be removed by the fifth day.

Place larger waterers and feed troughs in pens in addition to present waterers and feed flats on the fifth day. Some eliminate this step by starting out with the same waterers and feeders to be used throughout brooding.

7-14 days

Reduce brooder temperature to 95° F. on the seventh day.

Begin to remove small waterers, one a day, until only larger type remains.

Do not allow small waterers to become empty in an effort to train the birds to go to the larger waterers.

Remove feed flats, one a day, until only larger feed trough remains.

Allow the birds to venture farther from the heat, but use common sense in relation to weather conditions.

Confine birds to brooder area at night, but do not confine under brooder.

Clean jar or pail waterers at each filling. Clean waterers at least daily.

Place fresh feed before birds; remove dusty and powdery feed daily.

14-21 days

Reduce brooder temperature to 90° F. on the 14th day.

Keep feed and water before birds at all times.

Allow birds to go into runs on warm days and provide heat so they will have it if needed. Do not confine birds as closely to brooder at night.

Continue to clean waterers and to remove dusty powdery feed from troughs.

21 days and after

Reduce brooder temperature to 85° F. on the 21st day and continue to reduce the temperature 5° F. each week of brooding thereafter.

Continue sanitary procedures.

Do not fail to keep water and feed available at several areas within each pen.

5-6 weeks

Transfer to grow-out pens.

Cull and lightly debeak as you transfer.

Grow-out

After a brooding period of 4-6 weeks, depending on weather conditions, place birds in grow-out pens. Locate these grow-out pens away from your breeders and from common disturbances, such as road traffic, children's play area, etc.

Following these suggestions will assist successful grow-out:

Do not crowd the birds. Watch for cannibalism. A good time to debeak is when you move from area to area.
- Provide several feed and water stations. If growing out on ground or litter, place each feeder and waterer on wire. Birds will congregate in this area and it will be more messy. Wire water and feeder stands will keep birds from a concentration of droppings.
- Provide shelter and hiding places for protection from weather and from one another. Corn stalks in shocks, pine tops, panels, etc. will give birds a place to feel more secure.
- Wire floors are recommended for grow-out. Birds during this stage of growth are very susceptible to disease. If pens are above the ground put a drop curtain around the bottom of the pen to avoid drafts (Clemson University, 1978).

Maybe here would be a good place to say something about game bird medication. I would recommend that during this stage of growth you watch you birds carefully for signs of disease. It would not hurt to give regular medication as a disease preventive method. I do this with the drug Bacitracin especially during times of stress or wet weather. Never give antibiotics more than two weeks and less than seven days 10 days duration.

THE ASSEMBLY LINE METHOD

Every successful game bird breeder has through experience developed a method of raising game bird chicks of the species that he works with. We have done this by taking ideas from others and putting them with our own experience. Early on, we came up with a method of raising chicks that works for us. We call this method the **ASSEMBLY LINE METHOD**. It is not a new method, nor is it one that works only with a particular species. It can easily be adapted to raise the chicks of any game bird that is kept in captivity. This method will work with any game bird chicks. Waterfowl do quite well with this method if some minor adjustments are made. The game bird breeder should develop his own system which works for him.

The **ASSEMBLY LINE METHOD** involves the use of different *"environments"* (boxes) in which the chicks mature through each of the developmental stages of their lives. The needs of the chicks change as they mature, so this method changes with them. As the chicks pass through these different environments on their way to maturity, they resemble an automobile assembly line which places different parts on the chassis at the appropriate time.

This basic method of raising chicks can be used by anyone regardless of climatic conditions. The boxes are mobile and can be placed in a warm room if the outside temperature is not satisfactory.

Each hatch (usually 4 to 20 quail sized chicks) is placed in a box (can be a common cardboard box or one specially made from plywood material) which is modified to meet their basic needs at a particular age. We have a series of boxes that house the different age chicks. The larger chicks such as turkeys are placed in smaller numbers in larger boxes.

If more than 20 chicks are raised in a group, the boxes need to be larger to accommodate the greater number of occupants. The breeder may want to use ground brooding under a hover-type brooder instead of the individual boxes. The same principles apply whatever the type of box or pen used. Chicks of any age need the proper heat and humidity, feed and water, and protection from disease and predation.

The Nursery Box

This is the first box (environment) on the **ASSEMBLY LINE**. It is used to house the chicks as soon as they leave the incubator and serves as home for the first two weeks. The Nursery Box is about 15 by 20 inches in size and about 20 inches high. This box should be high enough so the chicks cannot easily jump out. Be sure to get a box that is longer than it is wide so the chicks can have a place to get out of the heat if they want to do so. The heat source is a 40-watt light bulb placed about two inches from the floor, but above the heads of the chicks. If this is not enough heat for the young chicks you may use a 60-watt bulb, but do not let it get too hot. Also be sure that the light bulb does not hang too close to the sides of the box as this presents a possible fire hazard. Many breeders use two light bulbs in case one should burn out during the night. We spray paint these light bulbs red which seems to stop *"glare blindness"* and reduces picking. Painting the light bulbs seems to shorten their life. If "infrared" heat lamps are used, great care should be taken to prevent overheating the box. Most of this type of lamp are manufactured in 150 or 250 watts which is too much for a small box. Watch the chicks to see if they are comfortable.

The Nursery Box has a cloth floor made out of an old towel that can be washed and reused. The towel offers good footing so leg problems are prevented. This towel bottom should be changed every day. The more chicks in the box, more often the towel, feed and water should be changed. Do not allow the towel to become wet or matted with droppings. Be careful to see that no loose strings are on the towel as they will be eaten and can strangle the chicks.

A real danger is to get the chicks too crowded. More than 20 quail size chicks in one of these boxes can cause problems. If you want to put more chicks than this together, the box should be greatly enlarged. Some species of game birds do much better if more than two or three chicks are raised together. There seems to be something to their liking if the youngsters are grouped in numbers that are natural to them in the wilds.

Starter feed is scattered around on the towel. We use starter feed with 28% to 30% protein. This can be turkey starter or game bird starter that is produced by any good feed company. The turkey starter has a medication which does not hurt game birds at all and helps control Coccidiosis and Blackhead. Do not worry about the feed on the floor as it will not hurt the chicks if they eat off the floor for a few days. It is necessary to have the feed available so they will learn to eat quickly and get a good start. Older chicks should never be fed off the floor. By the way, for small chicks, such as quail, it is necessary to grind up the starter feed so it will be small enough for the chicks to eat. We do this by simply putting a small amount into a saucer and putting pressure on it by mashing it down with the bottom of an ordinary mason jar.

The water fount is placed out from under the heat source so the water will not get hot. Warm water breeds bacteria and can be harmful. Very cold water should never be given as under certain circumstances the young chicks will die after drinking chilled water. The water kept out in the cool area also gets the chicks out running. They need exercise to build healthy bodies. There should be several water founts if you have many chicks. Two or even three are recommended.

Rocks or marbles can be placed in the water founts so the babies will not get wet and chill or even drown. The regular poultry water founts are too tall for baby quail, so jar lids can be used if care is used in placing the rocks in the lid. When small quail chicks are started, it is much better to buy specially molded plastic water bases. These fit on ordinary canning jars and can be bought from suppliers. Some type of medication should be put in the water the first two weeks. Bacitracin, Terramycin, or some other antibiotic works fine.

The top of the box should be covered with hardware cloth (welded wire) to keep the active chicks from jumping out. We put newspaper over a part of the top to keep the heat in the box. This newspaper can be adjusted to control the heat inside the box by leaving more or less space open. Again caution should be used to keep the bulb from being a fire hazard. We have found often that more chicks are lost due to overheating than by not having enough heat. If the chicks bunch together and chirp they are cold and should have more heat. If they scatter and sleep away from the heat, they have enough heat or maybe too much. Panting chicks suggest too much heat.

The Baby Box

After the chicks are about two weeks old, they can be graduated to the second box in the ASSEMBLY LINE. This box is the same size as the *"Nursery Box"* or it can even be larger. It has a special hardware cloth bottom that rests about 2 inches or so from the bottom of the box. It is designed this way to let the droppings fall below. It should be the goal of the breeder to keep the birds away from their own droppings as much as possible from this age through maturity as young birds are very susceptible to many diseases spread through droppings. The wire should be the small size, (¼ inch) as the small feet of the babies will go through the larger wire if you are raising quail. Larger wire (½ inch) wire is used for species of partridge, pheasants, and larger birds . The medicated water should be discontinued at this stage. Never give chicks medication longer than ten days as the good bacteria will be all killed and fungus and the like will get them. It will be alright to give medication again after a week of rest.

The light bulb should also be adjusted and the wattage changed to less heat output. If too much heat is given to the chicks at this age they will not feather out properly. *"Bare backs"* will result from too much heat. The rocks or marbles can be omitted from the water founts. Feeders should be given to the chicks. We use flat lids with some kind of wire guard to keep the birds from scratching out the feed. By this time the two week old chicks will be feathered enough to fly, so care should be given to prevent them from flying out when the wire top is removed for servicing the chicks. Each time we move the chicks, their wings are carefully clipped. The primary flights are clipped on one wing to prevent escape. (If the chicks are kept in *"low"* pens, there is no need to clip both wings. Clipping both wing primaries is done only if the chicks are kept in pens higher than three times their height).

I must again emphasize the importance of looking at the chicks every two hours or so to check their water, feed, and box temperature. This is also a good time to check for any other problems, such as cannibalism.

The Juvenile Box

This is the third box which is the same as the baby box with the exception of the larger wire on the floor to accommodate the birds' fast growing feet. To avoid crowding, we have several of these juvenile boxes so the chicks can be divided to have manageable groups.

Mixing different ages of chicks can be done if a few rules are followed. Generally it is best not to mix species. Never put chicks of other species with bobwhites as the *"odd species"* will **surely be killed**. Nose, toe and feather picking can all occur if new birds are mixed with the one batch. Mixing can be successful, among compatible species, if you do it when you move the birds from one box to another. It seems the different box is new to everyone and mixing can be done. Consequently we **arrange each box in a different way** so it will not look like the other boxes. By the time the chicks get used to the new box they are used to the new neighbors and all get along well. Never, never add a new batch of chicks to a box already occupied. The residents will take offense to the newcomers.

The Intermediate Pen

The fourth area in the ASSEMBLY LINE is put into use when the birds have feathered out enough to be without heat at night. It is much larger than the preceding boxes to give the birds more room. We make these pens out of ¼ or ½ inch plywood. Construction can be varied as long as the pen is usable. This simple pen is constructed as follows:

First cut two pieces of 4X8 plywood in half (going the long way) to get four pieces that are 2X8 feet. Cut one of these in half giving two pieces 2X4 feet which will be used for the ends of the pen. If the doorways of your building are less than four feet wide, make the ends narrow enough to pass through. Next, cut out windows in each of the long pieces of plywood approximately six inches by three feet. Cover these areas with small wire mesh to give light during the day. Cut a door in one end (or both ends), hinge it and put a latch on it (or have a sliding door system). Nail the pen together using 2X2's in the corners. Place strips of this 2X2 stock along the bottom edges so there will be a nailing place for the wire bottom. Cover the bottom with wire hardware cloth (welded wire mesh) ½ inch in size. You can get this in 48 inch widths or whatever width you make your pens. A piece of wire eight feet long will fit the pen area just right.

You should have a box-like pen with a wire bottom assembled. Since these pens can be stacked three or four high to save floor space, there needs to be a dropping board put on top of each pen. We use newspapers on this board, so keeping it clean is easy. If the pen is not placed out in the open where it can get wet from rain, we use heavy cardboard tops. We get the cardboard from discarded shipping cartons found at furniture stores. This cardboard makes excellent tops for the dropping boards and they are rather soft to help cut down on head injury if the birds fly up and hit the top of the pens. There are many good ideas out there just to be discovered so use your imagination in your pen designs.

Place a light in one end of the pen above the feed and water area. This will not be used for heat, but will be an attraction light for the birds at night. This night light not only encourages the birds to eat and drink during the night, but it also makes them calmer and less easily disturbed.

The birds can stay in a pen of this type until they are mature if not too crowded. A pen like this can handle up to 20 quail (fewer if used for partridge and pheasants or larger birds) if care is taken to prevent picking. We put alfalfa hay in the bottoms and keep the beaks seared off.

When the young birds are completely feathered and able to stand the climate without any heat they are placed in outside pens. We clip both wing primaries at this time to prevent "unbalanced" flying which can cause injury.

The Outside Ground Pen

The next step is to put the birds into an especially designed *"growing pen"* which in our case is built on the ground. If your climate is wet and humid you need to make some type of wire bottom outside pen. Do not put the birds on the ground unless the climate is dry. If you live in a very wet climate you could put your birds on the ground under a dry roof with six inches of river sand for ground covering. Of course, some species of the larger upland game birds are too large not to put in ground pens. This is a case where the breeder should be creative and design a system that meets his or her particular need. The dimensions of this outside ground pen can be about anything the breeder is comfortable with. Ours are eight feet wide by 24 feet long. The idea is to make the pens longer than wide to give the birds plenty of room to run back and forth for exercise and probably just as important, give them a place to retreat when they are threatened. Never put a bird into a pen where they are backed against a wall, such as a small square pen, if you do they will panic for sure and fly up. I have found that if the walk-in pen is much wider than eight feet it is difficult to catch up the birds as they can run around you before you can approach them. Never have the pen wider than the distance you can reach easily with your bird catching net. Have a shelter in one end of this pen where feed and water is kept out of the weather. We use platforms made out of 2X4's covered with wire mesh to keep the feed and water off the ground.

You may find that the birds refuse to get in the shelter and prefer to sleep out in the open. If this is the case, give them some branches out in the open. Put a 40-watt light in the shelter and leave it on in the evenings to attract the birds. They may come to the light to roost . In this case you can turn the light off after dark. We like to keep the ground bare with no vegetation at all. If the ground is wet enough to support vegetation, it also supports disease agents, earthworms, and other creatures. I know that this may sound like a contradiction to my philosophy of making the pens as natural as possible. However, you can put into these large pens vegetation in buckets or pots and give them enough water to support them. If they get droopy you can take them out and replace them with another. I use as a guide the desert conditions found in the southwestern states. It is dry as a bone most of the year but has lots of cover and even some types of vegetation for the birds to hide. This means that the pens should have lots of loose river sand which makes a wonderful area to keep clean.

The Breeder Pen

The final pen in the **ASSEMBLY LINE METHOD** is for *"adults only."* We sometimes use the same pens for breeding that we use for growing-out with some different furnishings. Brush, logs, and branches are added to make the place as natural as possible and to provide plenty of hidden nesting places. The natural setting applies to wire and ground pens alike. Actually, I believe that this is the key to getting birds to breed. If we can make them feel as comfortable as possible, they will get down to house-keeping in a shorter time than if they are stressed.

The very first pairs of Masked bobwhites we got several years ago were very wild and skittish. They were accidentally put in a pen that worked out just great. There was a *"bunch"* of tall grass growing in one end of the pen next to the outside door. We fed and watered them from the other end of the pen. Fortunately, the little hen chose to make her nest in the tall grass next to the outside door. It was an easy thing to gather her eggs each day without getting into the pen. We quietly reached through the door without disturbing the birds. This experience taught me a trick that has worked for many different species of upland game birds.

From this experience, we learned to design our other pens to allow very little disturbance. Nesting places were made that could be reached from the outside of the pens. I believe the less the birds are disturbed, the more chance of egg production. I arrange a place to nest that appeals to the birds as much as possible.

Maybe this would be a good time to discuss the subject of ground pens versus wire floored pens, as this is a real concern of many game bird breeders. It has always been my personal feeling that the more natural we can make the surroundings, the more likely the birds will lay eggs. As a rule, I still stick to this. However, the many game bird breeders that live in a damp climate or in severe cold conditions cannot successfully have outside ground pens. Some believe that Mountain quail cannot be enticed to lay on wire. This is not so. I think it can be said that if conditions are made desirable, most upland game birds will lay on wire provided their pens are made as natural as possible by using logs, tree limbs, grass etc..

Some breeders put the birds in ground pens during the laying season and then on wire for the rest of the year. This seems like a reasonable compromise. Try this method if you are having trouble keeping your birds alive on the ground. Be sure and not leave them on the ground during a long rainy season as they will pick up some disease that may be their end. Fortunately, some of the game birds in captivity have developed some immunity to certain disease problems.

As a rule, I would never brood rare and disease prone upland game birds on the ground. It appears that during maturation they have not built up immunity and seem to catch just about everything. Keeping them on wire certainly helps to control the excrement that they are exposed to during this critical time.

I have plans in the future to construct a special breeding pen on wire. It will be rather large (10x15) and will give the residents all of the advantages of being on the ground and the advantages of being on wire. It will have a wire bottom that is about two inches from the ground built like a *"porch."* Under this wire rye grass or some other type of fast growing grass is planted. As the grass grows up through the wire the birds snip it off and enjoy a salad every day without walking on possible contaminated ground. This idea could be used easily in building a very practical pen for any upland game bird. The more one thinks about this, the more ideas come to mind. This is an area for some experimentation. I cannot count all of the pen ideas that we have tried over the years. Some did not work at all. One breeder pen encouraged the quail to lay on the feed board and **every egg cracked**. Of course, I redesigned that pen. Other failures have led to the designing of very successful pens. If the breeder is at all creative, this is one area where he should have lots of fun.

I did design and build a very good pen for breeder Mearns quail several years ago. I was able to get six pairs of birds to lay almost 400 eggs. The design was like a rabbit hutch standing on legs. It was 30 inches wide and high and five feet long. It had a wire bottom, with a shelter built on the back half. Under the shelter I had a sand pan which was filled with four inches of clean river sand. In this shelter part I put large clumps of grass (the kind that grows about two feet high) which gave privacy. Dig up the grass leaving a large clump of roots attached to anchor it to the bottom of the pen. The hens built and laid in nests in the shelter area. I had a door on the back so I could quietly gather the eggs. The feed and water were placed in the fronts of the pens which was accessed by another door. The wire covered top and sides in the front gave the birds plenty of light and fresh air. I still have these pens and use them every year.

There you have the ASSEMBLY LINE METHOD. As you get experience you can probably make changes that work for you. The size, shape, furnishings and feed and water are flexible. Just so you meet the needs of the little residents, you can be successful. A great thing about our bird friends, they will live in a hut or a mansion and be happy and reproduce for us. Of course, we will make them as comfortable as we possibly can.

Ringneck pheasant hen and chicks.

Part 2

SOME FAVORITE QUAIL

SOME FAVORITE OLD WORLD QUAIL
(Tribe *perdicini*)

SOME FAVORITE QUAIL

The real fun of aviculture is getting *"hands on"* experience with birds. There is nothing quite like it in the world. We would like now to discuss some of our favorite ornamental quail for your consideration. All of the species in this section are available to the modern aviculturist. Rare quail and partridge are not easy to propagate. If they were, they would not be rare. However, we find that if good strong stock is available, these so called *"rare"* birds can be raised in captivity. Many countries where they are native have stopped legal shipment of these birds out of their country. This means the most sought after species are not available to the average game bird breeder.

We have tried to whet your appetites in such a way that you will want to try some of our favorites next breeding season. It would be a wonderful thing if the birds in this chapter could be in the aviaries of many people. This would do two things: 1) it would insure the breeder of many hours of pleasure and satisfaction, and 2) what is most important, it would insure the species of continued survival, as the natural habitat of several species is continually being destroyed. Udo Schultz, from New York, always says to the people after one of his talks about a certain species that he has had experience with, *"Everyone should have a pair or two of these."* I agree with him!

The writer has personally propagated most of his favorite species. There are still some species that we find appealing for some first hand experience. It is interesting how the progression through the species usually works. The first birds gotten usually are the more common inexpensive ones that are really *"guinea pigs."* If everything goes well, after a year or two, the breeder gets enough confidence to purchase a pair or two of the more expensive birds. Then, if all goes well, he graduates to the more rare birds. Within four or five years, he has had some experience with a few of the rare quail and partridge. If he lasts this long, he is hooked and can be classified as a true aviculturist. Most people are "drop outs" after the first season. They do something wrong, or fate hands them a disease problem and they get discouraged and quit. Only a few get beyond the first year or two to go on to the more rare birds. Again, the inexperienced aviculturist should not begin with the rare species, but should get a year or two of experience with some more common species before launching into the rare ornamentals. The chances of success are greatly multiplied when *"experience"* is added into the equation.

This book cannot answer all questions, but we hope it gives enough information to make the reader comfortable enough to try one of the species. If you do, be prepared for some mountain tops and some valleys as your emotions will be treated to a thrill beyond all imagination.

A Bobwhite quail family

THE

BOBWHITE QUAIL

FAMILY

(Colinus virginianus) Linnaeus 1758

This interesting and beautiful family of quail is a most fascinating group of birds. They are all small and each have their own beautiful color patterns. In the spring and early summer, the male bobwhite deserves his name. It not only is the most widely distributed species of quail but it is the best known mainly because of his familiar *"bob-white"* call. An interesting fact about the male bobwhite's call is if he does not have a mate he will call ***"bob-bob-white."*** When he gets a mate he will drop the extra *"bob"* in his call. Unlike other quail, bobwhites roost on the ground in low and fairly open cover where there is little obstruction of light by trees and rapid escape can be made by flight. When the covey is flushed the whir of wings is enough to give anyone *"heart failure"* as the birds usually fly up at the least expected moment.

When the conditions are suitable, this little bird will take up residence most anywhere. It even gets quite tame when living in fields next to populated areas. Wild house cats are cleaning out the pockets of this bird that lives in outlying areas of human population. This is a no-win situation. Many mornings, I have spotted pairs of this wonderful bobwhite in fields that were within the city limits.

The bobwhite takes on many color variations the further south they are found. Leopold says that the bobwhite is the most variable game species in Mexico. A male bobwhite from Chiapas, for example, would hardly be recognized as belonging to the same species as a specimen from Tamaulipas. Presumably each segment of the population is in some way adapted to the particular environment in which it lives (Leopold, 1959).

There are several subspecies of the bobwhite that are not known to be in captivity in the United States. Then too, there are many mutations developed in captivity that cannot be found in the wild. These color mutations are very popular and their propagation is the same as with any other bobwhite. All members of the bobwhite family can be handled much the same way. However, there should be some management adaptations that fit the temperament of each species being considered. These differences are discussed with each species.

Johnsgard gives a summary of the subspecies and their distribution:

> *C. v. Virginianus:* Eastern bobwhite. Resident to the southern Atlantic seaboard north to Virginia southwest to north central Georgia, southeastern Alabama, and northern Florida.
> *C. v. marilandicus (Linnaeus):* New England bobwhite. Resident of New England north to southwestern Maine southwest to east central New York, Pennsylvania, and central Virginia and south to southern Maryland and Delaware.
> *C. v. mexicanus (Linnaeus):* Interior bobwhite. Resident of much of eastern U.S. east of the Great Plains excepting the Atlantic Coast.
> *C. v. floridanus (Coues):* Florida bobwhite. Resident of most of Florida peninsular.

C. v. texanus (Lawrence): Texas bobwhite. Resident of most of southern Texas adjacent to New Mexico and northern Mexico including parts of Coahuila, Nuevo Leon, and Tamaulipas.

C. v. taylori Lincoln: Plains bobwhite. Resident of the Great Plains from South Dakota southward to northern Texas and eastward to western Missouri and northwestern Arkansas. Introduced populations in Washington, Oregon, and Idaho.

C. v. brewster: Masked bobwhite. Resident in central interior Sonora and formerly north to Southern Arizona.

C. v. cubanensis (Gray): Cuban bobwhite. Resident in Cuba and the Isle of Pines.

C. v. maculatus Nelson: Mottled or spotted bobwhite. Resident from central Tamaulipas south to northern Veracruz and west to southeastern San Luis Potosi.

C. v. aridus Aldrich: Jaumave bobwhite. Resident from the northern part of southeastern San Luis Potosi to central and central western Tamaulipas.

C. v. graysoni (Lawrence): Grayson bobwhite. Resident from south eastern Nayarit and southern Jalisco on the Mexican tableland south to the Valley of Mexico, Morelos, southern Hidalgo, and central southern San Luis Potosi.

C. v. nigripectus Nelson: Puebla bobwhite. Resident in the plans of Puebla, Morelos, and Mexico.

C. v. pectoralis (Gould): Black-breasted bobwhite. Resident in central Veracruz at elevations of from five hundred to five thousand feet along the eastern base of the Cordillera.

C. v. godmani Nelson: Godman bobwhite. Resident in the lowlands of Veracruz from sea level to fifteen hundred feet and intergrading with minor in Tabasco.

C. v. minor Nelson: Least bobwhite. Resident on grassy plans of northeastern Chiapas and adjacent Tabasco.

C. v. insignis Nelson: Guatemalan bobwhite. Resident in the valley of the Rio Chiapas in southern Chiapas and adjacent Guatemala.

C. v. salvini Nelson: Salvin bobwhite. Known only from the coastal plains of southern Chiapas near the Guatemalan border.

C. v. thayeri Bangs and Peters: Thayer bobwhite. Resident in Oaxaca.

C. v. atriceps (Ogilvie-Grant): Black-headed bobwhite. Resident from the interior of western Oaxaca northward along the coast to central Guerrero and probably south to the range of harrisoni.

C. v. nelsoni Brodkorb: Nelson bobwhite. Only in so. Chiapas.

C. v. harrisoni Orr and Webster: Recently described (1968) from southwestern Oaxaca near the coastal plain (Johnsgard, 1973).

C. v. coyolcos (Muller): Coyolcos bobwhite. Resident along the Pacific coast of Oaxaca in the vicinity of the Gulf of Tehuantepec.

Bobwhite quail family distribution

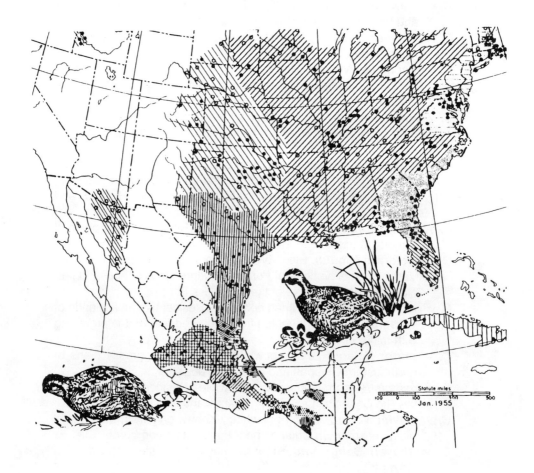

Common Bobwhite Quail

(Colinus virginianus virginianus)

When people hear the word **quail**, they think of the Common bobwhite. As a boy, these were the first quail that I raised. Those quail still live today (symbolically, of course) as it was through them that I caught the *"bird-in-blood disease,"* so to speak, and I still have it today! There is no known cure for this disease although it may come and go, the poor victim enjoys it forever.

Bobwhites have probably been bred in captivity longer in America than any other quail. There is a giant commercial industry supplying these quail to today's market. When any bird is raised in such great numbers, Mother Nature plays tricks with chromosome structure and mutations are produced. So, it is with the popular bobwhite. Some color mutations developed are albinism, melanism, red, fawn, silver, blue, yellow, and blond, to name only a few. Nearly every year one hears of a new color mutation. As popular as these color mutations are, some breeders are into the breeding of *"jumbo bobs"* which weigh more than 22 ounces (a wild bobwhite weighs seven to eight ounces). Several years ago we developed *"silver-jumbo"* bobwhites that were just beautiful. It took four years to get them to breed true.

If you are thinking about getting a pair or two of quail I would recommend either bobwhites or coturnix quail. I certainly must admit that because of my early years' experience I am partial to the bobwhite. Bobwhite quail are propagated easily, once the basics are mastered. They are a good beginner's bird and many breeders never get any other quail as they are truly *"hooked"* on the bobwhite.

I have found that my bobwhites do better when I pair them together. It is possible to mate them up as trios (one male; two females) or in larger groups, but in the wilds they mate as pairs so I prefer to leave them in the natural way. Some have put them in large colonies but I have never been successful doing this as the males will end up fighting and killing off each other in the middle of the laying season and many eggs are lost. They do well either on wire or in ground pens. However, if you live in a wet climate leave them on the ground only during laying season as they are likely to come down with some disease. There are advantages to both methods of raising quail. My advice to anyone raising any game bird is to find a system that works and use it. There is no **right** or **wrong** way if it works for you.

Bobwhites are readily available and can be had at a reasonable price. Many breeders sell eggs, chicks and mature birds, so the novice can get started either way. Many of us began with the bobwhite. People who live in areas where the bobwhite is native have an extraordinary fondness for his call and great personality. I know many breeders that have specialized in producing this species in great numbers for the commercial market. They would not have any other bird.

A male Bobwhite quail

The Black - throated Bobwhite Quail

(Colinus nigrogularis)

One of the more interesting quail that comes from "south of the border" is the **Black-throated bobwhite** or sometimes called the **Yucatan bobwhite**. The latter name describes the place where it is native.

There are two subspecies of this quail. Although there is some controversy as to the classification of it apart from the other bobwhites, the scientific community has been unable to make a unified decision about this. The nominate race comes from the Yucatan Peninsula of Mexico. The bird's range is limited to the south by northeastern Nicaragua and includes Belize and Honduras. All of the subspecies range in a small area and undoubtedly intermix with one another.

The two subspecies live in slightly different climatic conditions. They seem to thrive along the arid coastal areas where rainfall averages only 19 inches a year. They like the scrub forest and any open area where feed and cover occurs. This quail cannot survive the heavy rain forest.

Description

Male: Crest and crown brownish mottled border with white; forehead black lined with white stripe; beak black; face to throat area black with white line passing below the eye and ear to neck; neck front has scaly effect; neck back has rufous buff red mottling edged with gray; upper back, middle back and rump, mottled bobwhite pattern; breast whitish, heavily bordered with black (scaled effect); abdomen dull reddish brown; flanks and thighs scaly effect; upper tail coverts olive brown streaked with buff, brown and black; under tail coverts gray; wing coverts, primaries, and secondaries olive brown streaked with buff, brown, and black; legs (tarsus) dusky brown, unfeathered; feet dusky brown; size 7½ to 8½ inches.

Female: Crest, crown and forehead, dark brown streaked with buff; beak dark brown; eyes black; neck front buffy tan; neck back buffy tan edged with gray; upper back mottled brown, black and tan; middle back and rump mottled brown, black and tan; breast, abdomen, flanks and thighs, reddish brown heavily mottled with brown; tail grayish brown; wings: scapulars, coverts, primaries, secondaries, grayish brown; legs (tarsus) dusky brown; feet dusky brown, unfeathered; size 7½ to 8½ inches.

It is interesting to note that in spite of the small range they occupy, this small bird can rapidly colonize new forest openings that are opened up with the building of new roads and with the clearing of new farm land. It has been suggested that the birds follow these roads seeking new areas to populate (Leopold, 1972).

When they find a suitable area, they stay as long as the conditions meet with their liking. Like their North American cousins, these birds have good and bad years. Their mortality rate is high, but their rates of reproduction are also high which balances with their relatively short life span.

Wild Nature

These birds in captivity exhibit a wild nature that is common with many quail that come from Mexico and other areas of Latin America. This wild nature presents some problems that must be overcome by the propagator if he is to have any success. To generalize would be risky, as individuals in any race have varying temperaments. If any one has a Yucatan bobwhite that is *"finger-trained"* I have never heard of them. The Masked bobwhite and the Yucatan bobwhite have several common traits. Both have a high degree of wildness, severe cannibalism in captive conditions, and are susceptible to disease.

Breeding Requirements

Success in breeding this attractive little quail will depend largely on the stock one has to work with. If the stock is strong, there should be no problems in getting fertile eggs, strong chicks, and healthy mature birds. It can justifiably be said that *"all bobwhites are the same."* Basically, this is very true. Each of the many subspecies have the same characteristics. So, handle this bird the same way you handle the other bobwhites.

Breeder pens should be constructed to complement rather than irritate the *"wild"* nature of these birds. If the breeder birds are kept on wire, the pens should be long enough for the birds to get away from the keeper. If they cannot get away, they feel trapped and thus push the panic button. I use both wire bottom pens and ground pens and have found that the long and narrow pen is much preferred to the square pen despite the size. There should be a door on both ends.

Use plenty of brush in the pens and arrange it so that the eggs can be gathered with as little disturbance as possible. My breeder birds that are on wire just drop the egg when nature calls, but the pairs on the ground build nests and are faithful to lay in them. I always leave three eggs in the nest to encourage hard work to complete the clutch. The birds always lay more eggs using this technique.

If a breeder is fortunate enough to get some of these birds, if I were him, I believe that I would put them on the ground during breeding season to get them to lay. After the laying season is over, I would put them on wire.

I have never seen any of these birds that were not crossed with another species of bobwhite. The most common cross is using the Masked bobwhite as a partner with a Black-throated bobwhite. They are very close in appearance. In fact, it is very difficult to tell the females apart. There would be a great demand for fresh, pure stock if some new blood could be brought into this country. However, under the present laws this will be difficult.

Brooding the Chicks

These birds are notorious in the art of **cannibalism**. Some special tricks need to be used to have success with this species (and with the Masked bobwhites). Special precautions should be used to prevent this problem from cropping up in the chicks. I recently heard of a man that had success using foster hens (bantams) to brood the chicks. He reported no problem with cannibalism. Others have reported no problem with picking when a foster hen was used. The breeder should use all of the tricks up his sleeve to keep the birds from starting this habit.

Black-throated bobwhites are prone to fly up and hit the top of the pens because of their inherited wildness. The breeder should be sure to clip the wings and even put some soft padded material on the top of the pen if they continually fly up and hit the top with their heads. This is one thing that they will always do and there is nothing that can be done to prevent it. The remedy lies in preventing injury when they do it. I have noticed that as the chicks mature they become less likely to fly up. When they are well acquainted with their keeper, they will tame down considerably. This is still an irritating habit that the breeder must learn to live with. The chicks should be raised as any other quail chicks with success if the preventive measures are put into action. Use the **ASSEMBLY LINE METHOD** described earlier in this book. I, along with many other quail breeders, would love to try some of these little birds.

Bobwhite quail in flight

The Masked Bobwhite Quail

(Colinus v. ridgwayi)

The story of this beautiful little quail is a success story that involves two countries and many private breeders. Because of concern for the survival of the Masked bobwhite it has been delivered from the *"brink of extinction"* and is now being reintroduced to some of its former habitat. The demise of this quail in Arizona and in Mexico was the grazing of cattle (Bent, 1932). When this problem was corrected, the birds have now been reintroduced into its former home.

Herbert Brown was the first to discover and describe this quail, and we are indebted to him for most of our knowledge of its former habits and distribution. Brown says of this bird in 1904: *"It is not easy to describe the feelings of myself and my American companions when we first heard the call "bob-white." It was startling and unexpected, and that night nearly every man in the camp had some story to tell of Bobwhite and his boyhood days. It was to us Americans the one homelike thing in all Sonora and we felt thousands of miles nearer to our homes in the then far distant states"* (Bent, 1932).

William Brewster went to Mexico and collected a male specimen described in 1885 as a type of new species, which he gave the present scientific name. Brown writes of the early conditions before 1870 and describes the heavily grassed valleys and the notoriously bad Apache Indians which kept out people for many years. Several years of drought and overgrazing of cattle nearly wiped out this newly discovered little bird.

There is some variation in the coloring although the birds are pure stock. The eye-stripe is variable. It is very conspicuous in some mature males, but in others it is barely visible or absent. Also in some of the first year males there is some white on the head and neck which molts out the second year.

In captivity, the Masked bobwhite has two distinct personalities. Until it is settled into its home the bird is extremely wild, often battering his head on the top of the pen in an effort to escape. Spaulding says of his early experience (1947) with what he believed to be the last pair alive, *"One of the most pleasing characteristics of these two caged birds is their tameness and gentleness. Though wild when they came to me, they soon calmed down. In three months they were as quiet and tame in my presence as a pair of common Bobwhites might have been in the same situation"* (Spaulding, 1949).

Knowing the history of these beautiful little birds made us appreciate them much more. I suppose we raised over five hundred of them during the four years we worked with them. There is an inexplicable satisfaction in knowing that you have a part in the preservation of a species. This makes it more satisfying than ever.

Some Husbandry Tips

Although thousands of these birds have been raised in captivity, they are not easy to propagate. Once you have raised several they are not so difficult. Perhaps the biggest drawback in years before 1982, was the lack of good strong unrelated blood. After the U.S. Government released some bloodlines from their wild caught stock, the birds in the hands of private breeders began to multiply. At this writing there are many hundreds of these birds in captivity with many thousands having been reintroduced into the wild. I understand that the government has abandoned their project of reintroduction because of the great success in propagating these birds and because of limited funding.

At this writing, Tom Carter in Texas still has some of the original bloodlines that the Government gave to the Quail Breeder's Society back in the 80's. He is keeping the strain pure and not inbreeding or crossing the birds.

With strong bloodlines available, the problems that remain are connected to the disposition of the bird toward wildness and cannibalism. We soon discovered that as growing chicks they were as wild as a *"March hare."* Steps had to be made to cope with this wild nature. The brooder box was redesigned to allow more head room and places to hide. This helped some, but the little chicks would really go crazy until they developed confidence in their surroundings.

We soon discovered that they were notorious "pickers." Besides can- nibalism, we had to deal with their continual "flying up" when startled. As they matured, they seemed to get better about this, but we still had to deal with it in mature birds. There are several things that can be done to help the situation. First, we redesigned the pens to have **fiber board** tops. This material is rather soft and seemed to be easier on their heads when they bumped against it. Next, we kept the primary feathers in the wings clipped rather short. This had to be done every week or so as they grew very fast when the chicks were maturing. Lastly, we provided ample places for the chicks to hide. Our making no sudden movements or sounds seemed to help their calmness. It is a good thing that as the chicks matured they *"outgrew"* the habit to a degree. Our mature breeders would come up to get mealworms from us when in very large pens. Perhaps they feel threatened when they are in the small growing pens. Nevertheless, with all of their faults, they remain on our favorite list. More patience and understanding are required to get these birds to maturity than one realizes. As members of the bobwhite family they are basically easy to propagate. The problem comes from their many "vices" that must be overcome.

Of course, there is the problem of getting and maintaining Federal permits when dealing with these birds across state lines. I am sure this keeps many people from getting these birds. This is regrettable as the law was written to have just the opposite effect on the birds. This bird should be taken off of the *"endangered species list"* and put on the "threatened list" as it is so common now among private game bird breeders.

I had my first experience with a "sex change" with these birds. One of the cock birds that I originally got from Arizona changed into a hen the second year. I was amazed. The bird molted into the coloration of the opposite sex. I know of several other breeders that have had this same experience with them. I am not convinced that an internal change in the bird's sex takes place. Perhaps the coloration only changes. I wish now that I had kept up with this bird to see if it bred as a male or laid eggs in later years as a hen. A post- mortem would have been interesting to see just how the bird was built internally.

Columbia Crested quail *(Colinus cristatus)* from a painting from *The Manual of Neo-Tropical Birds* by Blake with permission of University of Chicago Press.

The Crested Bobwhite Quail

(Colinus cristatus)   **PLATE C**

The Crested bobwhite is a very striking bird. They range from Panama south through Central America into northern South America. It has been introduced to several islands in the neotropical zone. Blake, the noted ornithologist, recognizes fourteen species (races) of this interesting quail. It is not clear which of the races are now in captivity, but any of the subspecies should do well in the hands of capable breeders.

The fourteen races are as follows (Blake, 1977):

C. c. mariae: Darkest race of the species. More black markings over entire body and wings. Distribution, Western Chiriqui, Panama, from the southern slope to the coastal plain.

C. c. *panamensis:* Paler than mariae with upper parts brown, the black markings much more restricted with the breast bright brown, not black. Distribution, arid lowlands of the Pacific slope of western Panama.

C. c. *decoratus:* Similar to leucotis, but more richly colored. Distribution, humid tropical zone of the Caribbean coast of Columbia.

C. c. *littoralis:* Both sexes paler than decoratus. Distribution, semi-arid lowlands of northern Columbia.

C. c. *cristatus:* Distribution, Guajira Peninsula and the eastern base of the Santa Marta Mountains, northeastern Columbia.

C. c. *badius*: Both sexes darker than leucotis. Distribution, tropical and sub-tropical zones of Columbia.

C.c. *leucotis*: Without black mottling. Distribution, Valley of Magdalena, Columbia.

C. c. *bogotensis*: Smaller size, less white coloration. Distribution, above 7500 feet in eastern Andes, Columbia.

C. c. *parvicristatus:* Has shorter crest but larger in size than average measurements. Distribution, eastern Andes slope in Columbia, southwestern Venezuela.

C. c. *continentis*: Similar to horvathi. Distribution, tropical and subtropical zones of northwestern Venezuela.

C. c. *horvathi:* Distribution, northwestern Venezuela.

C. c. *barnesi:* Distinctly darker than average. Distribution, northern Central Venezuela.

C. c. *mocquerysi:* Crest long and paler. Distribution, northeastern Venezuela.

C. c. sonnini: Smaller with longer crest than parvicristatus. Distribution, northern Venezuela, the Guianas, extremely northern Brazil. Introduced on Mustique Island, Grenadines and St.Thomas, Virgin Islands.

Description

Sexes almost identical except female's pileum is mainly brown or buff, speckled or finely black streaked. General description: A short-tailed quail with large pointed crest, boldly spotted underparts. Sub-species variable as to size and coloration. Head and neck, whitish spot on side of head bordered by black or rufous stripe. Crest, white or pale buff, sometimes darker, feathers curved forward. Crown, white or pale buff. Forehead, spotted black and white. Beak, black. Eyes, brown iris. Throat, white, buff, or cinnamon sometimes spotted with black. Nape, tawny or cinnamon spotted: with black. Upper back, tawny buff, or brown with black spotted pattern, finely mottled gray. Middle back, same as upper back. Rump, patterned white. Breast, white, buff, cinnamon, dark spots making strong pattern. Abdomen, buffy. Flanks, mottled with black. Upper tail coverts, edged with black. Under tail coverts, buffy. Wings, edged with terminal black spots, feathers often edged with white. Legs and feet, clean legged, pale bluish gray. Size, 178-216 mm (Blake, 1977).

There are many more of these delightful birds available now as they have introduced some new blood. The bird breeders' that have them like them very much. They handle them like any other quail and take measures to overcome their nervous nature. When the birds mature, they become quite tame and show their beauty off more easily. It is hard really to appreciate the intricate coloring of these birds with their running up and down the edge of a pen. Really to enjoy them one must spend some time watching them.

I wish they raised more of these to ensure that they not become scarce and inbred. "Everyone should have a pair of these quail."

The Mountain Quail

(Oreortyx pictus) Douglas 1929

PLATE A

PLATE B

Probably one of the most striking of all the members of the quail family is the Mountain quail. It is by far the largest and has some of the most desirable characteristics of any quail kept in captivity. The Mountain quail is also known as Codorniz de montana, Mountain partridge, Painted quail, Plumed quail, and San Pedro quail.

An interesting thing about Mountain quail is the way the eggs hatch. We get hatches over a three day period which is unusual for any member of the quail family. Usually these birds pop right out of the egg. Another thing about Mountain quail is their reputation for not being regular producers. This is certainly true in the wild and most breeders have found they have an *"off year"* with these birds. The thing that most of us blame is the weather and I suppose that there is a lot of truth in that. Apparently, experience of the breeder has nothing to do with it. Bob Tybie of California is one of the most competent quail breeders today and just this week he wrote to say his birds did not do well this year while last year he got over 1000 eggs with high fertility.

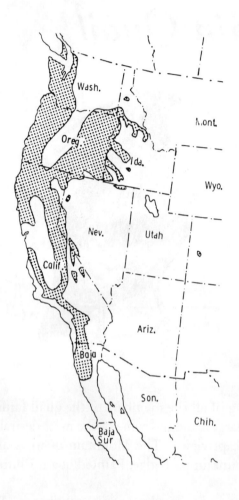

Range of the Mountain quail
(according to Johnsgard)

Implants have been successful in
Washington and Canada

Johnsgard lists the following subspecies:

O. p. pictus (Douglas): Sierra Mountain quail. Resident in mountain regions of extreme western Nevada west to the west side of the Cascade Range in southern Washington and south to the Sierra Nevada and inner Coast ranges of California.

O. p. palmeri (Oberholser): Coast Mountain quail. Resident from southwestern Washington south through western Oregon to northwestern San Luis Obispo County, California. Also, in southern Vancouver Island, British Columbia.

94   Some Favorite Quail

O. p. confinis (Anthony): San Pedro Mountain quail. Resident in lower California in the Sierra Juarez and Sierra San Pedro Martir.

O.p. eremophila (van Rossem): Desert Mountain quail. Resident in the mountains of southern and west central California in the Sierra Nevada south to the Baja California boundary and somewhat beyond and in extreme southwestern Nevada.

O. p. russelli (Miller): Pallid Mountain quail. Resident in the Little San Bernardino Mountains in Riverside and San Bernardino counties, California.

Description

Adults, 10.6-11.5 inches long. The sexes are very similar in appearance. This relatively large Western quail differs from all others in that both sexes have straight, narrow, and blackish crests composed of only two feathers, which appear with the juvenal plumage. The throat is chestnut, edged with black, and this is separated from the slate gray chest, neck, and head by a white line. Otherwise, the birds are plain olive gray on the back, wings, and tail. The flanks are a rich, dark brown, with conspicuous vertically oriented black and white bars (Johnsgard, 1973).

Management

One of the great things about our hobby is the fact that *"we never learn it all!"* In reality our birds become our tutors and show us many mysteries of life. I think, we learn more from birds when we specialize in a few species. In keeping with this conviction, we only had one species of quail in 1985 . . . *the Mountain quail.*

We chose the Mountain quail and kept only the Sierra race because they are larger, more brightly colored, and easier to sex using the *"nape method."* Using this method is relatively easy. The females' nape (back of the neck) has a brown colored area that goes up to the base of her scull. This is not always true, however, as many less mature birds never show this color distinction the first year. The males have a clear blue nape with no brown coloration. Again, this is not always true the first year. In fact, a few of the birds do not distinctly show this difference and we had to make an *"educated guess"* on what sex they were. The males usually have a heavier built head while the females often have a more delicate look about their head. Our stock has been bred for many generations in captivity which perhaps explains their very large size. To keep a good strong gene-pool we bred into our stock new blood every three or four years.

Hatching and Brooding

"Apparently there is no best way to hatch quail eggs. Some people swear by incubators; others by their favorite breed of bantam hen. I prefer the latter. By careful selection, I have produced a rather small run-of-the-barnyard bantam hen that averaged 415 grams by weight, and are excellent broodies. Rarely do they fail to give me a chick when I give them a fertile, hatchable egg. I don't mean to say that I never use incubators. I do. In fact, I start all of my eggs in a forced air incubator, but as soon as they can be candled, I transfer the good ones to the bantam hen where they stay until pipping begins. Then, the eggs go back to the incubator for hatching. This last move is primarily to avoid the ants (California is full of ants) which are death on hatching quail. Once the chicks are hatched and dry, they go back to Mama hen and most of my worries are over for the brood. Plenty of fresh vitamin-filled water, hard boiled egg yolk twice a day, a high protein game bird mix, and fresh lettuce are a must for starting my birds" (Orr, 1979).

We have found that smaller groups of chicks seem to do best. We use the debeaker to control cannabism and toe picking. Mountains are very bad about this and entire hatches have been lost to this terrible habit. Along with dulling the bills we use alfalfa hay in the bottom of the boxes extensively. We never put more than 18 chicks in each brooder box. I guess the temptation is too great to bite if the group is large. When the chicks are older, we do group them into groups of about 45 chicks. Great care must be exercised when putting different groups together or else the group whose territory is invaded will defend their property and losses will occur.

"We use a double socket in each brooder, using one 25-watt white light bulb and one 25-watt red bulb. The red bulb supplies the heat as the white bulb does not give off enough heat. Each brooder box is covered over about two-thirds of the way, depending on the weather. Watch closely the first couple weeks or so, for Mountain quail are sometimes notorious toe pickers. If toe picking does start to occur, we turn off the white light bulb, and it usually stops. We turn on the white bulb only when feeding the egg yolk and lettuce or worms, turning off when they are finished eating.

After a few days they become accustomed to the red bulb, and the white bulb can be stopped completely. Mountain quail never seem to feather pick as other game birds do" (Tybie, 1975).

One Breeder's Methods

"Mountain quail are not hard to raise once you get them hatched. But sometimes it is difficult to get them to lay fertile eggs, and hatching the eggs is a matter of personal preference I suppose. My hatching method is a bit unorthodox, but it seems to work for me. I use a forced air incubator set at 99 ¾° F. with the hygrometer wet bulb reading of 86° F. for the first seven to eight days and then candle the eggs and transfer the fertile ones to a banty hen to finish the job for me and to do the brooding. Humidity control is so difficult in my hot dry climate that I just don't trust incubators, so I rely heavily on my broody bantams.

With a good high protein food (27-28%) sprinkled generously with vitamins and electrolytes, lots of hard-boiled egg yolk, and some chopped lettuce occasionally, you'll rarely lose a young bird. Year old birds are something else they are especially susceptible to crop worms, and I have had only limited success with the prescribed remedies. Once a bird is far enough along to recognize the symptoms, it is frequently too late, and if the bird has already assumed the upright stance that you would associate with a penguin, you may as well bury it! I have used Piperzine, Wormal, Hygromycin, and Tramisol. None of these does the job that you would hope for, and since these worms are transmitted either directly or through an intermediate host, (such as earth worm etc.) strict sanitation including wire floors is probably your best bet. Fresh, clean water daily is important.

One thing I've learned about getting fertile eggs in the last couple of years is that large colony pens are better than smaller single pair pens. Last year of the 101 eggs from colony pens, 95% were fertile while only 13 of 32 were fertile from the smaller pens. This year 35 of 41 were good from colony pens, while a dismal 4 of 24 were fertile from individual pairs.

The ratio of males to hens in large pens is much less critical than in smaller areas. I just put all the birds that I plan to keep in a colony group in a 40 by 140 feet open pen and let nature do whatever it is that nature does, and wait for the egg laying to start.

There are a few things that you need to be especially mindful of in large areas. Watch for snakes, mice, rats, cats, coons, skunks, weasels, hawks, and owls. Snakes *can be the greatest hazard where eggs are concerned, so gather them as often as you can, at least four or five times a day. Besides animal predation, it is best not to allow eggs to be exposed to the direct sun for any length of time because the eggs can easily be ruined. Similarly, in large areas it is advisable to keep the flight feathers of one wing clipped to restrict flight to short distances. Contrary to what you might have heard, even the fabric netting that some of us are using now won't keep them from breaking their necks when they hit it at full flight, especially if they hit the nets at a sharp angle"* (Orr, 1984).

Some Final Thoughts

We have had many different species of quail through the years, and have enjoyed each of them immensely. I must say with all candidness, the Mountain quail is one of our favorites. It has a special charm about it that none of the others have. Well, to tell you the truth, I can't put my finger on the exact reason we like them. The very fact that they are **quail** makes us terribly prejudiced!

Mountain quail

The Blue Scale Quail

(Callipepla squamata) Vigors 1830

I first met it in the panhandle of Texas. This was many years ago but I still remember this "first introduction" as if it were yesterday. The carriage of this bird is one of its unique characteristics. Also, rather than sporting a distinct plume like some of its cousins, the Blue Scaled quail has an attractive crest that is topped by a white or light patch of feathers. Many people call this quail *"Cotton Top"* which is an appropriate name. It is also known as the *Blue Racer, Blue quail, or Top-knot quail.*

Our nickname for this quail is *"springs,"* as their call to us resembles the noise a spring makes. They have a habit of getting up on any high object and making their call. When the males call they fluff up their feathers and look twice as big as they really are. I like to hear them. A trick we use to get our birds to *"call"* is to place an extra bird in a pen that is out of sight of others of the same species. They will call back and forth to one another. I do believe they have a language all their own which is another story.

Johnsgard lists the subspecies and a distribution map:

C. s. squamata: Mexican scaled quail. Resident in Mexico from northern Sonora and Tamaulipas south to the Valley of Mexico.

C. s. pallida Brewster: Arizona scaled quail. Resident from northern Sonora and Chihuahua north to Arizona, New Mexico, Colorado, Kansas, Oklahoma, and western Texas; introduced into central Washington and Nevada.

C. s. castanogastris Brewster: Chestnut-bellied scaled quail. Resident in southern Texas south through Tamaulipas, Nuevo Leon, and eastern Coahuila, Mexico.

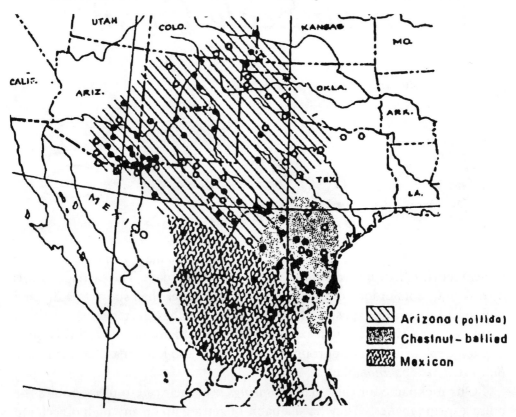

Arizona (pallida)
Chestnut-bellied
Mexican

Description

The Blue Scale is about 10½ inches long at maturity. The sexes are almost identical in plumage color. Their name comes from the delicate scale markings in their plumage which varies from slate blue to grayish in color. Both sexes have the cotton-topped crest. Males can be detected from females by the plain brownish chin coloration. The females will have light pin stripes in the chin area (Johnsgard, 1973).

A very popular subspecies of the Blue Scale is the *Chestnut-bellied Blue Scale*. The chestnut markings on the bellies are most evident on the males, but the females have the coloration also. This chestnut can be described as a burnt red color, and it sets off the slate blue color in a striking way. Some individuals do not have as much chestnut color as others. I have had some hens that were exactly like the normal Blue Scale, but they carried the genes, as their offspring were the chestnut-bellied variety.

Some breeders much prefer the Chestnut-Bellied Blue Scale. However, personal preference would be the determining factor. I like the "blue" coloration in the scale pattern of these birds. Besides being very beautiful in a "unique" way, they have wonderful personalities. They, like the other desert quail, are very verbal. This personality trait is a plus in having these wonderful birds around.

Raising Blue Scale Quail

Some people dislike this quail because of their nervous disposition. They are like the Gambel and the California Valley quail because they are an active, nervous, and somewhat timid bird. Although they are suspicious, I have found they can be tamed down and will come over to the fence for a treat of mixed grain. They have not yet eaten out of my hand but with a little patience and tender-loving-care they should tame down and become real friends.

Generally, Blue Scale quail are very good layers. One season, two of our hens, each laid over sixty eggs. The eggs are larger than the Bobwhite and are not so pointed on the little end. They are colored with light to dark brown spots that seem to be irregular. I have observed that the same hen will lay egg after egg that has the same color pattern. The eggs hatch best for me in a dry incubator. I run my forced air incubator at 83° F. wet bulb temperature. The dry bulb stays at almost 100° F.

I have found that the key to raising Blues is a large pen if you can put them on the ground. Blues can be raised on wire, but if your climate is dry and your soil is light, I would recommend they be put on the ground at least during the breeding season. My pens were 20 feet long by 8 feet wide. This size allows the birds to get plenty of exercise running up and down the pen. The pens were outside and unheated even in below zero weather. They like to roost off the ground in brush placed in the pens. I was afraid toes and feet would freeze, but no problem was observed. They had a place to get out of the weather (shelter) but would prefer to roost out in the open air. I worried about them when the temperature got 20° F. below zero.

Finally, I decided that I had done my duty and if they wanted to roost outside, that was up to them. We have had this same experience with other species of upland game birds. Ringneck pheasants in cold Montana about worried me sick until I got used to the idea of them running the show. If the birds want to be inside, they will go inside the enclosure.

Always get birds from at least three sources when you get into a new variety. This gives a good fresh blood to work with, and you do not have to worry about inbreeding. It also gives those who buy the young birds the knowledge that they not buying a brother and sister to mate together. Blues, like other quail, cannot take inbreeding for very long. Very soon the signs of inbreeding begin to show up. Infertility and lack of vitality are the most serious. Of course, the nature and conformation of the breed will gradually change as inbreeding gets its terrible grip on the stock.

Blue Scales are not aggressive. At least this was true with ours. I never saw them fight among themselves even during the breeding season and never saw them quarrel with their neighbors. I would not be afraid to put Blues with anything since the *"anything"* would not hurt them.

These quail are very susceptible to enteritis which must be prevented to keep them alive. We use a medication containing *"bacitracin"* which is extremely successful in preventing enteritis.

Sexing

Perhaps I should comment on the problem of sexing the Blues. The experienced breeder can tells the sexes by comparing the head of the birds. The head of the mature male will be more massive in appearance and will just have a *"masculine"* look. Heads of the mature female will not be as large, and the bill will be more delicate and feminine. If the heads do not give you a clue, then look at the throat. To examine the throat feathers, it is necessary to catch the bird. It is impossible to tell about the throat feathers while the birds are running up and down the pens. The hens will have tiny pin stripes while the male will have a clear bluish chin patch.

Do not be fooled by the size of the cotton top. Immature birds are very difficult to sex even by the *"throat patch"* method, as the last feathers to molt are those on and about the head. In this case, the breeder must be patient until the bird has reached maturity.

The Benson Quail

(Callipepla douglasii) Vigors 1829

There are at least three common names given to this bird by those who know it. This little quail is a "jewel" regardless of which name is used. Some authorities use "Benson," some "Elegant", while others use "Douglas" as a name. I suppose that for practical purposes all three names could apply to the same bird. Technically, the different names describe the nominate race and subspecies which come from different geographical locations in Mexico. From what I can determine, there is so little difference between the subspecies that it really does not matter which name is used. It is just a matter of choosing the name that you like. It probably would help if all of us used the same name so there would be no confusions which bird was being discussed. Since it appears that BENSON is the most commonly used name, I will use it.

Johnsgard gives these subspecies:

C. d. douglasii: Douglas elegant quail. Resident in extreme southern Sonora, south through Sinaloa and northwestern Durango.

C. d. bensoni (Ridgway): Benson elegant quail. Resident in Sonora, from close to its northern boundary to Guaymas and San Javier.

C. d. teres (Friedmann): Jalisco elegant quail. Resident in northwestern Jalisco, but not extending to Colima.

C. d. impedita (Friedmann): Nayarit elegant quail. Resident in Nayarit.quail

C. d. languens (Friedmann): Chihuahua elegant quail. Known only from western Chihuahua (Johnsgard, 1973).

Description

Male: Head gray, streaked with black on forehead and sides, speckled or dotted with black on the throat. Bushy, pale reddish crest. Sides and back of neck reddish brown flecked with gray. Back, rump, and tail gray. Wings brown, heavily mottled with russet and a little white on the coverts. Chest gray. Breast and abdomen gray with round white spots, large toward the rear. Sides streaked reddish brown and gray elongated spots. Under tail coverts dusky brown edged with tawny. Bill and feet blackish.

Female: Plumage mostly mottled grays and browns dorsally, with small dusky crest sometimes streaked with brown. Under parts gray with round white spots. Bill and feet blackish. Measurements: folded wing 106-115 mm.; tail 66-94 mm.; bill 13-16 mm.; tarsus 29-33 mm. Weight 160-190 gm. Males slightly larger than females (Leopold, 1972).

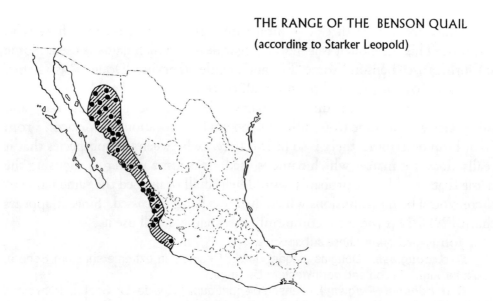

THE RANGE OF THE BENSON QUAIL

(according to Starker Leopold)

The first Benson quail that I personally saw were in the pens of a breeder in Arizona. He had long poles across the tops of the large walk-in ground pen. The birds were nervous and chattering and running along these poles. They did not try to fly but one could tell they were not too happy about being admired.

These birds had a red-orange tint to their feathers and the crest feathers were yellow-orange. They were quite a sight to see. This was many years ago and there were not that many Benson quail around. Right then and there I decided that I wanted to get some of these marvelous little quail someday. I am still waiting for that day.

Maybe another word about inbreeding should be said here. The captive Benson quail population went down hill to the point that very few fertile eggs were being laid all because of inbreeding. As a matter of fact, they almost died out in captivity until someone brought in some new blood. As of this writing breeders are telling me that they are getting 100% fertility and very strong and vigorous chicks hatching. Let's be careful of our pairing of our birds.

The demand for this bird is far greater than the supply, thus making the cost of the few birds available highly inflated. In 1985 there was some new blood introduced which turned around the status of this bird in captivity. The breeders that have this new blood are reporting 100% fertility and hatches, suggesting that inbreeding is no longer a problem with their birds.

Nervous Disposition

As with most of the desert quail (Gambel's, California Valley, Blue Scale, etc.) the Benson quail is rather nervous. They need a large space so they can get well away from anything that is a threat. These birds do best in long narrow pens where they can get away and feel secure.

Since quail are very susceptible to several diseases, to be successful I feel that besides a good program of sanitation, regular medication must be used. Coccidioses is a threat and must be controlled especially in young maturing birds. We use preventive medication with our birds. Some medication to combat "Enteritis" is essential. (Any commercial medication containing "bacitracin" is very effective) A program of giving worm medication should also be used, especially if the birds are kept on the ground. It is advisable to keep these birds on wire if possible.

Hatching and Rearing

Benson chicks can be handled like any of the other quail chicks. The **ASSEMBLY LINE METHOD** can be adapted to this quail. Extra precautions should be made to prevent some of their bad habits such as toe picking. This species is one that requires some experience to be successful (or a good dose of luck?). Not for beginners, the Benson offers not only a challenge but a reward to those who are successful in its propagation.

Mr. Joe Weeks, from Georgia, has raised many of these birds. He says, *"I have spent a lot of time and hard work trying to help keep the Douglas or Benson quail from dying out in captivity . . . I have been raising this attractive little quail for 15 years or more now. They are making a good comeback now in captivity.*

From my experience in Georgia, they seem to do very well in this part of the country and like most other quail probably get along fine under most conditions.

Benson quail especially need protection from damp, cold weather and frost in the winter. They seem to do better for me paired in pens 3X8 feet or 4X6 feet with a sand box and nest box. They like a place up high to roost and from which they can see out into the other pens. I put a round pole and a few tree limbs in each pen for them to perch and climb around on. This seems to make them feel more secure, and a calm, more relaxed bird makes a better breeder" (Weeks, 1986).

Benson quail are still rather expensive, but as more are produced the prices should come down. Prices of upland game birds are controlled by the free market of "supply and demand." This means that prices will vary from year to year depending on how many are raised.

THE GAMBEL'S QUAIL

(Callipepla gambelii)

The desert quail of the Southwest called the Gambel's probably has received more publicity than any other quail. His voice is the one that is heard in the background of the Western movies that are filmed in Arizona. From the quiet scenes around the campfire, to the scene in the gigantic canyon, one often hears the call of this quail. It sounds much the same as its cousin the California Valley quail but it has a clearer and deeper call. Movies filmed in Southern California probably *"star"* the California Valley quail for sound effects. The Gambel's is the favorite of many people. Not only are they attractive, but they are very verbal which gives them much character.

We have purposefully separated them so they would have *"discussions about the situation"* on which we could eavesdrop. The Gambel's quail has a very outstanding personality which makes it stand out among the crowd. One of these days someone will come up with a way to understand all of their "chattering".

Johnsgard lists the subspecies as follows:

C. g. gambelii: Southwestern Gambel's quail. Resident from southern Utah and southern Nevada south to the Colorado and Mojave deserts, northeastern Baja California, and introduced in north central Idaho.

C. g. fulvipectus Nelson: Fulvous-breasted Gambel's quail. Resident in north central to southwestern Sonora, and probable north to southeastern Arizona and southwestern New Mexico.

C. g. pembertoni (van Rossem): Tiburon Island Gambel's quail. Resident on Tiburon Island, Gulf of California.

C. g. sana (Mearns): Colorado Gambel's quail. Resident in western Colorado in the drainage areas the Uncompahgre, Gunnison, and Rio Grande rivers.

C. g. ignoscens (Friedmann): Texas Gambel's quail. Resident of desert areas in southern New Mexico and extreme western Texas.

C. g. stephensi (Phillips): Recently described (1959). Resident in Sonora, near the Sinaloa border (not yet verified).

quail**C. g. friedmanni (Moore):** Sinaloa Gambel's quail. Resident in coastal Sinaloa from Rio Fuerte south to Rio Culiacan (Johnsgard, 1973).

Description

The Gambel's quail may be confused with its cousin, the California Valley quail, but is slightly larger and has a different color pattern on its sides and breast. This beautiful quail has a black teardrop-shaped plume or crest which is carried forward on the head. It lacks completely the scale pattern found on the Valley quail. The males have a distinct red crest and black throat lined with a white border. The hens are drab grayish and lack the red or black in the head area. The call is similar to the Valley quail. My Gambel's have called up wild Valley quail to their pens, which leads me to conclude they can *"talk"*.

The Gambel's quail is a native desert quail of the Southwest. It is also called the **Arizona quail, Desert quail, Codorniz de Gambel, and Olanthe quail.** In the winter, very large numbers of these birds group together. I have seen as many as 150 to 200 in a covey north of the Phoenix area in Arizona. This was really a thrill to see these little quail come out from every little sprig of grass and cactus. Their range is from southern Nevada, southern Utah, and western Colorado south to northeastern Baja California, central Sonora, northwestern Chihuahua, and western Texas.

THE RANGE OF THE GAMBEL'S QUAIL
(according to Paul Johnsgard)

The Gambel's range overlaps with the
California Valley quail

In the wild, Gambel's quail are very prolific where the right conditions exist. Mating begins in April and continues until July. The Gambel's hen is among the most adept at concealing her nest of eggs. They are placed on the ground, usually beneath brush or grass clumps. The hen sits very close to the nest containing usually 12 to 14 eggs. If driven from the nest the hen will nest again two or three times, stopping only when it would be impossible to rear a covey before the onset of cold weather. This is reflected in their laying capacity in captivity which is probably beaten only by the Bobwhite.

The eggs are quite varied with the ground color ranging from light cream to dark tan, and the dots and splotches from reddish-tan to russet. The pattern laid by each hen is distinctive and may be identified from all other. The cock bird is not interested in helping with the incubation, but he is an excellent guard, watching from an outpost some twenty yards away (White, 1957).

Some Favorite Quail   109

The Gambel's offers the quail breeder an opportunity to discover the delights of easy propagation. It is prolific, and the hens will lay lots of eggs with a good fertility rate.

Pens

We have found that this quail does best when kept on the ground in large oblong pens. The type of pen has much to do with its well-being. Our pens are long and narrow which gives the birds a chance to run up and down the fence. This gives them the exercise they need and enjoy, while they have a chance to run off their high energy. These birds are highly nervous and active as a general rule. They will come to the hand for feed but are rather timid by nature.

To find out what breeding conditions work the best for Gambel's, we did some research one breeding season. We put three cock birds and five hens together in a breeding unit. In another, we put a trio, and in another, one pair. To our amazement the pen with the group of birds had trouble. One of the cock birds was killed by the others which left two cock birds to five hens. At the end of the laying season, it was discovered that the group matings did not produce as many fertile eggs as the pair mating. The pair laid 63 fertile eggs (plus five infertiles at the end of the season) while the group matings produced less than ½ the eggs with a corresponding ½ fertility. We thus concluded that while it is possible to colony mate them, they do much better in pairs.

These quail have maintained their popularity through the years. I know many breeders' that just have a pair or two around to enjoy them. One man called this week to say he had two pairs that laid over 80 eggs and were still laying.

Aggressive and Hardy

The aggressive nature of the cock birds and hens was a surprise to me. Any new bird that was introduced into a pen anytime during the year except during the winter months, when they naturally group in coveys, was harassed and in some cases killed. We soon learned not to introduce new birds because of this aggressive nature.

Gambel's quail are very hardy and seem to have disease resistance when mature. We are careful to avoid Coccidiosis and parasitic worms. Pen and cage cleanliness is very important in avoiding disease and parasites.

We found that Gambel's eggs hatched much better with a lower humidity. The hygrometer wet bulb was kept at 83° F. This is fine for a dry climate and high altitude. If the humidity is any higher the chicks seem to grow too large in the egg to turn while hatching. We mixed birds from three sources to get unrelated blood. Much care not to mate brother and sister, which would soon inbreed the stock, is taken on our farm.

The Gambel's quail is a great bird to have around. We enjoy their call early in the morning and late evening. It reminds us of the open desert. Gambel's are very verbal (like the California Valley and the Blue Scale quail). If you like your quail to talk try the following: separate the birds into pens across from one another where the birds can get up high and see each other. They will call back and forth and really talk over the daily news. This is a great way to enjoy your birds.

I am very impressed with several of the aviaries that I have visited which have been built for enjoyment of the birds. Rather than build the pens for the keeper, they are built for the comfort and well-being of the inhabitants. It is a great joy to see a farm built with the birds in mind.

Gambel's are easy to raise and can be tamed down a great deal with lots of gentle kindness. They are a favorite of many people including the writers.

We got our start with these birds by ordering eggs from a breeder in another state. We purchased 25 hatching eggs and to our amazement the breeder sent 26 with one cracked. To make the story still more astounding, we hatched all 25 of the eggs! This proved to be a cheap way to get a start of these lively birds. To be sure, I have ordered other hatching eggs and gotten very poor hatches. There is a risk in buying hatching eggs. There is a risk in selling hatching eggs. Because of these risks many breeders will not sell hatching eggs. They certainly will not sell any of the more rare birds in the form of hatching eggs.

If you have not yet tried any of these smart looking birds—do so. You will enjoy them I am sure.

A male California Valley Quail photographed in the wild by Lincoln Allen.

The California

Valley Quail

(Callipepla californicus)

Of all the birds native to the state of California, none is more universally enjoyed and appreciated than the California Valley quail. The handsome plumage, pert demeanor, and melodious calls are appealing to everyone fortunate enough to know the species, and it is not surprising that in 1931 the State Legislature by unanimous acclamation declared the California quail to be the State Bird of California (Leopold, 1977). Many names have been given to this attractive bird. Some of these are: California partridge, Catalina quail, Codorniz California, Crested quail, San Lucas quail, San Quintin quail, Topknot quail and Valley quail. Whatever name you use, next to the Bobwhite family, it is one of the most widely distributed quail in the Americas.

It is known commonly in California as the Valley quail, to distinguish it from the Mountain quail of the higher lands; but ornithologists now recognize two subspecies, the California quail and the Valley quail, both entirely distinct from the Mountain quail (Forbush, 1917).

The range of this quail is made up of varied topography and climatical conditions. It is found from Baja California, Mexico, up through the western states into Canada. Its eastward range goes as far as Nevada, Utah and Idaho with introductions in Colorado. This makes its range larger than any other desert quail probably because of its ability to adapt to varied conditions.

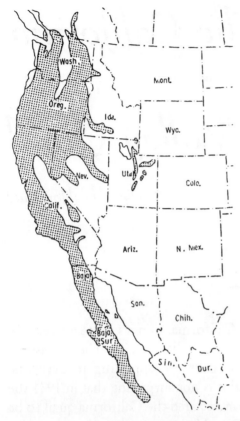

THE RANGE OF THE CALIFORNIA VALLEY QUAIL
(according to Johnsgard)

The range has been extended through successful implantations

A female Valley quail

As many as eight races have been named and described. All are very much alike. It is believed that the nearest relative is the famous Gambel's quail found in the Southwest. The uninformed can easily get the two confused. The difference that can be easily determined in the field, as the males of the California quail have a whitish rather than blackish forehead, have no black abdomen patch and have a scaled breast. The hens are quite alike but can easily be separated at maturity.

This quail is very colorful which adds to its popularity with breeders. The California quail is easily propagated and is found in many collections all over the world.

Subspecies

C. c. californica: Valley California quail. Resident from northern Oregon and western Nevada south to southern California and Los Coronados Islands of Baja California. Introduced in eastern Washington, central British Columbia, western Idaho, Oregon, Utah, and Colorado.

C. c. catalinensis **(Grinnell):** Catalina Island California quail. Resident on Santa Catalina Island and introduced on Santa Rosa and Santa Cruz islands, southern California.

C. c. plumbea **(Grinnell):** San Quintin California quail. Resident from San Diego County, California, through northwestern Baja California, Mexico.

C. c. achrustera **(Peters):** San Lucas California quail. Resident in southern Baja California, Mexico.

C. c. canfieldae **(van Rossem):** Inyo California quail. Resident in Owens River valley in east central California.

C. c. orecta **(Oberholser):** Great Basin California quail. Resident in the Warner Valley, southeastern Oregon.

C. c. decoloratus **(van Rossem):** Baja California quail. Resident in Baja California from 30° degrees north latitude to about 25° degrees north latitude.

C. c. brunnescens **Ridgway:** Coastal California quail. Resident in the humid coast area of California from near the Oregon boundary south to southern Santa Cruz County. Introduced on Vancouver Island, British Columbia.

Description

Adults 9½ to 11 inches long. This widespread quail of the western foothills resembles the Gambel's Quail inasmuch as both sexes have forward-tilting, blackish crests that are enlarged terminally into a *"comma"* or *"teardrop"* shape. Both sexes also have clear bluish gray to gray chests that become buffy toward the abdomen and have darker *"scaly"* markings reminiscent of scales. The flanks are brownish gray with lighter shaft-streaks, and the upper parts are generally gray to brownish gray, intricately marked with darker scaly markings. Males have black throats and a chestnut-tinged abdomen and are chocolate brown behind the plume, while the area in front of the eyes and above the bill is whitish. Females have dark brown rather than black crests and lack black throats. Immatures have buff-tipped greater primary coverts for the first year, and their outer two primaries are relatively pointed and frayed (Johnsgard, 1973).

A Typical Quail Day

This quail is highly gregarious during the "non-breeding" season. It spends most of the year in large coveys which seek daily feed and water as large groups. During the breeding season, the unit is the family. This family usually consists of the parents and any young which may survive natural predation. As the season progresses the little ones get fewer and fewer in number as they become victims of daily losses from predation. When very young, the chicks can all be lost by a sudden cool rain shower if they get wet and chill.

One of the striking social habits of the California quail is the sentry duty performed by cock birds throughout the year. When a pair withdraws from the covey and goes about the business of nesting, the cock bird becomes increasingly watchful for any possible threat to its mate, spending much time standing motionless, while the hen feeds or constructs her nest. This solicitous activity intensifies during the nesting period to the point where the cock bird spends relatively little time feeding and much time on the alert (Leopold 1977).

The parents and what young survive the early days make up the covey. As the families meet in their daily search for food they soon join up into larger coveys, and near the fall this may number several hundred individuals. As many as 600 birds have been observed in one covey. Probably the average covey would be under 100 birds. I have seen some coveys as small as six or eight birds. Apparently, the available feed and size of hatch determines the size of the coveys. During one winter when heavy snow had been on the ground for weeks, a large covey of these birds came to visit our Mountain quail. At that time we had several hundred of them in large pens. I cannot tell you the "sinking" feeling we had when we first saw all of those quail running around loose! We, of course, soon discovered that they were not our Mountain quail out for a stroll in the snow. We put out grain for our guests and they stayed with us for about three days and then moved on. What a beautiful experience! We still often talk about the feelings we had that day when we thought that we had lost all of our Mountain quail.

Each covey has its fixed range where it forages for food and roosts at night. This range will change when the food and water source changes. Early in the morning the covey goes out and fills up on food which consists of seeds when available and vegetable matter. After feeding, the birds make their way to the water where each one drinks. This is really a sight to see when they water at a pond. Each one finds a place along the bank to drink, and the edge of the water is lined with bobbing heads as they drink one beak full at a time. The day is spent preening and dusting near scrub cover or near the shelter of some thicket. It appears that the birds avoid very heavy cover by remaining on the edge of thickets. Late in the afternoon the covey makes its way back out to feed and fill their crops once again before drinking and going to roost. They spend the night in trees or small brush rather than staying on the ground. As the birds select their roosting place there is much chattering and talking. One wonders what they are discussing as they really get into the conversation with vigor. Such is the typical day in the life of typical California Valley quail.

Very Adaptable

History has proven that the species that can adapt to changes are the ones that survive. A very interesting quality about the California Valley quail, is the fact that it can survive in very extreme conditions. However, the one element that must be present for its survival is water. In extreme drought conditions the California Valley, among other quail, has been known to skip the reproduction cycle because of the lack of water and green vegetation necessary for the chicks to survive. Many of these quail have been known to die off during these extreme conditions, but because of their fast reproduction cycle they soon come back to the full number the area can support.

The California Department of Fish and Game has built underground holding tanks to catch the run-off rain water in the dry areas making it available to quail when they need it. It is reported that areas that had no quail populations before, now have birds due to this water source.

In western Oregon and Washington this quail is abundant. They have been able to adapt to the high amount of rainfall and have become well established. From the hot, dry desert to the rain soaked coast and even to the high desert this bird survives. In central Oregon, the California quail is the only one that can survive the climate. It can take the very cold winters and the hot summers. Many have tried to stock the Bobwhite in this area, but they cannot survive the conditions, yet the California quail appears to be here permanently. This is a marvelous example of what Nature can do with a species. Everyone that is familiar with this little quail is delighted that it has managed to survive in the desert conditions. What a great addition to the natural beauty of the wilderness and the populated areas! "May his tribe live on forever!"

Easy To Propagate

In captivity, the California quail is one of the easier quail to get to breed. They are by nature very nervous and thus do not do as well in small cages as some of the other quail. I believe they do much better on the ground if you have the drier climate conditions or if you make dry ground available for them. Many are raised on wire every year so there is no hard rule about them.

The chicks should be handled like any other quail. I have found them to be easy to raise and learn quickly to eat and drink. Once they reach maturity they seem to be hardy and disease resistant. The normal precautions should be made while raising them to avoid disease problems. We put an antibiotic product in their water to give them a good start, and then when they will be under stress add a little to their water.

When handling the adult breeders never add an odd bird to a colony or pair because the newcomer will be killed. They are pugnacious to outsiders during the mating season, but during the winter months they can be mixed with other birds with no trouble as they stay out of the way and are not at all aggressive.

Male and female
Valley Quail.

The Mearns Quail

(Cytonyx montezuma) Vigors 1830

PLATE B

One of the most sought after quail in North America is the Mearns. It sometimes is confused with another popular quail also sometimes called the Harlequin. The African Harlequin is not the Mearns Harlequin. The African Harlequin comes from South Africa while the Mearns comes from the southern United States and Mexico.

The confusing factor is that the Mearns has many names. It is called the Harlequin quail, Black quail, Cincoreal quail, Codorniz Encinara, Codorniz Pinta, (Pinto), crazy quail, fools hen, Massena quail, Mearns quail, Montezuma quail, Painted quail, Squat quail and many more. It could have more names than any other quail. Whatever name you use, it is the most adorable little quail that I know of. *"A rose by any other name is still a rose."*

Description

Mearns are the most unusual of the New World quail. They look like a committee put them together, as they are out of proportion when compared to any other quail. Their heads are extra large, and their eyes are big and compelling when they give you their famous *"melt your heart stare"*. The male has a bold black and white face and neck with feathers that form a hood over the back of his head down over the nape. The upper parts are marked with black, white and tan with a blend of gray and olive brown. The back and wings are streaked, mottled with elongated buff color. The sides and flanks are prominent with white spots lined with bluish black, The center line of the breast is a rich chestnut brown turning into coal black on the abdomen between his legs. It is about 8 to 9 ½ inches long at maturity.

The female is generally mottled with chestnut brown to gray. She has a crest and over-sized head and is generally not as outstanding as the male. My females had a light patch under the large eye giving them a very pretty facial expression. They appear to be squinting as if in bright sun light. The overall breast is shaded with a very beautiful pinkish cast. The color of the Mearns cannot adequately be described and needs to be seen to be appreciated (Leopold, 1972).

There are several subspecies of the **Mearns quail**. Some authorities list as many as five subspecies, but others question this many.

The Mearns quail subspecies:

C. m. montezumae: Massena Harlequin quail. Resident from Michoacan, Oaxaca, Distrito Federal, Hidalgo, and Puebla to Nuevo Leon and west central Tamaulipas.

C. m. mearnsi Nelson: Mearns Harlequin quail. Resident in western central Texas, central New Mexico, and central Arizona south to northwestern Mexico, including northern Coahuila.

C. m. merriami Nelson: Merriam Harlequin quail. Known only from the eastern slope of Mount Orizaba, Veracruz.

C. m. sallei Verreaux: Salle Harlequin quail. Resident from Michoacan south through Guerrero to east central Oaxaca.

quail**C. m. rowleyi Phillips:** Recently described from Guerrero (1966); not yet verified (Leopold, 1972).

In my opinion, the Mearns quail is the most interesting and beautiful of the gallinaceous birds, rivaling even the stately Mountain quail. The Mearns is always found in or near pine-oak growths where they keep busy digging and eating herbaceous bulbs. Without these bulbs the Mearns apparently cannot survive. It is said that populations of Mearns have disappeared when the range is grazed off by hungry cattle. The grasses that harbor insects are gone and thus a staple of the diet of the Mearns is gone too. Since the grazing of the habitat prejudices the welfare of the quail, it could be that in years to come the quail may die out in certain areas.

A male Mearns

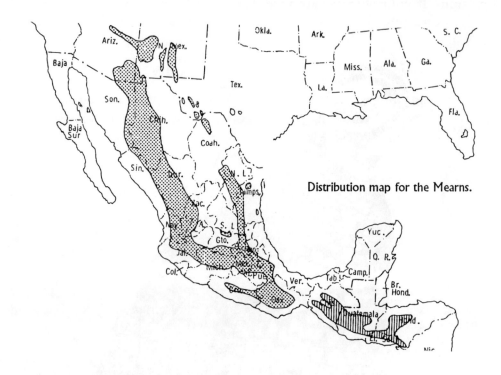

Distribution map for the Mearns.

An interesting phenomenon about the Mearns that are in captivity, is that there are very few females produced in given years. One breeder raised 24 males from two pairs one season. The next, he got no females either. The third year he did manage to get two females. When new blood was introduced, females were again produced at a ratio more than males. This perhaps was a result of inbreeding.

Getting the Eggs

I kept my Mearns on the ground during the breeding season when I lived in a dry climate. They seem to do much better and tend to be more content. However, in southern California it rains often during the winter. I never let them get on the ground and had good success keeping them on wire all of the time. Be sure they have plenty of good sand to dust and keep their feathers in condition. If your climate is too wet for ground pens, you can make special provisions for the breeding season. The ideal is to get some soil for the birds to dig and dust in. The breeders should be made as confortable and private as possible. Put plenty of logs, brush, and long grass for them to hide in. They will build dome-like nests built into a small hole scraped under the cover. Be sure that plenty of grass is available for them to make their nests.

Bob Tybie of Doyle, California, is the king of Mearns breeders. He writes about his husbandry of these birds. *"The Mearns is very susceptable to disease so good sanitary conditions are necessary. We raise ours on the ground as it is dry in this part of the country. But in more moist areas you probably would have to keep them on wire all the time. Only our young chicks are kept on wire. While the chicks are very young we use parakeet water fountains, as they have small lips to protect the small chicks. We sprinkle a little game bird mash on a sheet of burlap and put in a small lid with mash in it also as well as egg yolk and mealworms. We feed 30% protein supplemented with finely grated eggs and finely shredded lettuce. If they do not seem to be eating well, we cut mealworms in half and touch their beaks with them for the first few days, and then they usually begin eating them readily."*

"If picking occurs turn off the white light and turn on only when feeding egg yolk. Picking will stop if only red lights are used during the other times. After about two weeks chicks are put in larger boxes with the floors covered with stemmy alfalfa hay. We are never in a hurry to put the young birds outside until they are fully hardened off in wire bottomed brooders, for they are easily lost if the night is cold."

"After each hatch the incubators and brooders are disinfected carefully with a good sanitizer. This is a lot of work but very important so as not to spread any disease from one hatch to the next."

"Mearns quail are very hardy. Once they mature we seldom loose any birds. Anyone who can raise common quail can raise Mearns. However, they do require more attention to see that the chicks start eating" (Tybie 1976).

Mearns should be paired up. You may get by for a year or two running two hens with a cock bird but eventually the hens will fight and one or both will be lost. One of these years I want to see if the mother Mearns will hatch and rear her own young. It would be a very interesting study.

The pens should be as large as possible. Mine are about 15 by 10 feet. One end of the pen is covered and dry. The feed and water is kept in this sheltered area. The birds like to dig and dust in the dry dirt. The open end is planted with grass that gets about three feet high. This provides excellent cover and a nesting place for the hen. I let this grass get up about six inches or so before I put the birds in the pen each spring. The birds would nip off the grass when it is short and keep it from growing if put in too early. If you use wire bottom pens make them at least 4 by 8 and 4 feet high. One end needs some shelter and a dust box. Most Mearns when they are settled had rather hide than fly. When they do fly, they go straight up. If they hit the top of the pen just right they will break their necks. Many are lost because of this. To avoid this problem, I clip both wings so that all they can do is flutter up about two feet. They are balanced so no harm is done to them when they land. This is why it is important to have your pens high enough so that they cannot hit the top when they do fly. Another approach to the flying problem is to have the pens too low for the birds to pick up speed when they fly up. This technique is used with Coturnix quail. I personally feel that the high ceilings work better.

Hot Tempered

Some males are aggressive toward their hens. On the other hand the females are notorious for beating up on their mates. Some will even kill their mates if they are not separated. Their strong bill is used as a hammer on the top of the victim's head and can do real damage. I believe that many times one of the birds comes into breeding condition before the other. It is not always the male bird that is the aggressive one.

A Mearns breeder in California writes: *"More often it is the hen that gets "mad" at her male. When this happens they go for the head. They are just like a trip hammer. They will not let up until they have killed the one or the other. I have picked up an aggressive hen and held her for a few minutes, put her back with her mate, and she'd go after him again. When this happens, I have to separate them until she gets over her being "mad". The next day they are as good as can be. I put a board 6 or 8 inches by 4 feet up high enough for one of the birds to escape under it. I also have a nest box for them to hide in."* (personal correspondence from R. O. Taylor)

The major thing to do when this happens is to have some place for escape. There is no substitute for good cover for the Mearns. We have used clumps of grass, branches with leaves attached, and partitions or dividers in the pens which break up the line of sight. Some research needs to be done at this point.

Unusual Display

The display of the Mearns male is really something to see. It sets him apart from his quail cousins. He fluffs out his breast feathers which makes him appear twice his normal size. Standing on his tip toes with his neck stretched he utters his call. I could not believe it the first time I heard this mating cry. It sounded like some giant insect rather than a bird. It is a buzz which changes pitch as he utters his call. Some say that mated males seldom buzz in the wild, only the bachelors looking for mates make this call. Regardless of his motivation in making this call, it certainly provides his keeper with an unusual glimpse into his personal life.

Handling the Breeders

Usually Mearns lay the second year. This is not a hard rule as in captivity many lay the first year. If a young hen is put with a two year male, the eggs are more likely to be fertile if indeed she lays her first year. Mearns are late layers. In the wild they lay after the summer rains which trigger the grass and insects that the young feed upon. Without these the chicks cannot survive. In captivity I have known Mearns to lay as early as April and as late as August. Your climate and the romantic inclinations of the birds will determine when they will begin to set up house for a new generation. When the hen is ready to lay, she will scrape out a hole and line it with grass. Sometimes she will fashion a top for the nest which makes a cozy, well hidden sanctuary. Never take all of the eggs away as the hen will break up her nest if this is done. She will also break the eggs remaining. Mr. Tybie places infertile Bobwhite eggs in the nest to fool the hen. He leaves three nest eggs which I have found to be an ideal number. This is just enough to encourage the hen to complete her clutch but it is not too few to discourage her from trying. Many times using this method the hen will lay more eggs.

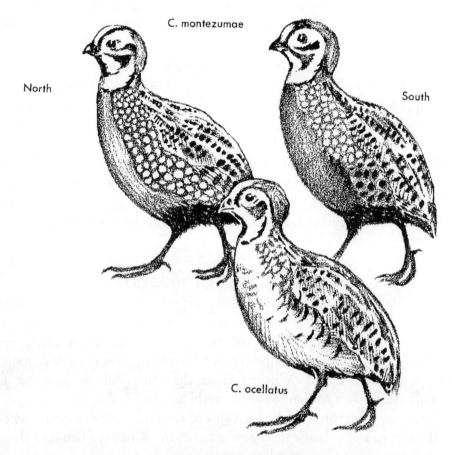

C. montezumae

North

South

C. ocellatus

Each of the three subspecies of the Mearns quail have distinct color variations.

From Eggs to Chicks

Most people have too much humidity in their incubators when hatching Mearns quail. If your hygrometer wet bulb is around 82° F. this will allow the chicks to remain smaller and seem to be stronger when they hatch.

Mearns chicks do not know how to eat by instinct. They must be taught. In the wild, the parents catch and feed insects to the chicks from their beaks.

Several methods have been used successfully to get the chicks to eat under captive conditions. The most popular is to feed small mealworms from tweezers to the chicks. (Never just throw mealworms into the pen for the chicks to pick up as they will begin to pick toes.) They soon learn that the mealworm tastes pretty good and will get on your hand for their food. Try anything you can think of to get them to eat or else they will die. We soon learned that about a third of the chicks never learn to eat for some reason. We tried everything, but some just starved to death. They will last about three days without eating. You can spot the ones that are not eating by their posture and the fact that some of them cry. We used "teacher chicks" which were older. Button quail chicks were also used as teachers. Some of these tricks work but the sad fact is that you will loose some of the little chicks. The hand raised chicks will be so tame they will eat off your hands. It is a gratifying experience for the bird breeder to work with birds that are as tame as the Mearns quail.

I wish there were more of these birds available to breeders today. They are very scarce and very expensive. We were looking back through old issues of the *Game Bird Breeder's Gazette* and found some advertisements for Mearns from a man in Texas. He was selling his Mearns for **FIVE PAIRS for $100.** This meant he was asking only $20 per pair. I have seen the price go up as high as $350 a pair. He had raised possibly over 200 birds that year. For years the price stayed around $90 to $100 per pair for these birds. In the last few years prices have tripled and there are not enough birds to go around at that price. In 1993 I sold unrelated pairs of Mearns for $200 a pair. Let's hope that there will be more of these wonderful birds bred in the future so the price will be within reach of most game bird breeders.

In 1993 I purchased six pairs of young Mearns quail. The situation was that I did not get my pens ready until March 1 which is rather late. I built special breeding pens which were designed especially for Mearns. While I was building the pens the birds were separated and the males kept separate from the females. They were in the same room but could not see each other. They did do a lot of talking. I began to lengthen the daylight about 30 minutes per day until I reached 15 hours of daylight. I put the lights on a timer and this job was done automatically with only minimum maintenance. This forced separation of the birds worked to my advantage. When the breeding pens were finished

I paired the birds up according to bloodlines. I had unrelated matings. The birds did not fight at all as they were in breeding condition. The males began to display and I had eggs in about 17 days. They continued to lay until the fall. I discovered some things about Mearns that helped me have success.

- Get the breeder birds in top physical condition. Feed lots of protein and calcium balanced feed.
- Keep the males and females separated until they are in breeding condition.
- Extend the light day to 15 hours before the birds are paired up.
- Give green grass every day. I pull up the "winter grass" by the roots and throw it into the pen on top of the wire pen bottom. The birds picked and ate the roots and all.
- Do not pair the birds up until they are both in top breeding condition.
- Have some private area with sand or dirt for them to dig out nesting cavities.
- Never leave less then three nest eggs in the nest. If you leave fewer eggs the hen will get mad and destroy the nest and start a new one. You will loose several days of eggs.
- Keep the breeders separate from the incubators and the brooding chicks. The danger of disease can be minimized.
- Check the young chicks every hour or so. You can avoid many problems by being on top of the situation.

If you want a challenge get a few pairs of Mearns quail. They will give you great pleasure and tax your patience for sure, but after it is all over you will count yourself fortunate to have had inj your collection some of these magnificent Mearns.

THE COTURNIX QUAIL FAMILY

(Coturnix)

This unique family of quails has found its way to America in grand style. Although the common species is much more popular than some others, this quail has made its way into the aviaries of many game bird breeders. Before World War II, this bird was unknown in the United States. After the war, the Coturnix quail became known to the American soldiers (that occupied Japan) as a part of every Japanese family and a staple in the diets of the Japanese people.

This family of quail has a wide range of color patterns and size, which gives something for nearly everyone. The general confirmation of this family holds true with all of its members and once seen they can easily be identified.

All of the Old World quails have similarities that can easily be seen. Climate, food, behavior, and general habits are very similar. One of the most interesting habits is migration during the winter months to feeding grounds. This migration was probably noticed and recorded first in the Old Testament of the Bible. Undoubtedly, this was the quail that fed the Israelites in the wilderness.

Dr. Bump gives us some interesting information on the terrain and habitat of some Old World quails (Bump, 1971).

Eurasian quail: Breeds in northern temperate to subtropical zones from northern Europe to central Asia south to Mediterranean countries, the Middle East, southern Asia east to Burma and up to 9,000 feet in Tibet. Winters from the southern breeding range south to tropical Africa almost to the equator. Spring precipitation within the breeding range may be from one to 4 inches per month.

Japanese quail: Breeds from southern Siberia and northern China to Korea and northern Japan. Winters mainly from central China and southern Japan south to Indochina, Burma and Assam. The spring rainfall is usually one to 5 inches per month.

African quail: The nomadic African representative of the Eurasian quail inhabiting the lower temperate to tropical zones. Breeds throughout the year with the rains in the tropics and normally in early summer in South Africa where precipitation is from ½ to 3 inches per month within its range.

Black-breasted quail or Rain quail: Resident but locally migratory from 6,000 feet in the southern Himalayas south throughout the Indian subcontinent. Precipitation during the breeding season may be from ½ to 5 inches monthly to 15 or more inches during the monsoon.

Harlequin quail: Predominantly a tropical to subtropical species though extending into the lower temperate zone in South Africa. Breeds throughout the year with the rains. An Arabian subspecies exists where there are no more than 4 inches of rain annually.

Australian quail: Mainly a lower temperate to subtropical species. Annual precipitation within its range is between 10 and 40 inches. Fall and winter may be dry. Snow is uncommon.

The Pharaoh Quail
(Coturnix *coturnix coturnix*)

The Pharaoh quail (Coturnix quail) is known in much of the ancient literature. This quail is so prolific it can be raised by the thousands in just a short period. It is widely distributed in Europe, Africa, and Asia where it migrates over large areas (Dement'ev and Gladkov, 1952). Apparently Coturnix quail were either domesticated in Japan about the Eleventh century or domestic Coturnix were brought to Japan from China at about this time. They were raised as pets and singing birds, but by 1900 Coturnix in Japan had become widely used for meat and egg production (Cain and Wormeli, 1973).

Game departments in the United States have made attempts in the past to establish this quail as they have successfully done with the Ringneck pheasant and other upland game birds. During a period of four to five years in the mid 1950's, at least one million of these birds were released in about a third of the U.S. None of these releases were successful.

Typical Pharaoh quail posture

Determining The Sex

At present there are at least five *"standard"* breeds of the Coturnix quail that are raised in captivity. According to the late Albert Marsh the easiest of these to sex are the Pharaoh and the Manchurian Golden breeds. The breast coloration can be used as a very accurate judge by the time the young birds are about two weeks old. At first we were not sure about the sex, but once you see the difference between the male and the female there is no question on most of the birds. However, we did have some *"fence straddlers"* at that young age and we had to wait until they matured before knowing for sure what sex they were.

The hens have a gray speckled breast sometimes tinged with brownish feathers. The males have a reddish cast on the breast with an absence of the speckled pattern that the hen has. They cannot be sexed accurately by watching them from a distance.

Another way to sex these birds is by using the vent sexing method. The mature male will exude a bubbly foam from a *"ball"* when he is in breeding condition. The sex organs are very distinguishable when extended by using the normal vent sexing methods. Marsh discovered that if the male does not have this ball near his vent he will not breed.

Another way to sex these interesting quail is by weight. The hen is generally larger than the male by as much as 20%. That is quite a difference. Our laying hens gained much more weight than their male partners.

A final method of sexing the Coturnix is by listening to the calls of the mature breeders. The males actually *"crow"* by standing on the tips of their toes. This upright position and the crowing sound *"Grr-rrr-rrr-rrr..."* is a dead give away! The females also make a call, but it is never like a crow. Their call is a high pitch *"cry"* and sounds like they may be lost. It sounds like *"Tik-ek-ek-tik-ek-ek..."* When they make their call they never assume the tall position of the cock but keep their heads rather low.

RANGE OF THE COTURNIX QUAIL

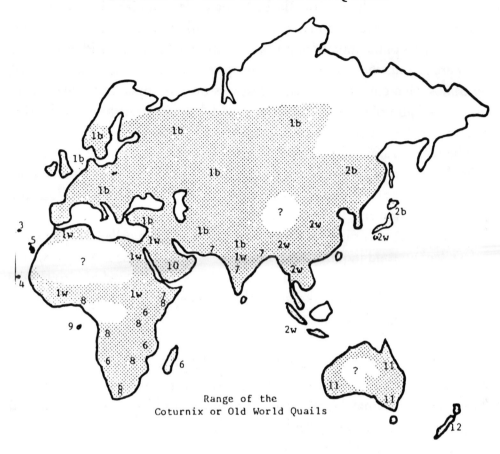

Range of the
Coturnix or Old World Quails

1. Eurasian migratory quail
     (C. c. Coturnix)
     1b. Breeding range
     1w. Wintering range
2. Eastern Siberian (Japanese) migratory quail
     (C. c. Japonica)
     2b. Breeding range
     2w. Wintering range
3. Azores quail
     (C. c. conturbans)
4. Cape verde quail
     (C. c. inopinata)
5. Canary Islands quail
     (C. c. confisa)

6. African quail
     (C. c. africana)
7. Black-breasted or rain
     (C. coromandelica)
8. Harlequin quail
     (C. d. delegorguei)
9. Sao Thome Island quail
     (C. d. histrionica)
10. Arabian quail
     (C. d. arabica)
11. Australian stubble
quail
     (C. pectoralis)
12. New Zealand quail
     (C. novae-zelandiae)

Several color mutations have been developed and have proven to be popular. There are the **Fawn, Black, Manchurian Golden, British Range, English White, Tuxedo,** and some other mutations. The late Albert Marsh developed most of the mutations and a large strain known as the **Pharaoh D-1**.

There is a distinct difference in the appearance of the sexes of this bird. **The males** have cinnamon colored feathers on the upper and lower breast region. His habit of standing on his toes and *"crowing"* sets him apart easily. This crowing begins at five weeks of age.

The females are similar to the males in coloration except that the feathers on the throat and upper breast are long, pointed, and much lighter cinnamon. Also, the tan breast feathers are characteristically black-stippled (Woodard, Abplanalp, Wilson and Vohra, 1973).

I must say that this is a very interesting bird. A man called me this week on the telephone and inquired if he should get some of these D-1 birds which got incredibly heavy which is ideal for meat birds. I informed him to handle these very large birds just like any others. They will probably have low fertility due to their large size.

Some Disadvantages

To achieve success with these birds there are some disadvantages that must be overcome. Fortunately, all these disadvantages can be adequately handled with good management adaptability.

Some of these disadvantages are:

1) The males are aggressive and fight,
2) They are excitable and will panic if suddenly disturbed, especially at night,
3) They fly straight up and injure their heads on the top of the pens,
4) Their droppings contain large amounts of ammonia that causes odor,
5) Eggs shells are dark and hard to write on, soft and can be damaged easily,

6) A rapid decline in productivity occurs at eight months of age,

7) Fertility is low on the average,

8) Low hatches as compared with some other birds, and

9) The chicks are delicate, require special care during the first two weeks.

A Great Beginner's Bird

For the novice breeder we would recommend this little quail. The coturnix has several advantages over the Bobwhite as a beginner's bird in that 1) they go through the life cycle at such a rapid pace, 2) they are readily available at a reasonable price, and 3) their eggs can be pickled and eaten. With any success, there will be large numbers of surplus birds and eggs. Years ago we got a trio (2 hens, 1 cock) of Coturnix, and in just four months we had over 80 birds (many laying eggs) all from just three birds. I quickly discovered that they ate like pigs rather than a delicate little bird. It was a great experience and we enjoyed it very much.

When you take the time to enjoy your birds, you will find these little quail have great personalities. Their ability to mature so fast makes them a very enjoyable bird. I recommend these and the bobwhite quail to all beginners.

Raising Coturnix Quail Commercially

This quail is a wonderful candidate for commercial production. Besides having a ready market for meat birds and for the eggs, the best thing going for the Pharaoh quail being raised on a commercial basis is the rapid rate of metabolism and maturity. This makes for lots of product in a short period of time. There are many successful commercial operations using this bird as the species. We found them to be very interesting and easy to propagate. A key to success would be in knowing some husbandry *"tricks of the trade"* in handling these birds. Once a general understanding of the species is gained, there should be no real problem in getting them to lay and lay and lay.

Below is a life cycle chart for the Coturnix quail with approximate body weight in grams: (1 oz. = 28.5 grams)

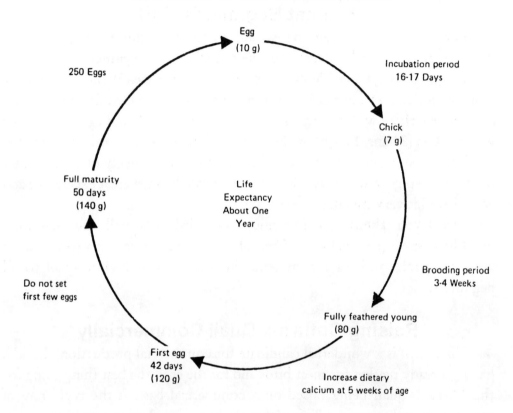

LIFE CYCLE OF THE COTURNIX QUAIL

Egg
(10 g)

250 Eggs

Incubation period
16-17 Days

Chick
(7 g)

Full maturity
50 days
(140 g)

Life
Expectancy
About One
Year

Brooding period
3-4 Weeks

Do not set
first few eggs

Fully feathered young
(80 g)

First egg
42 days
(120 g)

Increase dietary
calcium at 5 weeks of age

If you plan to raise these birds on a commercial I would recommend that you get some professional help. I would recommend Avian Consultants (see advertisement at back of book).

The African Harlequin Quail
(Coturnix delegorguei)

There seems to be some confusion about the "Harlequin quail". The problem comes from the fact that the **Mearns quail** is sometimes called the Harlequin quail. The Mearns quail is a New World bird while the true Harlequin is from South Africa. Perhaps it would be better for us to refer to the little Harlequin, as the **African Harlequin** quail.

Description

The cock African Harlequin is about six inches long and is very distinguished in his attractive coloring. It has a black-brown crown with a lighter center stripe. A black stripe runs through the eye spreading behind the ear coverts. A white stripe runs above the eye to the nape. The cheeks and throat are white which makes a very attractive contrast. The breast is black in the center with red-brown stripes running lengthwise along the sides. The belly and under parts are red-brown.

The female is mostly brown with lighter stripes and mottling. She is much duller than the male, thus enabling her to raise the family more safely (Rutgers, 1965). I have noticed that the females of the species become very tame while the males remain suspicious of their keeper. This is true of several other closely related quail. Our hens would take mealworms from our fingers in our walk-in aviary. There is just nothing anymore satisfying than making friends with such a *"sweet"* little bird. It is also very interesting to watch the male feed his hen mealworms when he gets brave enough to come out from hiding and get one. These birds are very attractive and their wonderful personality makes them even more attractive.

Handling

This quail should be handled like the more common Chinese Painted quail, more often called mistakenly the *"Button"* quail. It is advisable to keep pairs together, but separate from others of the same species. During breeding, they become quite vicious towards one another. Perhaps this is the instinct to protect their breeding territory from rivals. It is interesting that they are quite tolerant of other species but will not abide their own kind. While some breeders have had the females get broody and set on their own eggs, most find that the best way to multiply these birds is the hatching in an incubator and then brooding the chicks like other quail.

A Bad Habit

As mentioned before they have a bad habit of fighting with each other during the breeding season. A more objectional habit that they share with all of the members of their genus is flying straight up and hitting the top of the pen. Many a head has been scalped by this and sometimes necks have been broken. There are several methods to take care of this that I have used through the years. A most obvious one is to put them in tall pens and keep their wing primary feathers clipped. Be sure to clip both wings evenly so they will not be unbalanced and thus fly up out of control. If the clipping is done about twice a year and the pens are tall, they will not be able to reach the top of the pens and thus avoid being brained or scalped. Another method to keep them calm is to have plenty of brush for them to hide in and under. They had much rather hide than panic in flight if given a choice. If they are not crowded, they will hide and when feeling secure begin to tame up to their keeper. After a few weeks even mature birds tame down and become very friendly.

The hen produces two clutches a season in the wild, each containing up to 10 eggs, which are laid in a slight hollow in the ground. If the breeder will leave three nest eggs in the nest the hen will continue to lay an enormous number of eggs. At four weeks of age the young resemble the adult and their sex is apparent as the males will begin to show their colors. I believe that my young hens laid at eight or nine weeks which makes them very prolific.

In the past few years these birds have become hard to find. A few years back, you could hardly give these birds away. Now, the situation has greatly changed. Every once n a while a pair or two of these birds shows up at the swap-meets that are held around the country. They are quickly bought by those that see how cute and pretty they are. With the scarcity of these birds in captivity their captive future is in question. Always, one must guard again inbreeding when only a few birds are available. The temptation of selling to prospective breeders a brother and sister as a pair is too great.

I really did enjoy the pair that I had. The hen laid well and she even went "broody" but I did not let her raise her own young. The nights are very cold in central Oregon and the little chicks would not have survived the cold nights. I am sure in milder climates the pair could hatch and raise their own chicks in a larger ground aviary.

These little birds should be popular with the hook-bill breeders as they can survive in the bottom of a large walk-in aviary just as the Button quail do. Larger, they can take care of themselves better and not be intimidated by any of the larger birds.

The Chinese Painted Quail

(Coturnix chinensis)
(Excalifactoria chinensis)

This smart looking little quail is commonly known as the **Button quail** in America. It is better known in Asia and Europe as the Blue-breasted Quail. It's scientific name is *Excalifactoria chinensis* and it is found in India, Ceylon, Indo-China and Formosa. Some classify him as *Coturnix chinensis* when it occurs in Nepal, but both are probably the same little bird.

The Painted quail is the smallest of all the quail. Consequently, they are unique and a joy to keep. Very common in pet shops, it is kept by those who like cage birds as it does well in the bottom of a large aviary.

The cock bird is the brightly colored one in the family. His breast is covered with blue-gray and burnt-red markings. His face has a blackish area that is outlined by a black line extending from the beak, below the eyes and joining the black patch on his throat. It has a broad white crescent below the black throat extending back to the ear coverts bordered with black. He is a beautiful little bird and must be examined closely to be appreciated.

The hen is mottled brown and lacks the black and white markings. She is rather dull in appearance compared to the cock bird, but her markings are subtle and very beautiful upon close examination. Her under parts are not as dark a brown as is her upper parts (Rutgers, 1965).

There is a silver mutation now bred that is very beautiful. The silver on these mutations almost covers up the pattern around the neck but it still shows very faintly which makes them striking. We had some silver Buttons and liked them very much. They are certainly not as colorful as the normal colored birds but they are still very beautifully colored. There are some other mutations coming out now which I have never seen. As time goes on, there will be as many mutations with these birds as there are with the Bobwhite quail.

If the reader wishes more information on this little quail he or she is urged to get a copy of the author's book *"The Chinese Painted Quail."* This is the only book in the world exclusively about this little bird. It contains 150 pages filled with good, basic information that the experienced and novice breeder will enjoy. See Appendix for ordering information.

Some Faults

These quail have some bad habits that are shared with many of the Coturnix family. They are flyers. They fly straight up and will brain themselves on the top of the pen unless precautions are taken. Often in the night when they are disturbed they will fly straight up as hard as they can and keep this up until they knock themselves silly or break their necks. The least that can happen is they scalp their heads. To remedy this, we put ours in very tall pens and clip the primary feathers on both wings. At best they could only flutter three feet and thus could not reach the top of the pens regardless how hard they tried. Another tactic, put them in very low pens so that they barely have head room. This keeps them from getting up the speed when they fly.

Another fault which is common is the males sometimes are aggressive to other Button quail males. This is really not a fault, but is a good trait that simply means the male has a strong protective instinct toward his family. Many times several pairs can be kept together if the pen is large enough for each pair to stake out their own area but they should be watched carefully to see if they will adjust. If fighting should break out, separate the pairs immediately and be thankful that no permanent damage occurred. These little birds will do each other great harm if left unattended to their own ways.

A Word of Warning

Many years ago we had these beautiful little birds and tried to keep them in a large outside aviary in Montana. We soon learned that they could not tolerate very cold weather. Worse than that, we lost some more from some very aggressive Bobwhites. It seems that these little quail are vicious to each other during breeding season, but they are real cowards and show their size during other times of the year. This was a heartbreaking experience for us. Sometimes I wonder why I love Bobwhites so much considering some of their terrible habits. Please be very careful in putting these tiny quail in pens with others. They are so small, they need help sometimes.

Interesting To Raise

These quail are easy to raise provided you have strong parent stock. Often, this problem of inbreeding is common. The most often heard complaint is the eggs are infertile or the chicks are weak and die. This could be a problem of inbreeding. It would be wise to get your birds from several sources. As a rule, the ones available in pet shops are not the ones to get. It is better to get birds from a breeder. You can see what parents they come from and find out how they breed.

Chicks not hatching could also indicate a problem with the incubation process. One of the problems with Button quail eggs is they are very difficult to candle to check how the humidity is working. About the best we can do is to open up the unhatched egg and try to determine what the trouble was. See the section of egg incubation for more information.

Treat the tiny chicks like any other quail. Be sure that the wire is small enough to hold them. We have had them slip through ½ inch hardware cloth. Once they get their first meal or two, they are hardy and take to life vigorously. They feather out fast and can fly in just a few days. These tiny birds are strong and quick, care must be taken when the pen door is open.

Believe It Or Not

We discovered that these little birds have some kind of predetermined instinct about when to hatch. They call to one another, and when one gives the signal they all hatch out together. It is fascinating to catch them just when one hatchs and then they all hatch within a few minutes of each other. Some of the other birds do this too, I am told. It is a very interesting thing to watch and just to see this happen is worth keeping the birds. I am not totally convinced that they can regulate their hatching time but I must admit that ours **all hatched within 30 minutes** and those that did not hatch within this time frame were infertile.

Raising The Chicks Naturally

Some breeders let them incubate and brood their own youngsters. For many years it was thought that it would be impossible to get the tiny chicks started in a brooder artificially. When the birds were first imported they were allowed to hatch and raise their own young. To do this they need to be on the ground and have some grass tufts growing or planted for them to nest in. The hen does all the incubating and the caring of the young. If the male will not let the hen alone when she gets broody, he should be removed.

It is safer to take him out when the chicks hatch as he may pick at them. At four weeks the chicks will be old enough to be independent. If the cock bird is placed back in the pen when the chicks are removed, the hen will likely lay another clutch of eggs.

There is nothing more exciting than the watching of parent birds raise their own young naturally. However, there is much more risk of losing chicks when this is done. Nothing can beat the TLC of the aviculturist.

These little quail are high on the preferred list for the beginner. All of us who have raised them have had a treat. Some breeders get hooked on the many mutations that these little birds are throwing these days. If one tries to get a few pairs of each available mutation his pens would soon be full of many pairs of these birds.

Final Thoughts

We are often asked which is our all-time favorite quail. We have difficulty answering this question as the species that we are currently working with usually has our attention. However, it can be said with all honesty that these little *"Buttons"* holds a place on our all-time favorite list.

The Rain Quail
(*Coturnix coromandelica*)

Another name for this very little quail is **BLACK-BREASTED QUAIL** which it goes by in many circles. A native of India and surrounding areas, this quail cannot take terribly cold weather. It is a migratory bird and is resident and nomadic during monsoons, spreading out widely over otherwise parched areas with availability of grass cover and food (Ali and Ripley, 1980).

It is more popular in the Southern California area than any other area in the United States. I suppose this is because it makes such a good aviary bird when housed with parrot-type birds. Then too, this is a bird that likes hot weather, so it fits well into the warmer climates. During the winter months if they are severe, care should be given to provide adequate heat. It will live entirely off the spilled seeds (if allowed to do so) and even will nest if grass tufts are placed in the pen. Some breeders have had good success in letting the pairs hatch and raise their own chicks.

The male is six inches long and resembles the common quail but has black markings at the throat and there is a large black spot in the center of the breast, sides of the head are black with white margins. Wings brown, eyes brown, bill horn colored, legs flesh colored. **The female** has no spot on the breast and no black markings on white throat (Rutgers, 1965).

In size, the Rain quail is just slightly larger than the Chinese Painted quail (Button quail). I know of one breeder that has an odd bird and cannot find a mate for it. There seems to be a real scarcity of these birds at the present time although a number of years they were offered for sale on a regular basis. It would be a good thing if someone could bring into the United States a new shipment of these birds. They are much more popular in Europe than in the United States. Perhaps the reason that few are imported into the U.S. in recent years is the very strict and difficult laws. This is a shame as this could be a real asset to any aviary.

The Rain quail fits very well in a mixed aviary. The pair will build a neat nest hidden in a clump of grass. The cock bird will carry every delicacy to his hen and give it to her with a *"lovers'"* tenderness. A box of damp, sharp river sand in which they can take a dust bath should be made available. This is especially true if they are kept on wire. In the evening the pair will huddle comfortably together in or near the sand and preen their feathers before roosting in the sand box. It is said to be somewhat aggressive to members of its own species (as are others in this family) during breeding season. Pairs should be kept away from other pairs of the same species. The small outside aviary should be partly covered with river sand and partly covered with a fairly dense undergrowth. The roof should have some type of covering to keep out inclement weather but open enough to let in some rain for bathing. The hen will lay ten to twelve eggs in a hidden nest which can be found if the breeder will look carefully when one of the pair is missing. Incubation lasts for 16-17 days. When the chicks are old enough to be on their own, the old cock bird may show aggression toward them if he is planning on having another family. Either he or the chicks should be removed to avoid any injury to the young chicks.

There is nothing any more pleasing to the eye than to see the family strolling around the pen in search of small seeds. The little chicks seem more tiny than ever when tottering behind the parents. Fine seed should be made available along with some type of live food. The parents will call the chicks to come running for the discovered treat.

Some breeders insist that one of the "live foods" be used in raising chicks. Mealworms, fly larvae, crickets, or some other insect food should help the chicks to learn to eat. It is a good idea to try anything that can be tried to get them to eat on their own. Once they have gotten used to the commercial feed they seem to have no trouble surviving. As with many other rare quail, the *"trick"* is to get the young chicks eating before they loose their energy from the egg yoke and become too weak to eat.

Part 3

SOME FAVORITE PARTRIDGE

THE PARTRIDGE FAMILY

(Phasianidae perdicini)

Some Helpful Generalities

Generally speaking, anyone with some basic knowledge of avian propagation can have success with the more common varieties of partridges. The ASSEMBLY LINE METHOD of raising the chicks works very well with all of the partridge species. Of course, there must be some adaptations as on the whole, the partridges are larger birds than the quail and adjustments must be made. The feeders and the waterers must be adjusted to accommodate the size of the birds. This is really an advantage in some ways as the readily available supplies manufactured for the poultry industry work well for partridge without any modifications.

Choose the species you want to work with carefully. Take some time to do some reading and learn all you can about the birds that are available to you. It is our habit to get articles from old issues of the *Game Bird Breeders' Gazette* and see what has been written about the species in question. We provide these back articles for a small cost. The book, *The Gazette Index* has complete information. I always read the *"ads"* in the magazine to see what is available and the general market price. If the price is too low, then I am suspicious. Read about each species and learn how to propagate it before you buy any birds. Not only interesting, the ads are very educational.

There is not a bird breeder alive that does not *"drool"* over the list of the 47 species of partridges. The reason is that only about 12 of the species are kept in captivity. Of the 12, there are about four that are not kept in the U.S., but are kept in Europe and Asia. We are sure that zoos have some of the species that are native to their land in captivity.

We will discuss some of the partridges that can be obtained in the U.S. for those that may get some, or wish to know something about them.

Lucky for those of us who love aviculture, the world is full of some wonderful birds called **PARTRIDGES**. There are 47 species of partridges in the world. Here is a listing (Robbins, 1984):

Rock partridge *(Alectoris graeca)*
Chukar partridge *(A. chukar)*
Przewalski Rock partridge *(A. magna)*
Philby's Rock partridge *(A. philbyi)*
Barbary partridge *(A. barbara)*
Red-legged Partridge *(A. rufa)*
Arabian Chukar partridge *(A. melanocephala)*
Seesee partridge *(Ammoperdix griseogularis)*
Sand partridge *(A. heyi)*
Common Hill partridge *(Arborophila torqueola)*
Rufous-throated Hill partridge *(A. rufogularis)*
White-cheeked Hill partridge *(A. atrogularis)*
White-throated Hill partridge *(A. crudigularis)*
Red-breasted Hill partridge *(A. mandellii)*
Brown-breasted Hill partridge *(A.brunneopectus)*
Boulton's Hill partridge *(A. rufipectus)*
Rickett's Hill partridge *(A. gingica)*
David's Tree partridge *(A. davidi)*
Chestnut-headed Tree partridge *(A. cambodiana)*
Sumatran Hill partridge *(A. orientalis)*
Chestnut-bellied Tree partridge *(A. javanica)*
Red-bellied Tree partridge *(A. rubrirostris)*
Red-breasted Tree partridge *(A. hyperythra)*
Hainan Hill partridge *(A. ardens)*
Bamboo partridge *(Bambusicola fytchii)*
Chinese Bamboo partridge *(B. thoracica)*
Ferruginous Wood partridge *(Caloperdix oculea)*
Crimson-headed Wood partridge *(Haematortyx sanguiniteps)*
Snow partridge *(Lerwa lerwa)*

Madagascar partridge *(Margaroperdix madagascariensis)*
Black Wood partridge *(Melanoperdix nigra)*
Grey partridge *(Perdix perdix)*
Daurian partridge *(P. dauricae)*
Tibetan partridge *(P. hodgsoniae)*
Stone partridge *(Ptilopachus petrosus)*
Long-billed Wood partridge *(Rhizothera longirostris)*
Crested Wood partridge *(Rollulus roulroul)*
Caucasian Snow partridge *(Tetragallus caucasicus)*
Caspian Snowcock *(T. caspius)*
Tibetan Snowcock *(T. tibetanus)*
Altai Snowcock *(T. altaicus)*
Himalayan Snowcock *(T. himalayensis)*
Verreaux's Monal partridge *(Tetraophasis obscurus)*
Szechenyi's Monal partridge *(T. szechenyii)*
Chestnut-breasted Tree partridge *(Tropicoperdix)*
Green-legged Hill partridge *(T. chloropus)*
Annamese Hill partridge *(T. merlini)*

The list of partridges above gives the reader some idea of the scope of this unique family of birds. There are so very many species of the partridge family that the Western world has not even seen, much less even heard of. Much work needs to be done through research in husbandry methods, reproductive cycles, feeds, and environmental conditions needed by this family of birds. The reason for this can be seen in the statistics about many of their native countries. A natural habitat is being destroyed at an alarming rate. Fewer and fewer of the species are being seen in the wild which indicates that their numbers are declining.

It must be said again, the breeder with no experience should not start with one of the rare species of partridges. He should get some practical experience with one of the members of the Rock partridge family (chukars, etc.) before he makes a large investment in the rare ones. It is a great temptation to take home many of the beautiful partridges. The best advice that one could give is to specialize in one or two members of the family for a year or two and then get into some of the others. I must confess, this is the most unheeded advice that I give.

Partridges are a hardy species. It can be said that they are much more hardy than most of the quails and some of the pheasants and turkeys. For this reason it is no doubt why they are so popular. Of course their beautiful coloring helps one admire them. It is my intent to get heavily into this wonderful group of birds.

This family of upland game birds offers the aviculturist perhaps more challenges than any other that we will discuss in this book. Many of these are truly exotic because of the mystery surrounding the very countries from which they come. Many of these countries are *"closed"* to outsiders or very restrictive on the exporting of native fauna. Some of these countries are so isolated that trapping birds would be life threatening. Never-the-less, I am thinking about importing some through our quarantine services. The sooner this is done, the better, as conditions will surely get worse in the future. This is a very expensive venture and one that has much financial risk. As the saying goes, *"Someone's got to do it"* if we are to get any new blood and new species into the United States.

Himalayan Snowcock

(Tetraogallus himalayensis himalayensis) Gray 1842

This bird is the most striking of all of the members of the partridge family kept in captivity. The coloration is not as striking as the size and carriage of the bird. Adult males weigh up to six pounds and have a strong curved bill which is used for digging for food.

The Himalayan Snowcock is a resident of the western Himalayan mountains (Ali and Ripley, 1980) and lives at an altitude of up to 18,000 feet and descends to lower altitudes in severe winters. It likes to inhabit rocky ledges above the timber line and is often seen on outcrops of rock surveying its territory.

In the breeding season the cock bird is particularly noisy. He utters a loud prolonged penetrating whistle or pipe of four or five notes rising in scale and repeated with persistence from a rock or mounds.

Robbins describes the bird as follows: Adults: 28 in. Largely grey, white, chestnut and black streaked and vermiculated plumage. A white throat separated by a broken chestnut collar from dark grey underparts and white under tail coverts are diagnostic. Yellow eye stripes during breeding season (Robbins, 1984).

For years the Himalayan snow cock has been sought after by aviculturists. Until recently, the state of Nevada, had the only stock in the U.S. which was brought from Afghanistan in a program to introduce the species into the wilds of Nevada. In the fall of 1980, a hunting season was opened. The project was dropped a few years later for lack of funds.

In the wild the bird is apparently monogamous (Dement'ev and Gladkov, 1952). These birds usually keep in pairs, or parties of three to five, though coveys of more than 20 birds are frequently observed. The birds shoot down the hillsides in the early morning to drink, and slowly work their way upwards feeding as the day warms up, scratching the ground and digging vigorously with their stout bills. They hardly ever fly uphill or flap their wings in flight accept just before alighting. When alarmed the bird invariably runs uphill with a waddling goose-like gait, its coloration blending to perfection with the barren environment. The partly erected tail is jerked now and again in the moor hen

154   Some Favorite Partridge

The partly erected tail is jerked now and again in the moor hen manner, flashing the white under coverts. It mounts a rock before taking off, plummeting at great speed straight down a steep hillside or round its contours or across a ravine, often traveling long distances without a single wing beat, the wind whining through the pinions. They are noisy birds, continually uttering clucking calls as they feed, and shrill cackles of alarm when flushed, as well as on the wing (Ali and Ripley, 1980).

In the 1960's, The Nevada Department of Fish and Game imported some of these beautiful birds with the idea of release into the wilds of Nevada. The department released nineteen birds in 1963 that were wild trapped in India. Every year they released many birds. By 1976 they had put a total of 464 birds into the wilds. However, due to financial restraints, the department abandoned the project and sent the remaining birds they had to the state of Oregon. Now, I do not know what has happened to these birds.

The few aviculturists that have had these birds did well until the stock became very badly inbred. Several years of sibling matings deteriorated the stock. I understand that just recently some new blood has been imported from England which should give the captive birds a boost. The birds that I have seen are just spectacular. Everyone should get a pair of these birds — ha!

Chicks can be handled like other partridge, but should be raised on wire at least until mature. I have seen many of these birds kept in ground pens with success after they matured and would recommend that the young be raised in as sterile environment as possible to avoid disease problems.

These birds are still being advertised in the *Gazette* on a regular basis. So it seems that a few are being raised. All of the stock are decendents of the birds that were originally imported by the state of Nevada. These birds should be carefully bred so as not to inbreed the limited gene-pool.

An artist's conception of Rock partridge, it looks almost the same as a Chukar but with a more nearly white throat and face, narrower bands on the flanks, with a generally more bluish-grey body.

The Rock Partridge Family

(Alectoris)

Rock partridges are a very interesting and beautiful family of partridges. They are perhaps the best known to aviculture. There are several subspecies that have not made their way to the United States which would be very interesting to propagate. Because of politics and the remoteness of their natural habitats, their importation at the present time seems rather remote.

The very popular *"Chukar partridge"* is a member of this well known family. They are all much alike in conformation, but are distinctly different in coloration. This is a case where the breeder can raise the particular member of the family that he likes the best.

As a general rule this family is easy to propagate using the ASSEMBLY LINE METHOD with adaptations as to the size of the boxes, wire, etc. We found the several species that we have had to be very enjoyable birds. Their personalities vary within the species. Our youngsters became tame enough to eat from our hands. The birds that we had to work with gave us many hours of enjoyment. The personalities of each species are quite different. This makes propagating each of them a joy. Were they all the same, it would not be nearly as much fun to work with them. They are all about the same size and can be raised in the same type of equipment. Even the eggs are about the same size.

Since chukars and the other Rock partridges are very closely related they should not be allowed to hybridize. There are commercial breeders in the U.S. that are producing a *"hybrid"* between the Red legged partridge and the common Chukar partridge. *"At present there has been some mixup over the pure and hybrids that are now being produced. Both have a white throat patch with a black border. In the common chukar the border is clean cut, while in pure Red-legged partridge the bottom edge of the band becomes more or less broken and gradually merges into the upper breast feathers, giving a speckled effect to the neck and upper breast area. This is one of the most obvious ways of determining whether a bird is a pure specimen. Hybrids have proved to be very good game farm birds because they are docile in captivity, lay a large number of eggs, feather picking is almost unknown, and they are quite easy to raise."*

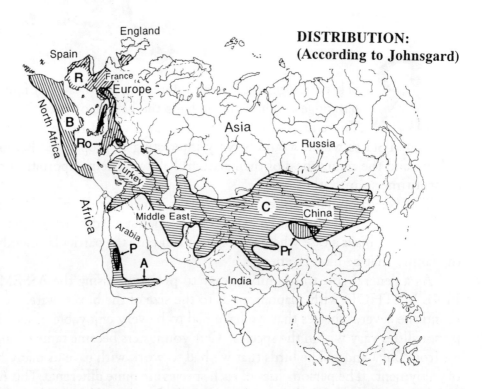

DISTRIBUTION:
(According to Johnsgard)

A. Arabian Red-legged; B. Barbary partridge; C. Chukar partridge; P. Phylby's partridge; Pr. Przhevalski's Rock partridge; R. Red-legged partridge; Ro. Rock partridge

Chukar Partridge

(Alectoris chukar) Grey 1830

There are at least 13 subspecies of this popular bird. In 1965 there was a reclassification of the genus and the Rock partridge was placed as a separate species. All are so much alike that from a distance it is impossible to tell them apart. On close examination there is a difference in appearance and in the habitat that supports each species.

The species that has been so successfully introduced in the United States is the Indian Chukar and it is hunted for sport in several of the western states. There is a separate species, the Great partridge that has a limited range in China. This is a fascinating bird. They inhabit even more desolate regions than do the common Chukars. There has been no introductions in the U.S. of the Great partridge by any of the state game departments. The giant chukars that are raised in captivity are probably bred up from the common Indian Chukar and do not represent the Great partridge. There are many aviculturists that would give most anything to have some of these birds. One of these days, with some good fortune, someone may be able to bring into the United States some of these *"Great partridges."*

Distribution

The distribution chart (below) for the Chukar partridge family shows that they are as widely distributed across Europe as the Hungarian partridge. Apparently, they are quite common over their range.

Distribution of the Chukar Partridges

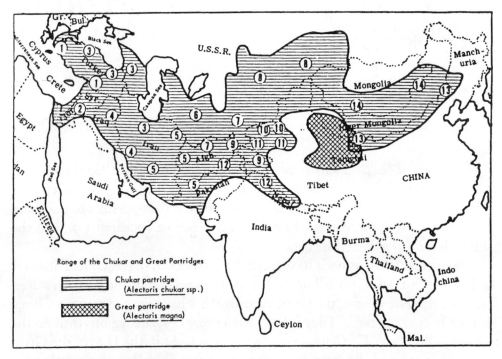

Chukar Partridges
1. (Alectoris c. cypriotes)
2. (Alectoris c. sinaica)
3. (Alectoris c. kurdestanica)
4. (Alectoris c. werae)
5. (Alectoris c. koroviakovi)
6. (Alectoris c. subpallida)
7. (Alectoris c. falki)

8. (Alectoris c. dzungarica)
9. (Alectoris c. pallescens)
10. (Alectoris c. pallida)
11. (Alectoris c. fallax)
12. (Alectoris c. chukar)
13. (Alectoris c. pubescens)
14. (Alectoris c. potanini)

Great Partridge
   (Alectoris magna)

Easy to Raise

The Chukar partridge is so easy to raise that thousands of them are produced annually on a commercial basis. Very strong bloodlines are available and they are not overly priced. Many thousands of these birds are raised each year. The breeding of so many has led some mutations to appear. Some mutations are quite pretty and are interesting to work with.

In my opinion chukars are easy as well as a lot of fun to raise. They are hardy and seem resistant to disease. I discovered that the eggs must be turned regularly the first week of incubation. The germ tends to stick to the lining of the egg. Some small breeders start their Chukar eggs under bantam hens for the first week and then transfer them to an incubator. The results are very good using this method but it is a lot of work and could not be done on a large scale. Some of the rare Rock partridges would be worth doing this to get better hatches. The young can be raised on wire or on the ground. I always raise my birds on wire to maturity before putting them on the ground. The local climate will dictate your situation. However you choose to raise chukars, you should make every effort to keep the area clean and dry. Be careful about letting damp places in the litter go untended. Keep the litter as dry as possible. You should medicate for Coccidiosis and Blackhead if the birds are raised on the ground. It is best not to raise other species with the chukar unless they are closely related. To do so would be asking for problems.

Chukars are somewhat pugnacious and cannot be mixed with other birds during the nesting season. Males will often fight, although I have seen some that got along well with many neighbors with no problems. If you plan to colony breed your birds raise the male birds together so they will develop a pecking order early on. This will make them more compatible during the breeding season. To help avoid this and other problems do not overcrowd the birds. Give them plenty of room and lots of brush and grass to get out of the way of their picky neighbors. I suppose it is the particular strain that makes the difference in some of the bad habits. Use the wire or ground method for the breeders. They will usually do well on any type of feed, but do best on a high protein ration. If you are interested in getting some experience with the partridge family, try some chukars. They are inexpensive and will prove to be a source of valuable experience in dealing with this interesting family of birds.

A Chukar partridge

Philby's Partridge
(Alectoris philbyi Lowe 1934)

PLATE B

This partridge is comparable in most instances to the chukar except for the dark black chin. Its general confirmation is slimmer and it is perhaps taller then the common Chukar partridge. The unique black chin area sets it apart immediately.

The Arabian peninsula in a rather limited area is the native habitat of this partridge. Like the rest of the Rock partridge family, the Philby's is very adaptable to the dry, hostile desert and is said to be plentiful in its range.

Several of these birds have been imported in recent years by some Zoos and private breeders. The San Diego Zoo has raised quite a few of these birds and have even let some of them out to private breeders who are members of bird clubs. They have reproduced quite well in the hands of these private breeders and the surplus birds are available in very limited numbers. It would be good if some breeder would specialize in these birds to insure that they not become inbred.

The two pairs on display at the present time at San Diego Zoo appear to be nervous. However, housed in a pen area conducive to breeding, they will calm down and be more gentle. Often one sees them up high on a tree branch looking out over the area. Those in the wild like to get to high places.

The breeders and chicks should be handled like the other Rock partridges. The breeder should watch for cannibalism should it occur and be prepared to stop it immediately. The chicks grow rapidly on a high protein diet and at maturity will make an excellent addition to anyone's aviary.

Barbary Partridge

(Alectoris barbara)

Within the Rock partridge family I would have to say that this one is my favorite. I think the thing that I like the most about the appearance of these birds is the very delicate lacing pattern around the neck which is offset by a beautiful brown background color. Their Build is generally like other members of the family.

A description of these birds shows their beauty: Adults; 13" (33cm). Crown, nape and collar on lower neck deep chestnut, last nearly black at sides with white spots, rest of upper parts grey-brown. Scapular slate-blue with wide rufous margins, as in the Chukar A. chukar. Long supercilium, lores, cheeks and throat pale grey. Pink chestnut eye stripe, overlaid with long orange-buff feathers behind the eye, extends to join collar. Chest pink-grey. Flanks basically pale slate, overlaid with bars of black, sandy-buff or white. Buff on front of belly and vent more obvious than on other Alectoris. Male slightly larger then female. Iris, light brown or red-brown. Bill, crimson or orange-red. Legs, strawberry-red (Robbins, 1984).

There are probably five subspecies living in Morocco, Algeria, Tunisia, Libya and on the Canary Islands. The birds live in altitudes as high as 10,000 feet and along the coastal sand dunes which shows their versatility.

Not only are these perhaps the most beautiful in the *"Rock"* family, it is difficult to obtain good pure breeding stock. This is a shame as the few breeders that have them are very pleased. There have been some releases of this bird into the wilds by state game departments in California and Hawaii back around 1960. The success was nominal and the program was dropped. Although never very numerous, their original range has made them known to a great many travelers. The eggs and nest are very similar to the chukar, differing only that the eggs are slightly smaller and possible containing a trifle more pigmentation in the color of the shell.

The ones that I had were badly inbred and I did not get any fertile eggs although one hen laid more than 30 eggs. It was a disappointment not to hatch any of these beautiful birds. Before we were able to get any new, stronger, blood we had a major tragedy. Some predator (we think a Badger) literally pulled off the wire from the top of the pen and of course the poor birds did not have a chance. We were very saddened about this as the Barbarys were our favorites. The unwritten rule, *"the favorite or most expensive birds will always be the ones to go to a predator"* certainly worked once again. Soon after, we installed an electric fence around all of our pens and from that day to this, we have never lost a bird to a predator. That electric fence unit went continuously for more than ten years before it wore out. The cost figured about $5 per year including electricity.

The extraordinary thing about these birds is the beautiful delicately laced neck area. The coloration is very striking. Their confirmation is like the chukar except they are built a little heavier. There is no doubt that they are a member of the Rock partridge family.

Chicks are easy to raise provided that good strong blood is available. This is one of the many species that deteriorate with inbreeding. I do not know when the last new blood was imported, but it seems to me that if you are working with these birds you should be careful to get strong bloodlines. I have talked with several breeders who complained that their fertility rate was low and the hatching was poor. This is a sign of inbreeding and that is where to start in correcting the problem.

I find that small groups of these partridges do best. There seems to be more contentment with the chicks when they have around ten others to grow up with. One or two chicks together alone will be nervous and not do as well. Be careful and not to mix these chicks with other species that may fight with them. They are not aggressive toward others so need to be protected until mature.

These birds will crossbreed with other members of the Rock partridge family. I have never found it advantageous to do this. It is a real temptation when a breeder does not have a mate for a bird to try crossbreeding. If you think of what you will do with the offspring, then you may change your minds and not crossbreed.

Red-legged partridges

Red-legged Partridge

(Alectoris rufa)

This member of the Rock partridge family is truly a beautiful bird and one that will bring pleasure into the life of the aviculturists. The thing that makes them so distinctive is the black markings around the neck and head. These extra black markings are what attracts many breeders to them as compared to the Chukar partridge.

The Red legged partridges are the western European representatives of the group of Rock or Chukar partridges. Unlike the latter, they are predominantly lowland or hill loving birds that adapt well to scrub, grasslands and cultivated fields. Earlier found in western and southern Germany, their current range is restricted to central France south to northwestern Italy and west throughout the Iberian peninsula. They have been successfully introduced into England and several island groups. There is one species and five subspecies of this bird in Europe where they are native. Some taxonomists consider the Corsican as doubtfully different from the French red-leg.

Description

Forepart of crown blue-gray becoming brown on top of head and nape. Throat white, edged with black. A mantle of black and white; over the neck and upper breast. Back and upper covert olive brown. Middle breast blue-gray. Upper flanks barred with black, white and chestnut. Belly buff. Tail feathers cinnamon except for the buff central pair. Beak and legs coral red. Male with blunt spurs. Female similar to male, but slightly smaller and without spurs. Subspecies with minor color variations. Length 13½ inches. Weight about a pound. May be separated from the Chukar by the speckled mantle and from the Barbary Partridge by the white rather than blue-gray cheeks and throat bordered by black rather than brown.

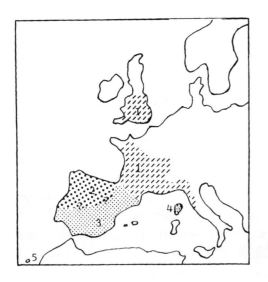

Range of the Red-legged Partridges

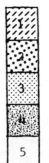

1. French redleg
   (A. r. rufa)
2. Northern Spanish redleg
   (A. r. hispanica)
3. Southern Spanish redleg
   (A. r. intercedens)
4. Corsican redleg
   (A. r. corsa)
5. Canary Island redleg
   (A. r. australis)

Habitat

Unlike the Chukars, the Red-leggeds show no preference for steep, rocky slopes or rugged, mountainous terrain. They are partial to flat or rolling country and to the adjacent, often rough hills and valleys between. They occur from sea level to 7,000 feet though are much less abundant at the higher elevations. Preferred habitats include cultivated fields, open meadows, moderately grazed pastures, scrubby areas and savanna-like wooded patches usually without dense cover beneath. Fairly open brush lands, especially if adjacent to cultivation are often utilized as roosting or escape cover. Lush meadows, thick brush and well-forested areas are generally avoided except for edge cover. Swampy and wet meadows are generally avoided. The natural vegetation within their ranges is similar to that occurring in parts of the Pacific States and from eastern Colorado and Texas eastward through the unforested parts of the South (Allen, 1984).

The species most often found in captivity are the French red-legged. These have been raised for a number of years. Another subspecies that we are personally familiar with is the Spanish red-legged. We feel that they are more attractive.

A problem with the Spanish red-legged partridge is that most of them are badly inbred. I understand that there has recently been some new blood imported which should help the captive stock considerably. These are my favorite of the two subspecies. They are larger than the French and are more brightly colored. It seems that through the years, the French have been used as breeding stock of the commercial breeders. It may be difficult to get a pure strain of these now. It is a shame when breeding stock does not stay pure. A cross here and one there is all it takes to ruin a strain of game birds. I would hope that someone would get hold of pure Spanish and keep them going for the next generation of game bird breeders.

Some have trouble sexing these birds. They can be sexed easily when mature, but the immature are sometimes difficult to deal with. The size of the head is a good indicator. Also, the vent sexing method can be used.

Breeders and young should be managed like any other member of the family. They should pose no special problems and should be easy to raise if the stock is strong and not inbred.

Red-legged partridge

Arabian Red-legged Partridge
(Alectoris melanocephala)

Photo on cover upper right

This is one of the most beautiful partridges that is native to the Arabian peninsula. It inhabits southern Saudi Arabia from Jiddah east to Muscat in Oman and south to the Aden Protectorate (Johnsgard, 1988). There is only one subspecies, *A. M. Quichardi* which is native from El Hajar and eastern Habramaut in Saudi Arabia. Some authorities say it is intergrading with *Melanocephala* (Meinertzhagen 1954).

Like the other Rock partridges this is a gregarious species traveling in small groups of five to eight wondering the desert looking for food. In the wild they nest from March to August depending on weather conditions.

Several years ago the San Diego Zoo imported some of these birds and have moderate success in raising some young. I believe that only five specimens were imported and only one of these pairs had reproduced thus giving only siblings from which to make up new pairs. The other pair could have laid eggs by now which would be very good to keep the gene-pool strong. There are several private breeders that have them in their collection. They are handled like the other partridges and are delicate the first few days of life.

At the Wild Animal Park in Escondido, I have spend some time observing a pair of these birds. The male was aggressive to his keeper and was very tame. He would come over to the wire and threaten or beg. I never was sure which was the case. I was told that this pair on display was siblings and the Park did not set any of their eggs which were in a nest under a bush.

These are very distinctive birds and should be in great demand. As you see in the cover photograph they are very beautiful with rich marble blue patterns on the back with a beautifully laced neck.

See-see Partridge

(Ammoperdix griseogularis)

Many *"old timers"* will remember this bird from many years ago when several states were propagating it. This bird was a candidate for release in Nevada and maybe one or two other western states at one time. When the project was judged to be unworthy, the birds were released to some private breeders.

For some reason this pretty bird never caught on with aviculturists. There are a few still left, but it has been years since any have been offered for sale. This is rather sad as there are many good things about the See-see which make him desirable. His beauty is striking.

The males have an ashy-grey foreneck. A white band runs from lore's through eye and ear coverts ending posteriorly in a Rufus patch, bordered above and below by black lines. The black line above is broader and stretches from across forehead backward to the nape. The outer tail feathers are chestnut. Underparts are pinkish-buff, horizontally streaked on the flanks with black and chestnut. Orange bill and yellow legs set him off (Ali and Ripley, 1969).

Their call, constantly heard in the spring, is a clear double note, "soo-see" which is coupled with a whistling chirp (Strange, 1958).

Chicks should be raised like other partridge chicks. If the breeder has trouble getting the chicks to eat, it may be necessary to resort to some tricks described in earlier sections.

This is a very interesting species of partridge and one that should be given more attention. Personally, I would like to get some of these to do some research on their habits as they are very interesting birds.

Several years ago, I had a late night phone call regarding these birds. The caller wanted to know what he had and told me some things about them. I immediately recognized them by his description as See-see partridge. The gentleman was very impressed with the birds and was glad to know what he had. He went into great detail about their uncanny characteristic of never flying into the side of the flight pen. They would circle the top of the pens. Apparently, these were some birds that the state of Nevada had worked with in years past as the man lived in that state. After some restocking efforts Nevada abandoned the efforts as the birds did not take well like the Hungarian Partridge and other introduced species. He got them from some vendor who did not really know what they were. The low price caused the buyer to be somewhat suspicious as he should have been. However, after getting the birds home he was delighted with them.

I have wished often that I had gotten the telephone number of the man so I could follow up on his experiences with the birds. Also, he would be a potential supplier of some breeding stock if he had success with them. If any reader has some of these birds, let me urge them to keep the gene-pool as strong as possible.

One of the curious aspects about aviculture is **why some birds become popular and others do not.** I have studied this for more than thirty years and have come up with not a bit of concrete evidence about what the real cause is. Perhaps breeders like the way the bird **looks,** or the **ease of propagation.**

Our case in point, the **See-see** is a very beautiful bird with lots of personality. Why it did not catch on is still a mystery! Perhaps someone can look back into history one of these days and see some trends in the world of aviculture.

Arabian Sand Partridge

(*Ammoperdix heyi* Temminck 1825)

This partridge is really an interesting little bird. It is one of the smallest of the partridges which makes him cute. They are not much larger than a Bobwhite quail and have distinguished bars along their sides as is typical in the Rock partridge family. The nominate race, *A. h. heyi*, lives in the arid and stoney areas from the Jordan Valley of Israel south to southeastern Saudi Arabia, and west to Egypt and Sudan east of the Nile (Johnsgard, 1899).

Johnsgard lists three subspecies:

> **A. h. intermedia**: western Saudi Arabia, south of heyi, south to Aden and Muscat.
> **A. h. nicolli**: Egypt east of the Nile, south to about 27°N latitude.
> **A. h. chomleyi**: Egypt, south of *nicolli*, south to northern Sudan and east to the Red Sea.

Description: Adults. 8½ in. - 9¼ in. Male. Plumage basically vinous with an obvious plumage pattern only on the head and flanks, except for grey tone on head. Thin frontal bank over base of bill to eye pale chestnut; back, wing and center of tail tinged brown and closely barred grey; flanks appear pink-grey, striped with black and chestnut; outer tail feathers red-brown; bill, dull yellow. Female, sandier and greyer, lacking pale patch on ear coverts. Bill yellow-horn or dull yellow. In both, legs dull yellow or yellow (Robbins, 1984).

I saw my first Sand partridge several years ago at the San Diego Wild Animal Park which is an extension of the San Diego Zoo. The pair was in a large walk in aviary at the entrance to the park. They would run back and forth along the upper edge of the enclosure in an effort to get some privacy. They never did tame down but I would be wild with all of those noisy people daily disturbing my privacy. The Zoo has a pair on exhibit down town which are in a sand bottomed aviary about 12 feet by 10 feet and they seem to be quite a bit calmer than those in the larger pen. Perhaps they could be tamed down as they get confidence in their surrounding.

During the spring mating season, the male would get quite aggressive toward some of the other birds in the mixed collection. He would fluff out his sidebar and stand tall and utter a threatening call as he would chase the other birds away from his mate. On one occasion he was doing this and got within a few feet from us which was a thrill. To make a long story short, along the outer edges of the enclosure from the outside one could peer into the heavy vegetation and see their nest. They continued to lay until more than 18 eggs were in the nest.

The Zoo reports that success in hatching these birds has been mixed. It seems that being from a dry and hot area the normal humidity is somewhat lower and the Zoo was having trouble finding out exactly what it should be. The last time I talked to a keeper they were still working on the problem.

The chicks are handled like any other partridge once they are hatched. They are a bit wild and must be handled to avoid problems that come with this characteristic. I would recommend that the breeding pen be on the ground and as large and private as possible at least until the birds get calmer. They do best with no other birds in their breeding pen. Some work and careful research needs to be done with these birds. This would be a real challenge and very rewarding. It would be nice to have these available to private breeders. At this writing, I do not know of anyone except the Zoo that has any. I have hear rumors that there are some private breeders that have brought them into the United States.

Hungarian Partridge

(Perdix perdix)

This is truly one of the most interesting of the more common kept partridges. Some people call this bird the **Grey Partridge**. More often than not, this bird is raised in small numbers by private breeders. Some states, such as Oregon, are raising this bird in large numbers for release in a suitable habitat. The *"Hun"* was introduced to western Oregon in 1900 and to eastern Oregon in 1912. Initial stock was imported from central Europe while later releases came from birds raised on game farms (Masson and Mace, 1974). Several Western states have a similar restocking program although the birds at liberty can raise families and reproduce in their new environment.

Sexes can be distinguished most accurately in the **Grey Partridge** by the markings on wing coverts and scapulars. In the adult male, a single longitudinal buff stripe extends from the tip of the feather to the quill; in the female, cross bars run out from the longitudinal stripe (Yocom, 1943).

Description

Forehead and cheeks pale chestnut. Crown dark brown. Back brown streaked with buff on sides. Upper tail coverts light brown with darker bars. Neck and breast gray with a conspicuous dark chestnut horseshoe mark on lower breast. Flanks barred with chestnut. Tail feathers chestnut. Females and

juveniles lacking or with an indistinct dark or sometimes whitish horseshoe.
Length 12 inches. Weight almost a pound.

Habitat and Climate

Adaptable to a variety of open land habitats from extensive cultivation
with little cover to alpine meadows, heaths, bogs and brush lands. Not a forest
dweller.

Central Russian gray (*P.p. lucida*)
Azerbaijan gray (*P.p. canescens*)
Siberian gray (*P.p. robusta*)

RANGE OF THE EASTERN GRAY PARTRIDGES

Native Range

The Hungarian (Grey Partridge) is one of the most common game birds in Europe. Its range extends from France in the West to Siberia in the East. The Hungarian Partridge for practical purposes has been divided into the Western and Eastern subspecies.

Huns are not easy to propagate. I should qualify this by saying it is not easy to get fertile eggs. It seems that they are one of the few upland game birds that must choose their own mates. If a mate is chosen for them that they do not like they will not mate up as pairs. The hens will lay, but of course all her eggs will be infertile without the services of her *"drafted"* partner. My feeling is that most of the private breeders do not go to all of this trouble to get true mated pairs.

WESTERN RANGES OF THE GRAY PARTRIDGES

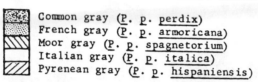

Common gray (P. p. perdix)
French gray (P. p. armoricana)
Moor gray (P. p. spagnetorium)
Italian gray (P. p. italica)
Pyrenean gray (P. p. hispaniensis)

The following gives some insight on a method of handling young Hungarian partridge (Hoffman, 1974). *"Before transferring to the brooder house, the unit was on for at least 24 hours at a temperature of 98° F. The floor of the house was covered with small gravel, large enough to prevent the chicks from eating it. A brooding and rearing unit consisting of a 10 feet by 12 feet brooder house, a 10 feet by 12 feet sheltered cover".*

"Newly hatched, chicks were started in brooder houses with a 20 inch high metal draft guard in an oblong circular arrangement around electric brooders. Game bird starter feed was scattered on several newspapers on the floor and waterers were scattered freely over the area. Care was taken not to make any abrupt changes in this feeder-waterer arrangement."

Male Hungarian (Gray) partridge

Madagascar Partridge

(Margaroperdix madagascariensis) Scopoli 1786

Recently some of these beautiful birds were brought to North America and there is much hope that they can become well established in captivity. Coming from the island of Madagascar, they are not found in great numbers in the wild due to the small size of the island.

A description shows how beautiful these birds are:

Adults 10". **Male**. Upper parts reddish-brown with shaft stripes of white and mostly with rufous or buff crossbars; a line of black feathers with whitish shaft stripes down the middle of the head; sides of the head and throat black, with white stripes over the eye and along the sides of the throat; foreneck and middle of chest chestnut; sides grey; middle of breast and belly black with oval white spots; sides and flanks mostly chestnut; tail black barred with reddish-white; bill black. **Female**. Black generally above, mixed with olive-brown with pale shaft stripes and bars as in the male; throat, sides of head and underparts mostly rufous-buff, the latter with concentric black lines on each feather; sides and flanks barred with black (Robbins, 1984).

It is too early to have any data on the propagation of these newly imported birds. If they can be established in captivity, they promise to make a very suitable addition to the aviary.

I have not had correspondence with the men that are working with them, but have talked by phone to a gentleman in England that has had much success with them. He indicated that they were fairly hardy little birds and that there would probably be no more imported from the island of Madagascar because of political reasons. The birds were becoming very scarce in the wild and the government had or was planning to ban all exportations.

This family of upland game birds would make a wonderful project for some keen game bird breeder. Not much work has been done with these birds in the United States. They are readily available in Europe and could be imported if the funds were available. All of these birds have such rich coloration one falls for them immediately.

Common Hill-partridge
(Arborophila torqueola torqueola) Valenciennes

This family of partridges is little known to the average breeder in the United States. Their common names contain *"Hill"* partridges. Davison (1982) shows that there are 16 species of this unique and beautiful family. All have the same general size and body conformation and are distinct only by color markings and origin. All of the Hill partridges are strikingly beautiful because of their rich coloration. To really appreciate their beautiful color they must be looked at from the hand. These birds are about the size of the Chukar partridge, but built closer to the ground, and live in forests in the tropical to temperate areas of eastern and southeastern Asia and Taiwan. This area includes a vast geographical difference. Generally, the sexes are alike and none have spurs (1988). This family is a challenge to the true aviculturist. Very few species are known to be in captivity anywhere in the world.

These partridges have well-developed bills and legs for pecking and scratching on the ground. All have rounded wings and short tails. Male plumage is usually colorful, sometimes spectacular; females are mostly drab. They tend to be shy in places where hunted. They usually feed in the morning and late afternoon. Their crops allow them to store food between meals (Fleming, Fleming and Bangdel, 1979).

There are three forms recognized: the gray-breasted group, the brown-breasted group, and the scaly-breasted group. This family of partridges differ from Perdix (Chukars) in habits and important structural detail. There is a supraorbital row of bones in the skull extending from the lachrymal to the postorbital process such as is found in the Tinamous of the Neotropical region. The Common Hill-partridge is the bird that has found its way most often into the pens of the private bird breeder. It has been available at a high price for many years. This genus ranges from the Western Himalayas right across to eastern Assam and through the Indochinese and Indo-malayan regions.

In the wilds, they live in ravines and hillsides that are not too steep and clad in dense forest of oak, laurel, and other evergreen trees and shrubs. They are gregarious and keep in coveys of five to 10 birds in dense undergrowth, scratching for food among the rich mulch and humus on the forest floor. It trusts its legs for escape, but when suddenly come upon or flushed by a dog, it will fly strongly, moving easily through the maze of tree trunks and other obstacles. They often take refuge up in a leafy branch. They roost at night in trees with the covey sitting huddled together along the branch.

Robbins gives their description:

Adults 11". Sexes very similar. Short tailed, dumpy olive-brown partridge. Crown and nape bright chestnut, with the nape also spotted with black, narrow forehead and broad supercilium black. A black spotted chestnut line under supercilium, cheeks black, ear coverts bright chestnut, bare crimson skin around the eye, upperparts golden olive-brown finely barred with black and broadly mottled with chestnut and black. Chin, throat and neck black. Remainder of underparts grey and white with broad chestnut streaks and white drops on flanks, vent rufous-white with black bars, under tail coverts black and white. Eyes brown to crimson-brown, bill dark brown (Robbins, 1984).

Ali and Ripley give some interesting information about the voice and calls. They make a single low mournful whistle (1½ seconds long), repeated every two or three seconds, reminiscent of the awkward intake effort of a school child learning to whistle. This is repeated slowly two or three times and followed by a series of three to six mellow double whistles in ascending scale, vaguely reminiscent of the hawk-cuckoo. They have been rendered as **bobwhite, bobwhite, bobwhite, or do-eat, do-eat, do-eat** (first syllable short, second prolonged). Frequently one bird leads off with a shrill continuous call by way of invitation and accompaniment; a second bird promptly joins in with a crescendo call, the duet ending rather abruptly when the climax is reached. The birds answer one another from different directions and are particularly vocal in the mornings and evenings (Ali and Ripley, 1980).

Care of the chicks should be "intensive" by checking on the little fellows every hour or two. They will need more care than the ordinary Chukar chick. A high protein diet should be fed the chicks to help them develop during their quick growth. Some breeders use a bantam hen to brood the delicate chicks at first. They are sometimes difficult to get to eat on their own and the bantam does a good job teaching them to eat. Be sure the chicken does not have any parasites either internal or external as they will surely infest the little chicks. A program of preventive medication should be adapted to keep down infection until a natural resistance can be built up. Watch for the more common diseases such as Coccidiosis and Blackhead. Medication for these problems usually are very effective. With rare birds I usually have a regular medication procedure. I give a low preventive dosage of Solu-tracin 200 for the first 10 days which gives them a good start. I then go off all medication for at least two weeks. This allows the good bacteria to regrow in the systems of the little birds. If medication is given regularly, the bacteria are not allowed to built up and the resistance of the chick is reduced. They often get fungal and other problems. I usually put these rare chicks on medication one week out of each month until they mature. This extra protection often gives them the boost they need to get through the period of their lives when they are highly nonresistant to disease.

Watch for an outbreak of Coccidiosis. If this occurs take immediate action by giving the proper medication. Be sure there is no buildup of excrement which is an invitation to Coccidiosis.

Several years ago some Common Hill Partridge were imported and are occasionally available for purchase, but the price remains very high as the supply is limited. There are quite a few breeders in the U.K. that are raising these beautiful birds, but they have never been bred by many in America. This is a real shame as they are a very beautiful bird. I would hope that someone would import several pairs of these birds before the doors of importation are completely closed. This would make them more available to more breeders and their popularity should go up as a result.

Not recommended for the beginner, they are a real challenge for the experienced aviculturist.

Javan Hill-partridge

A.K.A. Chestnut-bellied Hill-partridge

(Arborophila javanica (Gmelin) 1789

The Javan Hill-partridge falls into the group known as the gray-breasted which show generally the color patterns they sport. This bird is native to the island of Java and is said to live as high as 3500 feet in the mountains of this island. It is known in the United States by two vernacular names, Javan and Chestnut-bellied. In several other countries it is known as Brown-breasted tree-partridge.

In the wilds, the breeding season is quite extended, with records for January through to April, and from July through to November (Johnsgard 1988).

About four years ago I noticed that some of these birds were offered for sale by a bird importer for $600 a pair. Only two pairs were available in this shipment. I have often wished that I had got these birds as I have admired them each time I go to the San Diego Zoo and Wild Animal Park where they are on display. I have not seen them available since, and I suppose that none will be brought into the U.S. since the passage of the new Bird Law. There are several breeders in Europe that are having success with these birds.

A few pairs of these birds have found their way to our local zoo where a few chicks are being hatched and raised. The zoo also has the Sumatra Hill-partridge. From a conversation with Allen Liebermann, Curator of Birds at the San Diego Zoo at the time, I learned that these birds are not easy to raise to maturity. If one can raise Roulrouls, Mr. Liebermann feels that these can be successfully raised. The zoo keeps their pairs in mixed aviaries planted with tropical plants and of course get the misting regularly for high humidity. I became good friends with the pair at the Wild Animal Park as I visited them nearly every week. The female of the pair is very gentle but her mate is quite nervous by nature. I mentioned this to Mr. Liebermann and he informed me that the hen was hand-raised and the cock bird was brought from Germany and probably was a wild caught bird. This would explain the difference.

Fertility is very high from the zoo birds. The problem is the mortality of the chicks. They start easily enough, but they often die during maturation probably before their immune system has started. Out of four chicks hatched probably only one will make it to maturity. The mortality rate could possibly be lowered by spending more time with the chicks to see that all goes well with them. A bantam hen could raise more of the chicks in the opinion of Mr. Liebermann.

It would be a good thing to get more of these birds into the hands of the private breeders as they are one of the most attractive partridges in the Hill family. The breeders that have them are facing the difficulty of badly inbred birds as there is not that much diversified blood around.

Every time I go to the San Diego Zoo, I make a point of seeing the pair there on display. They are always busy scratching in the leaf-mold for insect tidbits. They are fairly tame once they settle into their quarters. When first introduced into a new environment they appear quite nervous. The cock bird will find an insect and call his lady over to enjoy the treat. What a great sight! I plan to get into these wonderful birds when possible.

Javan Hill partridge *(Arborophila javanica)*.

Ferruginous Wood Partridge

PLATE C

(Caloperdix oculea) Temminck 1815

This is another rare bird in captivity. They are *"tropical"* in habitat and must be kept in frost free aviaries. The birds that I know of all are in Southern California and are not producing in great numbers although they are quite hardy and are adaptable to captive conditions.

A description would be as follows:

Adults 10½." Sexes alike. Rufus-buff head with dark chestnut crown and a black line behind the eye. Black lower hindneck, back and sides of body are with white to rufus-buff scales; upper belly and breast is unmarked, bright ferruginous. Rump and upper tail coverts black with light rufous `V' shaped marks; tail, black; eyes, dark olive-brown; bill black; feet, olive-green (Robbins, 1984).

The eggs are a glossy white and hatch in about 20 days. These interesting partridges build a domed nest on the ground that has a side entrance about one inch off the ground. (Much the same as the Roulroul Partridge). The chicks are delicate and require special attention until they are older. Since this is a tropical bird there should be fruit and vegetables added to the diet along with mealworms. Small mealworms are helpful in getting the chicks started.

Fràncis Billie, a renowned authority on birds, provides the following information about the keeping and breeding of this species. *"In captivity the problems of keeping and breeding Ferruginous Wood Partridge are distinctly different from and much greater than those of propagating other partridges and quails, and as a result, few people have succeeded in keeping and raising them in any real numbers."*

"Some of the problems associated with their management in captivity are their sensitivity to the various poultry diseases and parasites transmitted by ground contact, forcing the breeder to keep the birds on wire-bottomed cages so they have no direct contact with the ground or their own droppings. This however is not a good

idea because on wire they will get feet and leg problems. The worst enemy of these birds in captivity is Crop Worm. Another infection they are quite susceptible to is Pullorum disease, a bacterial infection caused by Salmonella. Still another is Aspergillosis, a fungus disease of the respiratory tract."

"Most breeders take the eggs and incubate them. If this method is to be used, eggs should not be held longer than a week before being placed in the incubator, and during storage they should be kept at a temperature of between 50° F. and 60° F. and relative humidity of around 80-90 percent. They should be stored with the pointed ends down. Tilting them or turning them daily during the pre-incubation storage period is also desirable. Incubation may be done in either a still air or forced air incubator with the latter generally preferred although considerably more expensive. In either case the eggs should be rotated ninety degrees every three to six hours or at a similar regime until the last few days of incubation when they are moved to hatching trays."

"Ideal incubation temperatures differ with the type of incubator being used. The best for incubating eggs in a still air is 103° F. with 60-65 percent relative humidity for the first two weeks and 99½° F. in a forced air machine with similar relative humidity as for the still air method. For best results there should be an increase in the availability of fresh air. The final humidity should be somewhat higher than earlier in incubation. The incubation period is 18-20 days."

"Following hatching, chicks must be provided with heat and artificial brooders are best since bantam hens are too large for these very small chicks. The initial temperature of the brooder should be 90° F. which is then gradually reduced for the next two weeks to around 80°."

"Newly hatched chicks should be provided with high protein food such as chick starter, and in addition may benefit from finely cut fresh green leaves from lettuce, endive or dandelion leaves. With Ferruginous live insect food such as mealworms, may be critical in inducing the young to begin eating. Also by sprinkling Purina Startina with hard-boiled eggs and finely chopped greens along with small live and chopped up mealworms will get them started and provide extra nutrition for a good, healthy start in life."

"For water I recommend jar lids filled with water and marbles. Also add one teaspoon of Terramycin per gallon or maybe ½ teaspoon of Head Start per quart of water, as a disease preventative (Billie, 1985)."

Roulroul Partridge

(Rollulus roulroul)

PLATE D

GEO. W. NOREEN

The Roulroul (**Red-crested Wood Partridge**) has no known subspecies. They range from south Thailand, Malaysia, Sumatra, to Borneo. Lowland forests, bamboo groves and clearings within an old forest seem to suit them as a habitat. Large fruits, seed, various insects, including wood ants make up their diet in the wild.

Description

Adults. 10" (25.4cm) Sexes different. Typical Wood partridge. **Male**: Maroon crest, red orbital skin and patch on bill, white patch on crown; dark glossy plumage (appears black in poor light) reddish feet, wings dark brown. Eyes red; bill, upper mandible red; rest black. **Female**: Glossy green plumage with chestnut scapulars and rusty brown wings, dark grey head and reddish legs and orbital skin diagnostic. Eyes, red; bill, black; legs, red (Robbins, 1984).

Some Interesting Observations

As late as 1971, aviculturists began to take notice of this interesting species of partridge. Several research projects were conducted with them at the Washington, D.C. Zoo, The Los Angeles Zoo, and one or two private breeders.

Probably the most interesting habit about this little Southeast Asian game bird is its nesting. Both sexes seem to help gather litter from around the nest site, and they pile it up, the female doing most of the work according to Frank Todd. They then make a hole leading into about the middle where an area is enlarged big enough for a nest. Mr. Todd tells us that they remove the eggs, and in this way they've had hens lay 20 to 30 eggs. He says in Southern California, the Roulroul egg laying season begins in April and extends into September. After producing 15 eggs or so, a hen will often begin laying again in a month or so. They are sometimes getting Roulroul eggs as late as September. He says the incubation period is 18 days, and the chicks hatch quickly once they pip and begin eating well from the beginning, and they have no trouble raising them. He describes the egg as most interesting and unique. It is pure white and very pointed, sort of triangular in shape, but of course with rounded edges. It is what you might say abnormally large in proportion to the species. The L. A. Zoo used a forced air incubator, and a temperature of 99½° F. and 87 percent humidity seems to be ideal for Roulroul eggs under their atmospheric conditions there in Southern California. Because of their natural nesting conditions in the humid rain forests, running a machine with slightly higher humidity than is used for many other types of game birds is probably necessary for best results.

I was recently in touch with Dr. Michael E. Dam, Jr., another famous bird breeder familiar to everyone in the fancy, and he added a couple more interesting bits of information about Roulroul management for this story. He mentions that this species will produce their first year and that the clutch is four or five eggs which they will incubate themselves, but if removed, you can get several times this many. Apparently either or both sexes construct the nest, for while Frank Todd reported the hens at the L. A. Zoo do most of it, Dr. Dam says his cock birds have done most of the nest building at his collection. Also Dr. Dam points out the *"gallant"* behavior of the cock bird that Mr. Charles Sivelle mentioned of picking up food and feeding it to his mate by putting it in her beak. Dr. Dam thinks that feeding Roulroul chopped peanuts and mealworms, which they love, is a good way to stimulate their sexual instincts and get them to breed. He also recommends that you feed them lots of fruit like peaches, pear, apples, oranges, etc.

Roulrouls appear to be monogamous in their mating. It is reported that during the part of the year they are not engaged in reproduction activities, they group up in what you might call coveys like Valley and some other kinds of quail do. They live most of their lives on the ground, foraging around for food and caring for their broods during the breeding season and seldom fly unless pressed to do so. They probably roost in trees or bushes at night in their natural environment since in pens they'll sleep on a limb or perch (Allen, 1971).

"Even though they are susceptible to cold weather, we have found that if they are well acclimated, they do well. Our temperature here occasionally drops to the high twenties, and they weathered that with no apparent ill effects. However, we provide a great deal of ground cover and litter, such as pine needles that might offer some protection. It is important to put the birds outside in the spring if one is going to winter them outside to allow proper acclimation."

"I reported earlier that the female does most of the nest building. Although this is the case most of the time, we have one pair where the male is more active. The hen tosses a pine needle over her back to the male who then tosses it over his back and piles it up to form the dome into which they make a cavity for the nest. In our experience, we have found pine needles are the most suitable nesting material (Todd, 1971)."

In 1993, I got three pairs of these very beautiful birds. The males were very beautiful with their very stately or kingly carriage. However, I must say, the hens were much prettier with the irredecent greenish color of their bodies. They were much more tame than the males and all would come to your finger for mealworms or for bird scratch.

Their pens were about seven feet long by 30 inches wide and about two feet high. The sides were made of plywood and the bottoms were half covered with hardware cloth. The other half of the bottom was plywood to hold the four inches of river sand in the rear of the pen. I had a door at both ends to service their needs. Tall grass clumps were placed in the back of the pen on the sand to give cover and security. When we came into the room where they were located they would dash up to the from of the pen to get their treats fed by hand. They liked green grass pulled up by the roots and of course they loved green lettuce. Chopped apples were fed in season and we even tried fresh oranges cut into little pieces which they sampled if nothing else was available. Their regular diet was game bird crumbles which were before them at all times. The nest was built in the back corner of the pen.

I had one pair per pen. Other breeders colony breed these birds in pairs in large ground pens around 12 by 12 feet per three pairs. The birds soon establish their area and do not bother the other pairs. Brush and other cover should be placed heavily in this pen arrangement to give ample security from the neighbors.

Breeders report that once the pairs start to lay, the eggs keep rolling out. Some hens lay up to 60 eggs per clutch. They are very prolific layers. The problems comes with getting the chicks to start right. The parent birds feed the chicks from their beaks. The breeder might have to try all sorts of tricks to get the chicks started eating. Teacher chicks are the most popular. These can be older Roulrouls or a Coturnix chick about the same size. The young chicks should be kept on wire if at all possible to enhance their chance of survival. I have heard of some breeders using bantam hens to hatch and raise the young chicks. This seems to work well for some but not for others. I suppose it is in the management of the broody hen that makes the difference. Coccidiosis and Blackhead disease should be medicated against as the young are very susceptible to these problems. This is especially important if they are kept in ground pens.

I have never figured out why these partridges are not more popular. They have gotten a bad name as some are known to be hard to raise. Their price is very high. I paid something like $400 per pair but the birds were unrelated which made them worth the price to me.

Bamboo Partridge

(Bambusicola thoracica)

This interesting little partridge has not become too popular and this is a shame. It is a very colorful bird, but many birds that were once in the United States have now died out.

There are actually two species of Bamboo partridges. The first is not well known. A common name is **Mountain Bamboo partridge**. It's native land is western China, northern Vietnam, east Pakistan, and Burma. The native range is not restricted to bamboo forests as the name suggests (Robbins, 1984).

It is doubtful that any of these birds have ever been imported into the United States. It is thought that Jean Delacour had some at one time.

The **Chinese Bamboo partridge** is the little bird that is in U.S. aviaries. There are two subspecies, one from mainland China and the other from Formosa.

Robbins (1984) gives us a description of this pretty little bird:

Adults. 10½ in. "Forehead to back of neck dusky grey, lighter from base of bill over eye to side of neck. Side of head below eye, throat and side of neck rufous, color extending irregularly to upper back. Upper parts mottled deep ruddy and fulvous on slaty olive-grey. The feathers are finely marked darker. Primaries dusky, edged lighter; tertiaries tipped fulvous, lower back without mottlings. Tail deep rufous, finely barred with broken black. Breast from throat bluish-grey, color extending to shoulders, bordered on barred lower side by rich ruddy-rufous; underparts yellowish-rufous, spotted with dark brown and ruddy; center of belly unmarked; bill and feet, dark brown (Robbins)."

The Formosian bamboo partridge is much like the Chinese except much darker. I have heard that most prefer the lighter, brighter Chinese species. Both species display the charm and beauty of this unique little partridge. I enjoyed the pair that I had many years ago.

The chicks are not easy to raise for they are fed from the beak by the parent birds (Strange, 1958). We can testify to this fact as we had trouble with one or two of our chicks not eating. They would cry during the night and my wife would get up and put a mealworm down their throat and they would be quiet for a few more hours. After two or three days of hand feeding and using all the tricks in the book the chicks will learn to eat on their own. We found that more than one chick raised together caused them to learn to eat much faster than a single chick raised alone.

If the chicks don't eat readily on their own, there are some tricks that can be used to get them to eat. The most common one is to put in another chick (Button quail or Coturnix quail) that sets an example in eating. The *"teaching chick"* must be a variety that is not aggressive to other chicks. Also, to get the chicks to eat you can mix some of the feed into a mash and simply **throw** some of it against the sides of the brooder box. The chicks will be heard pecking the sides of the box as they investigate the spots of feed on the wall of the box.

Our hand raised chicks were quite tame. They would take mealworms out of our hands and seemed to be content with us about their pen. We kept them in a large walk in type pen and would work with them every day. Although wild at first, these birds could be tamed to make very gentle inhabitants of an aviary provided that enough time was given to the taming process.

The mating cry of this partridge is **outstanding**. The noise would rule them out of any **civilized neighborhood**. If you are thinking about getting these birds, be aware of the weird mating cry they make. Tip your neighbors off ahead of time so they won't call the Cops and accuse you of wife beating. The call starts low and gradually goes up the scale and continues for up to a minute or longer. The first time we heard it no one knew what it was. Frankly, we grew fond of the call and looked forward to hearing it. When you know what it is, it is rather musical.

Part 4

SOME FAVORITE PHEASANTS

Japanese Green pheasant.

196　Some Favorite Pheasant

THE PHEASANT FAMILY

(Pheasianidae)

The Pheasant family is not native to North America. However, most people are familiar with the game pheasants known as *"Ringnecks"* and assume that they are native Americans. Probably, no other family is more colorful and striking in appearance as the *Phasianidae genus.*

All members of this genus have the same traits such as: 1) the hen always is the nest builder 2) she is also the setter and raises the family without the assistance of the male 3) she is always the more plain in coloration (Gerrits, 1974).

Pheasants can provide a challenge of a lifetime. There is still much more to be learned about them both in the wild and in captivity. Pheasants are excellent aviary birds. They spend most of their time on the ground and thus they adapt well to large ground type pens. Their diets are easily adjusted to captivity as they are omnivorous with seeds, berries and the like forming most of their daily diet. They will also eat insects, mealworms, and other animal matter. Nothing is more thrilling than to see a *"clipped or pinioned"* pheasant loose in an uncovered pen. Some species are quite adaptive to this type of situation provided that predators are controlled. Every pheasant fancier should acquaint himself with the habits and nature of the species that he intends to work with as some of the species are quite different and must be handled accordingly.

Since these are rather large birds, it is best that they are kept in large ground pens to keep their feathers in good condition. I do know of a breeder that keeps his birds in large wire bottomed pens because of the wet climate, but this is unusual.

Ornamental pheasants can offer the aviculturist many hours of enjoyment. Many are very tame and make friends with their keeper. I have had them jump up on my hand for a peanut treat that delighted me to no end. When kept in large pens they keep their feathers in excellent shape and are very beautiful.

The **ASSEMBLY LINE METHOD** of brooding works well with pheasants of any species. The general care that all game birds require works well with this family.

Pheasants have a very large following among the *"show people"* who exhibit their birds at bird shows such as fairs and club events. The birds must conform to the descriptions of the same species in the wild.

Some Favorite Pheasant

We will only discuss our **favorite** pheasants. Coincidentally, some are quite common while others are quite rare pheasants. All of them are striking in their own way. Each one has its own particular personality which makes them not only an interesting group, but very beautiful.

Any one of **our favorite pheasant** would be an excellent bird for the aviculturist. Most are readily available through the ads in the *Gazette*, they are hardy in varying climates, they are good layers, good strong bloodlines are available, and some have built up some disease resistance.

New in this revised edition is a discussion of the Tragopan family of pheasants. Some of the subspecies are not readily available to the average breeder, but are included anyway to add to your "want list". I must admit that this family of pheasants offers challenge and interest to most pheasant breeders. Some of the information on the "Trags" is not given from personal experience but from the experience of successful breeders of this species.

Ringneck Pheasant

(Phasianus colchicus)

This is the most commonly known pheasant in America because of its great numbers in the wild in the middle and western states. There are 32 different subspecies of this very beautiful bird. The description gives the general appearance of the family. They all are very similar with some minor differences.

Male: Crown: greyish, bronze-green with distinct white eyebrow. Head and neck: dark bluish-green with distinct purple cast. Eye: very dark brown. Ring: Wide, being slightly narrower in front and rear, having a narrow, but distinct break or interruption of approximately ¼ to ½ inch in front. Breast: A rich purplish-red with black edged markings. Belly: The belly or abdomen is blackish-brown. Upper back: light golden yellow feathers with black edging. Shoulders: maroon-chestnut with black and light buff centers. Flanks: very light golden-yellow with large black markings. Wing: the wing has a bluish-grey patch changing to reddish-chestnut and grey markings in the lesser and secondary coverts. Rump: light bluish-grey with a few of the upper feathers being marked with small black and white, green sheened markings. The lower outer fringes are rusty red. Tail: heavy black bars extending part way towards outer fringe, followed by dark brown shadow into fringe. Legs: medium grey approximately three inches in length from knee to pad of foot. Weight: Yearling two to two ¼ pounds. Two year two ¼ to two ½ pounds (Gazette, 1962).

The hen is much smaller than the male with brown mottled markings over entire body. Body confirmation similar to male with markings variable.

We raised Ringnecks in Montana and had quite an enjoyable experience with them. We purchased day old chicks out of Idaho. They were handled like any game bird and were brooded on the floor under a hover type brooder with success. The neighbor's dog got in one night and scattered them all over the field. It turned out better than we thought, we simply netted them and put them back into their pen. Luckily, they were not wild and we got all but about 12 of them back.

I pinioned them and let them out in an open topped pen grown up in grass and brush. It turned out that the neighborhood owls were very fat that year. I discovered that the birds were disappearing one a night, so the experiment was abandoned.

An interesting thing was to study the color variations in the cock birds. Some had a very beautiful blue saddle while others had bright green saddles. Besides being interesting to see, this variation is probably evident in the wilds as I have heard hunters claim that only a very old bird will have a blue saddle. Mine were first year birds that had the blue saddles, but I never told the guy he was wrong about this.

These pheasants gave me the first experience with **mass cannibalism** when they were growing in their long tail feathers. I struggled with the problem for about two weeks before their feathers grew out long enough to hide the *"pickable"* area. Everything was tried, and finally, we worked through this stage in their maturing. No disease problem was encountered and they took the cold climate very well after maturity. They preferred to roost out in the open on the ground even during storms.

Besides the Chinese ringneck, there is a type of Ringneck that is very popular called **Jumbo ringneck**. This bird was developed beginning just after the War by Mr. and Mrs. I. J. Perkins of Oconomowoc, Wisconsin. They began by mating just the larger birds with the best qualities each year (Allen, 1969). The resulting birds weigh over 7 pounds and have become the mainstay for many commercial game bird farms.

We should mention that many years ago our first experience with pheasants was with the **Mongolian pheasant**. When I first saw the size and brilliant colors as compared to the Chinese ringneck, I knew that I had to have these birds. I had some wonderful *"first time"* experiences with this stock. These birds caused me to begin my long study of pen design. It did not take long for me to learn that the best type of pen for my situation was a **movable** pen that allowed about 15 square feet per breeder bird. The exact dimensions were 10X12 and 6 feet high. The sides were boarded up to about 24 inches to keep outside sights from distracting the inhabitants. The pen was light enough for two people to move it to new grass every week or so. This not only kept the ground clean, but it gave the birds new greens each week. In a few weeks it was possible to rotate the pen back to the original spot as the grass had by then grown up again. The pen was completely covered with wire poultry netting. I remember that I had trouble with predators digging under the sides of the pen and getting to the birds. Finally, I put a 12-inch strip of wire flat on the ground along the outside the four sides. This was enough to keep the predators from trying to dig into the pen. This was back before I discovered the value of an **electric fence charger**. If you have any kind of predator problem with animals, this is the thing to get. Sorrowfully, it will not work on hawks and owls. Every one of my aviaries is now protected by one of these "gadgets."

I had my first experience in marketing game birds as I sold all of the birds to a group that put on a banquet. They were very pleased with the nice plump *"Pheasant Under Glass"*.

Reeve's pheasants have a beautiful long tail and get quite tame.

Reeve's Pheasant

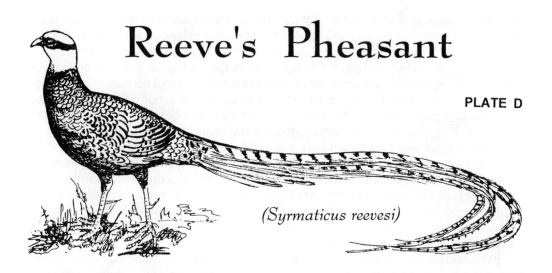

PLATE D

(Syrmaticus reevesi)

These rather large pheasants not only have a beautiful color pattern, but have *"personality plus."* The males can be rather aggressive toward their keepers. Our mature male was always watched very carefully. Our children would not go into the pen with him and when we had to feed and water it was a stand-off on who would intimidate whom. I like to think that we won as we never got **jumped on**, but I am sure that the male pheasant thought that he got the best of us. We had a trio in a very large pen and they kept their tail feathers in good condition. To do justice to a beautiful long-tailed bird like the Reeve's one should have them in a large pen. Never put in another bird of any species with them or the poor thing will surely be killed. The young chicks are also aggressive toward others and will even fight among themselves. They are hardy and a pleasure to have around.

It is interesting to note that years ago these birds were released into the wilds by some Western states. The introduction did not succeed which was a disappointment. The flight of these birds was slow and deliberate which proved not to be much sport to the hunters, although much powder was wasted until the right *"lead"* was learned. Also, the Reeve's are very territorial and they ran out all of the other pheasants from their territory. It was learned that the Ringneck could not live in the same area with the Reeve's. There is said to be a few left in the wilds.

The male has a white crown surrounded by a black band which also covers the forehead, cheeks, ear coverts and nape. A white patch extends from beneath the eye onto the throat and neck; the facial skin and a narrow band above the eye are red.

The mantle, back and rump are mustard-colored, each feather having a deep black border; the wing coverts are white with brown black and chestnut borders, the tertiaries and secondaries barred white, chestnut and black with a broad mustard-yellow tip bordered with black and dark chestnut. The primaries are blackish, barred with brown; the tail, of twenty rectrices, is extremely long, the two central pairs of feathers being silver with curved black and dark brown bars along the shaft and broad yellow margins. The outer tail feathers graduate from silver, with black and dark brown barring, to yellowish-cinnamon, vermiculated with black on the outer feathers. Upper breast has black and chestnut collar separating the white neck from a narrow band of mustard-yellow, black-bordered feathers; the remainder of the breast and flanks are chestnut, barred with black and white, graduating to mustard-yellow and deep cinnamon lower down. The abdomen, vent, thighs and under tail coverts are black.

The female has a reddish-brown crown, the rest of the head being buff with blackish nuchal band and ear coverts; the mantle is mottled black and dark chestnut with large arrow-shaped white markings. The back and rump are greyish-brown finely marked with black, the wing coverts mottled greyish-brown, white and buff with large black spots and primaries and secondaries reddish-brown barred with black. The tail is long and pointed, irregularly barred with buff and dark brown; the shorter feathers are plain chestnut and black with white tip. The lower breast, sides and flanks are boldly mottled pale chestnut, grey and white, while the abdomen and under tail coverts are pale-buff (Wayre, 1969).

One way to tell the strength and purity of the stock is to note the coloration of the white crown on the male. If it has dark streaks in it is said not to be as good as a bird with a pure white crown. Judges in shows look for the white crown and give extra points for this feature.

If you have a large-covered pen and want to fill it with some very interesting birds, try some Reeve's pheasants. You will enjoy them immensely and will spend many hours of enjoyment working with them. Be sure and not mix the chicks or even mature breeding birds with other species.

THE RUFFED PHEASANTS
(Chrysolophus)

Only two species are in the **Ruffed pheasant** family that are probably the most beautiful and popular of all the more common pheasants. These are the **Golden pheasant** and the **Lady Amherst's pheasant**. Very little needs to be said about these beautiful pheasants since they are well known and popular, not only among pheasant fanciers, but with the general public as well, because they are so widely displayed in zoos, parks, other public attractions and private collections (Allen, 1969).

When it comes to these pheasants, there has been a great tragedy happen to the breeding stock in America. Breeders have *"crossed"* these two species to come up with birds with different colors. This process has all but wiped out the **pure** wild bloodlines of these birds. What a shame! There are very few breeders who would know the difference between a **pure** bird and a bird crossed. Interest is building among game bird breeders to propagate the *"pure" and "wild"* representatives of the species. Several breeders are maintaining pure stock which sells for a premium. This is always a controversial subject. What is really pure stock? Just because the stock came from the native country does not mean, it is pure and from the wild. It is sad how easy it is to cross these pheasants up.

Not only will these two species interbreed, but they are very much alike in habits and temperament. Usually, when one species is raised successfully, the other can be treated the same with success. We like both species very much because of their tremendous beauty. Besides being colorful and pleasing to the eyes, they make very nice aviary birds.

Ask any pheasant breeder and he will probably tell you that these two pheasants are by far the most beautiful in their own way. This is great, as they are the least expensive of all the pheasants. Every game bird breeder should consider one of these outstanding pheasants to add to his collection.

Our Ruffed pheasants became quite tame when settled down to our aviary. At first they were extremely wild natured, but soon they became our friends.

Anyone that loves birds will really enjoy having a pair or two of these birds in their collection. Many parks have pinioned Ruffed pheasants roaming free on their grounds. They make a terrific show and the only problem this poses is the danger of predators, especially large owls and hawks. I would develop a plan to pen them up at night if I were doing this again. Their feed and water could be in a shelter and when they go into it each evening they could be penned up. They could be trained to do this on their own as my experience has been they are very intelligent birds and learn fast. Under these conditions they will become quite tame and really put on a show especially during the breeding season. The male will strut his stuff and delight all those that see his antics.

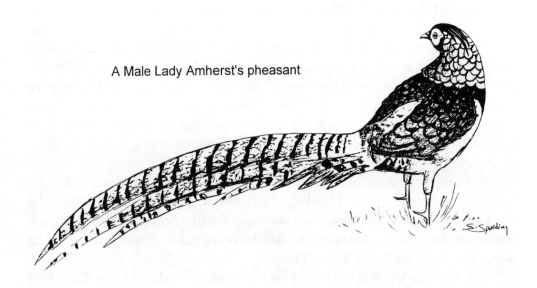

A Male Lady Amherst's pheasant

Lady Amherst's Pheasant

(Chrysolophus amherstiae)

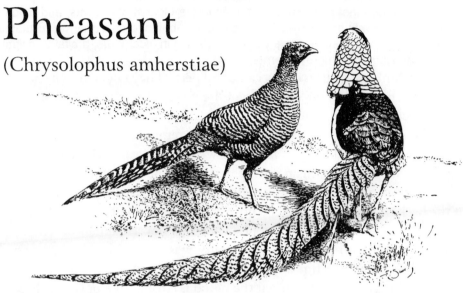

These birds always draw a crowd when the males are mature and have long perfect tails. Their carriage is majestic and rather *"Royal"* and the admiration is well deserved. The following description will give you an idea of their appearance.

Male: Crown covered with short metallic-green feathers; narrow nuchal crest of stiff, elongated crimson feathers; ruff of rounded feathers, white with a blue-and-black border; mantle and scapulars of rounded feathers, metallic bluish-green with a black border edged with scintillant green; feathers of back broad and square, black with a green bar and a wide, buffy yellow fringe; those of the rump with a vermilion fringe; tail-coverts mottled black and white with long orange-vermilion tips; central rectrices irregularly lined black and white with black crossbars; other rectrices similar on the narrow inner web, silver-grey passing to brown outside, with curved black bars on the outer web; wings dark metallic blue with black borders, the primaries only blackish brown sparsely barred with buff; face and throat black, with metallic-green spots, breast like the mantle, the borders of the feathers wider and brighter; rest of the under-parts pure white, the base of the feathers grey, except the lower flanks and vent, which are barred with black and brownish grey; thighs mottled white, black and brown; under-tail-coverts black and dark green more or less barred with white. Iris pale yellow; bare facial skin and lappet bluish or greenish white; bill and feet bluish grey.

Hen: Similar to the Golden pheasant hen, but larger, the dark barring blacker, with a green sheen; crown, sides of head, neck, mantle, lower throat and upper breast strongly washed with reddish chestnut; upper throat and abdomen pale, sometimes white; lores, cheeks and ear-coverts silvery grey spotted with black; back strongly vermiculated; tail feathers rounded, not pointed at the tip, as in the Golden pheasants, and much more strongly marked with broad irregular bars of black, buff and pale grey vermiculated with black. Iris brown, sometimes pale yellow or greyish in older birds; orbital skin light slaty blue; bill and legs bluish grey (Gerrits, 1974).

Our Amherst's pheasants became real pets. They tamed down shortly after we got them as one year old birds. Of course, each strain of these birds will have different personalities.

These birds can take cold weather! The temperature went down to -25 F. and stayed around -10 F. for about six weeks one year and the birds managed just fine. We had them in an open pen that was next to an old horse shed into which they could get during the night and when it snowed. There was a ledge at the back of the shed where the little hen made her nest. We worried that she would push her eggs out of the nest, but this never happened. The nest was built under a box-like structure. It really was an old chicken hen nest that I found. It worked just fine and the hen seemed to appreciate her privacy.

The chicks are easy to raise if the blood is strong. We only got three fertile eggs the first year and only one hatched. Really, to tell the truth, we did not expect them to lay at all the first year. The little chick was raised with some Golden pheasant cousins and did just fine. It was no trouble telling the two species apart although the females are quite similar in appearance. The Amherst's hen is lighter in color than the Golden hen. Also, our *"Ladies"* were a little larger too. There is a different coloration to the feathering. We were careful not to let the two hybridize.

The chicks are somewhat delicate the first few days after they hatch. Care should be taken to be sure that they do not chill until they are eating well to keep up their body heat. We did not notice any special problem with cannibalism with our birds, but we debeaked them when they were about a week old.

Many pheasant breeders use brooding hens to care for the chicks. Since the chicks are about the same size as the mother's own chicks would be, this works just fine. Be sure to see that the broody hen is free from internal and external parasites. Chickens are carriers of several diseases that game birds easily catch.

208   Some Favorite Pheasant

Golden Pheasant

(Chrysolophus pictus)

PLATE E

If you like bright colors, you will like the male Golden pheasant. There is no other bird that can compare to his brightness and attractive appearance. The following description will give an idea of his beauty.

Male: On the crown of the head is a crest of elongated, silky, bright golden-yellow feathers. The ear-band is a brownish grey, the other parts of the face, the chin, the throat and the neck are brownish red. The tippet is formed of broad, rectangular feathers, the visible part of which is light orange in colour. Every feather in the tippet has two dark-blue bars across the tip. The upper part of the back is deep green, and every feather is margined with velvet black. The lower part of the back and the rump are of a deep golden-yellow colour. The tail feathers are mottled predominantly black and brown. The wings feature the colours dark red on the wingtip; deep blue tertiaries; black and brown bands on the primary and secondary quills. The entire under-part of the bird is scarlet, merging into a light chestnut in the middle of the abdomen and the thigh-parts. Under-tail coverts are red. The iris and the naked skin round the eyes are light yellow; the bill and legs are a horny yellow.

Hen: The plumage of the hen is much plainer than that of the cock. The colours are mainly light, medium and a very dark brown, with an occasional pale-yellow feather. The feathers show a black mottled or barred design. It should be noted in passing that among the hens variations in the intensity of colour do occur. The iris is brown, the skin round the eyes is yellow, the bill and the legs are a horny yellow (Gerrits, 1974).

We raised these marvelous little pheasants when we lived in Montana. They were kept outside in the very cold winters with no trouble. We did offer them a covered shelter for the feed and water and most of the time they did not stay there except to eat and drink. We had a very tame little male that would roost on top of the gate frame. This kept me awake many nights as I could imagine how cold he was and how vulnerable to a predator reaching through the wire to grab him. No harm ever came to him. Most of our Golden pheasants roosted as high as they could get in their large outside pens.

If the breeder has good strong bloodlines, these pheasants are easy to breed and raise. We had some of our hens get broody and even set on a clutch of eggs. The nest was located up on a rock ledge about five feet high. When the chicks hatched, they ran off the ledge and got chilled before we found them. I suppose that if the nest had been located on the ground the chicks would have stayed under their mother and survived. We were disappointed at the loss and vowed to let the hen raise the following year with some good tight wire around her to hold in the tiny chicks.

About 45 years ago before the big war, Professor Alessandro Ghigi of Bologna, Italy, created the Yellow Golden mutation . See color plate E for a picture of the yellow and the normal to compare the two species. The species breeds true and is called *(Chrysolophus pictus luteus)*. It is very popular in the United States and other countries. They have a beauty all of their own but to my mind do not compare to the coloration of the true pure Golden pheasant.

If you are interested in getting into pheasants, this is the one to begin with. It was the first pheasant that I ever saw as a boy. Somehow this makes them very special to me.

Silver Pheasant

(Lophura nycthemera)

These are beautiful and interesting birds. The mature male is really something to see. Following is a description of these pheasants.

Male: He is large and white. The upper body has a chalk-white colour with three to four narrow black lines running across in a wavy pattern. The under-parts, the chin, the throat and the long crest are a magnificent, glossy, deep bluish-black. The rectrices are very striking because of their great length. The central pair is pure white and is decorated on the outer web by a few narrow broken black lines.

The cock Silver pheasant assumes the adult plumage only in the second year. Because the immature dress is considerably different from the full dress, a short description will be given.

The young cock does not have the pure white upper body, but is finely vermiculated white, reddish yellow and black. The tail has not yet attained its full length and resembles the tail of the hen, though it is already somewhat longer and more coarsely vermiculated. The crest and the under-parts are a dull black. V-shaped white lines run across the under-parts.

Hen: Though the hens show a great deal of individual variation, it may safely be said that they are mainly olive-brown with more or less inconspicuous black vermiculation. Chin and throat are spotted with grey and the crest is tipped with black (Gerrits, 1974).

There are several subspecies of these birds in captivity. I really do not know which we had. They were very beautiful and made good aviary birds. We had a pair that was several years old. The old male stood on a log and *"whirred"* his wings which made a strange, but interesting noise. He would do this early in the morning and late in the evening during breeding season. Not only was he a large bird, but he was somewhat aggressive toward us. He never got violent, but you be can sure that we watched him when we went into his pen.

Painting of true Silver pheasant in their natural habitat of Eastern China by C.R. Knight.

212 Some Favorite Pheasant

THE TRAGOPANS
(Tragopan)

Many upland game bird fanciers say that the Ruffed pheasants, the Golden and Amherst's, are the most spectacular of the pheasants, but the gorgeous and highly ornamental Tragopans are, indeed, exquisite creatures and surely rival even the stunning appearance which the Ruffed pheasants put on with their dashing behavior as they "strut their stuff" during courtship display (Allen, 1969). I believe this to be true, but the fact that not many people have had the advantage of seeing a perfect feather Tragopan cock display has led to the unfair comparison with the Ruffed pheasants.

The primary reason, I think, is the tragopans do not lay nearly as many eggs as most of the other pheasants. An average number of eggs in a clutch of a tragopan is perhaps five while the other pheasants can lay as many as 30 or more in a clutch and they even in some cases double clutch in a year. Also, the price of the birds determines their popularity.

Tragopans are rugged and tough birds in their wild state, but not nearly so strong and long-lived in captivity, unless good facilities are provided. They seem to need lots of space. Every successful breeder will house his birds in large spacious open runs and sheltered areas. If you are short on pen space, then you should probably not consider getting into these birds. There are many exceptions to this I know. I hear of breeders all the time having success with pen areas that are not nearly as large as recommended. Most successful breeders have pens in excess of 80 square feet per breeding pair.

The tragopans are found from "Kashmir in the west, along the Himalayan range, through Burma to Central China." It is immediately evident that they come from the highest altitude in the world and are definitely cold weather birds. Breeders all agree that they cannot tolerate very hot weather. If your climate is hot, you should make provisions to keep the birds as cool as possible for their protection. Also, they do not step on the same piece of ground ever in the wild so they have not built up a tolerance for disease as some of the other pheasants.

In the wild they eat most anything, including leaves, seeds, berries and other kinds of vegetable matter, as well as live food such as insects, larvae, worms etc. Because of this, the wise breeder will supply them, a variety of food stuffs to be sure that they get the needed nutrients.

Egg production has been increased in Europe. Generally higher production probably is the result of their more spacious pens, cooler weather, and even better care. The young require more time to raise than do other pheasants and these European breeders seem to have caretakers to give the time. The better husbandry here in America is having an effect on the production of these birds. Several breeders are reporting as many as 17 to 20 eggs per clutch from birds are several generations out of the wild. Better care and housing is probably the reason.

There are five distinct species of Tragopan or Horned pheasants. Their plumage is predominantly red, buff, brown and black, spotted and speckled with white or grey (Wayre, 1969).

Breeding Tragopans

The logical place to begin in keeping these birds is a discussion on aviaries or housing. As said earlier, these birds require very large spaces in which to live and breed. Temminck's probably can stand closer quarters than the Satyrs. The danger in the smaller enclosures is not only discomfort on behalf of the birds but their general health and condition. A fat breeder bird will not be a good one. The enclosure should be as high as seven to ten feet if possible to give the birds a feeling of openness. One breeder has long flight pens 100 feet by 10 feet wide (Holmgren, 1972). Needless to say, the larger the better when it comes to pen size for these birds.

Holmgren gives us a good idea about these outside flight pens. He was bothered for years by wild birds such as sparrows and starlings getting into his pens thus eating food and spreading potential disease germs. The original wire was two inch mesh. He solved this by dividing off a portion of the pen and enclosing it with one inch wire netting. This stopped the wildbirds from getting in. To allow the pheasants to use the other side made of the larger two-inch wire, Holmgren put a passageway entry at the bottom corner that was covered with brush and trees for the pheasants to go in and out to use both sides of the pen. This was a very inexpensive way to do it as it cut the amount of more expensive wire in half.

Most breeders isolate each pair. The male tragopan seeks out a private place behind a tree or shrub to put on his display. The breeder could put plywood boards placed vertically to give him privacy. Every effort must be made to give these birds everything possible that they have in the wild if we are to get good strong breeders.

It is interesting that the tragopans are very particular about their matings and in some cases need to choose their own mates. The Hungarian partridge is another game birds with this characteristic. Perhaps a lack of understanding of this fact has led to many infertile eggs when the cock bird is not really interested in his hen that the breeder chose for him. Many stories can be related about the simple matter of switching a hen which turned the cock into a real "lover" when before he was not interested in the least in displaying or even mating. Even though both were sexually ready for mating the fact is one of the couple did not like the other for whatever reason.

One of the problems with the tragopans as with some other game birds is getting the male and female to come into breeding condition at the same time. Either the male is ready and the female not; or the female is ready and the male not. One solution is to use artificial lighting. Most always, the male is longer in getting ready to breed than the female. Lighting could be given to the male three to four weeks before the female and they would come into condition at the same time. This has been proven to work in the commercial breeding of Ringneck pheasants. So if one has an unproductive pair, perhaps it is because they do not like each other or they are not both in breeding condition. The wise breeder would spend lots of time finding the answers to these questions.

It would be a good idea to have some extra young cock birds in waiting when mating first year birds. When tragopans mate, they usually will stay together for life. Finding the right mate is very important. Most breeders have not had good constant success with mating trios. It may work for a time, but eventually it does not work out. Although in the wild, monogamous matings is the rule, when captive conditions prevail, game birds can be changed to meet the demands of the breeder. Some breeders find that the stamina of the male goes down fast as the breeding season progresses, thus giving fewer chicks near the end of the Summer.

Hatching and brooding chicks

Like other pheasants, the tragopan hen lays her egg in late afternoon or evening. Holmgren says he tries to gather the eggs shortly after laying to avoid the cold nights in the early breeding season. He used to use chickens to hatch his tragopans, but due to the intensive labor required he has gone to the more modern incubator. There is still nothing that will get healthier, more perfect chicks, than a broody hen whether she be chicken or natural mother. However, dangers are many, and great care must be given to avoid the many accidents that can happen using a broody.

These game bird chicks can be brooded using THE ASSEMBLY LINE METHOD described earlier in this book. They are difficult to get to eat and must be given special care in this matter. The usual teacher chick and other tricks can be used to entice the chick to begin eating. Once they learn to eat if they are given a good balanced ration they will be hardy and strong when mature.

Young chicks are very susceptible to disease and should be brooded on wire mesh to keep them as clean as possible. The chicks should not be kept in close-quarter brooding for more than three weeks as they need lots of exercise as they develop. However, do not put them outdoors too soon as if they chill they will die. Some plan must be worked out to give them as constant heat as possible at night when they are in danger of chilling. Also, if they are put outdoors too soon, they may succumb to their weakness to intestinal disorders until they can build up the immunities that they need.

The chicks should be taught to roost at an early age. Some breeders feel that the toe exercise the chicks get while perching helps their toes to remain straight. Crooked toes can be caused by faulty incubation, nutrition, and exercise. Tragopans are prone to crooked toes for whatever reason and must be given special care to avoid this problem. Not only does the value of the bird go down with crooked toes, it is not humane to let the toes go crooked if it can be avoided.

Feeding Young Tragopans

As with all young chicks, tragopans should be given a soft and easily digested food to get off to a good start. Some breeders start their chicks exclusively on finely chopped greens for the first two weeks and then get them on some sort of game bird starter. However, this is a bit extreme and a compromise should be worked out to give them the needed greens along with the other protein food. Grated hard-boiled egg, a good chick starter, some protein such as mealworms, and anything else you can think of will make a good variety diet. Put the feed on the floor at first to get them used to eating. Later, graduate them to feeders. Probably tragopans should be fed more green vegetables than the high protein. Some breeders feel that too much protein can cause leg problems while others have not had any trouble with this. A good vitamin should be available two or three times a week so the chicks will have every opportunity to get the balanced diet that they need. The more green grass the growing chicks get the better feather and body they will have. Some breeders claim they can see a difference in the condition of the chicks when they are out on green grass for a few weeks. I would advise feeding grit to help in the digestion process.

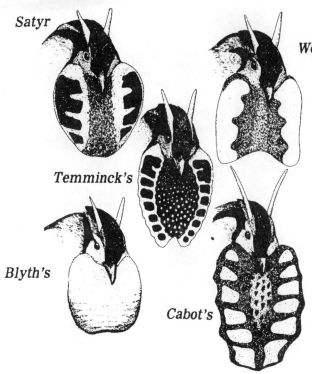

Satyr

Western

Temminck's

Blyth's

Cabot's

Tragopan cocks showing the relative size and patterns of their horns and bibs (lappets) during courtship when fully inflated and distended to their fullest. Drawings by Paul A. Johnsgard and reproduced from his new book, *PHEASANTS OF THE WORLD* (now available from the GAZETTE Book Department).

Some Favorite Pheasant 217

Western

Blyth's

Satyr

Cabot's

Temminck's

218 Some Favorite Pheasant

Satyr Tragopan

(Tragopan satyra)

PLATE F

More than likely, the Satyr tragopan is the most often seen of all the tragopans. Their price is more reasonable and many are offered for sale. Satyrs are very beautiful game birds. The *Pheasant Standards* produced by the American Game Bird Breeders' Cooperative Federation gives good descriptions of the tragopans.

MALE

HEAD AND NECK:

    Head, black, almost completely feathered.

    Crest, black, with a deep crimson-red band on each side.

    Neck, deep crimson-red.

    Iris, brown.

    Fleshy Horns, blue

    Bare Skin of Throat, dark blue.

    Lappet, blue in the middle, pale green on the margins, with four or five triangular scarlet patches on each side.

    Bill, black.

Body:

> **Mantle and Shoulders**, deep crimson red, with small black-lined white ocelli.
>
> **Lower Back and Rump**, brown, vermiculated with black and rufous, with white large olive ocelli bordered with black, and a small terminal lined white ocelli.
>
> **Upper Breast**, deep crimson-red, with small black-lined white ocelli.
>
> **Lower Breast, Flanks and Abdomen**, crimson, with black and white ocelli becoming larger and greyish on the abdomen and flanks.

WINGS:

> **Scapulars and Wing Coverts**, brown, marked with red, vermiculated with black and rufous, a small terminal black-lined white ocelli.
>
> **Scapulars and Wing Coverts**, brown, marked with red, vermiculated with black and rufous, a small terminal black-lined white ocelli.
>
> **Tertiaries and Inner Secondaries**, brown, vermiculated with black and rufous with large olive ocelli bordered with black.
>
> **Primaries,** black, with irregular buff bars.

TAIL:

> **Small Upper Tail Coverts**, brown, vermiculated with black and rufous, with large olive ocelli bordered with black, and a small terminal black-lined white ocelli.
>
> **Long Upper Tail Coverts**, brown, with subterminal black bands.
>
> **Under Tail Coverts**, brown, with brown-lined white ocelli and black fringes.
>
> **Tail**, mottled dark brown and buff, black at the tip.
>
> **Length**: 9¾ - 13½ inches.

LEGS AND FEET:

> **Legs and Feet**, pink.

SIZE:

> **Length:** 26¼ - inches 28¼ inches.

FEMALE

Head and Neck:

> **Chin and Throat**, pale brown or buff, lined with black.
>
> **Iris**, brown.
>
> **Orbital Skin**, bluish.
>
> **Bill,** horn brown.

BODY:

> **Upper Body**, rufous to dull brown, according to individual variation, with pale buff central markings and blackish vermiculation and patches. On the whole more reddish than Temminck's.
>
> **Lower Body**, like the back, but much lighter, particularly the abdomen where the pale center expands into a whitish spot.

WINGS:

> **Wings,** rufous to bright brown, according to individual variation, with pale buff central markings and blackish vermiculation and patches. Almost always their wing bend is tinged with orange-crimson.

TAIL:

> **Tail,** rufous brown, with irregular black and buff bars.
> **Length,** 7⅝ inches.

LEGS AND FEET:

> **Legs and Feet,** whitish grey.

SIZE:

> **Length:** 22½ inches.

The Satyr cock is larger and obviously of a darker hue, more reddish than the Temminck's cock (Holmgren, 1972). The hens are rather alike in both the Satyr and Temminck's species. The Satyrs are somewhat more nervous and less trusting than the other species. *"I can bespeak the intelligence of a Satyr chick. When fairly well feathered it was my practice in the morning to remove this chick from a brooder inside to an outside enclosure. Only to be returned in the evening, sometimes late. Upon opening the door with a 'come on,' the chick would promptly appear from the shadows, hop onto the palm of my hand and remain there until I got to the brooder inside. This bird, proved to be a cock, has always displayed phenomenal tameness and has been a productive breeder (Holmgren, 1972)."*

The Satyr or the Temminck's would be a good species to raise to get into tragopans. The Satyr is more brightly colored and has a distinctly different personality than the Temminck's. It would be hard to chose between the two. Some breeders would heartily recommend the Temminck's for their personality. Other breeders recommend the Satyr for thier outstanding bright plumage. A Satyr cock bird that jumped up into my hand to get a peanut really stole my heart many years ago. I have liked them ever since solely on their tameness and their astounding beauty.

Temminck's Tragopans

(Tragopan temmincki)

PLATE F

"*The courting display of the Tragopan cock deserves special mention. Apart from the lateral form of display as found in all tragopan species, there is another display of wondrous import which not only defies description but conjures up thoughts of the great marvels of Creation.*"

"*Observing his mate some distance away the cock, seemingly in coy-like mien, poses low behind an object—in the wild perhaps a fallen log—and, with eyes focused on the object of his adoration, he emits a series of sharp clicking sounds and at the same time unfolds, from below his throat, a bib-like lappet on which is blazoned in vivid resplendency a pattern of design truly unique, a phenomenon which baffles human understanding and invokes the whole evolution of ages (Holmgren, 1972).*"

Breeders have reported these birds to be so tame that they will tug on a pants leg to get the attention of their keeper, nibble on an ear, and otherwise show affection that one would expect from the family pet dog. I can truly say that the tameness of these birds is an outstanding characteristic. These birds show off better in a walk-in type aviary where the keeper and others can go into their environment. Kindness will be rewarded if the birds are given some of their favorite treats such as peanuts or other tidbit. The kinder one is to these birds the better they respond. The cocks are tamer than the hens.

Description of Male

HEAD AND NECK:

Crest and Neck, deep orange-red.

Head, black, including a wide bank around the lappet and nuchal collar.

Bare Face and Chin, bright blue.

Horns, greenish blue.

Lappet, dark blue, spotted all over with pale blue and eight arrow shaped scarlet marks on each side.

Iris, brown.

Bill, black, with the tip horny.

BODY:

Mantle and shoulders, deep orange red, with numerous small pearl-grey ocelli lined with black, the base of the feathers blackish and buff.

Back and Rump, Indian red, more crimson on the lower back and rump, with numerous small pearl-grey ocelli lined with black, the base blackish and buff.

Upper Breast, deep orange-red.

Lower Breast, Flanks, and Abdomen, clear Indian red, with pearl-grey centers forming large spots, which become larger on the flanks and abdomen.

WINGS:

Coverts, deep orange-red, with large pearl-grey ocelli lined with black, the base blackish buff.

Inner Secondaries, black, mottled with grey and buff.

Outer secondaries, black with mottled grey bars.

Primaries, black, with mottled buff bars.

TAIL:

Longest Tail Coverts, light red, with pale grey centers.

Rectrices, pale buff, mottled and barred with black, with a wide terminal black band.

LEGS AND FEET:

Thighs, orange red.

Legs and Feet, pinkish to reddish.

SIZE:

Length: 25⅛ inches.

FEMALE

HEAD AND NECK:

Crown, black with grey or buff shaft stripes.

Chin and Throat, buff to whitish, with black lines.

Nape, buff or grey and black, tinged with rufous.

Iris, brown

Orbital Skin, bluish.

Bill, horny.

BODY:

    Upper Body, rufous to greyish brown (usually Fulvous brown), according to individual variation, strongly mottled with blackish and with arrow shaped pale buff to greyish white markings. Never as reddish as some Satyr, nor as grey as Cabot's and more coarsely marked above than Satyr.

WINGS:

    Primaries, marked with irregular bars on the outer and mottled on the inner webs.

TAIL:

    Rectrices, irregularly barred with mottling of grey or rufous.

    Length, 6⅞ inches.

LEGS AND FEET:

    Legs and Feet, fleshy grey.

As you can see from the descriptions, the Satyr and the Temminck's are very much alike but are very different. It is very difficult not having both of these species in one's collection to enjoy the differences.

This bird could hold the record for the highest altitude home, living up to 14,000 feet above sea level. It is confined to dense mountain forest during the winter, ascending in the summer to the higher wooded slopes. One often wonders how any bird could survive the extremes in this area.

Temminck's cock display.

Cabot's Tragopans
(Tragopan caboti)

Although less brilliantly coloured than the other tragopans, the male Cabot's is nevertheless a striking bird (Wayre, 1969). This species is the most easterly of the genus found as high as 5,000 feet in the Chinese provinces of Fukien and Kwangtung.

These birds were not at all uncommon in French collections before World War I but all died out after the effects of World War II. It is said that Cabot's is in danger of extension in the wild. During the last few years these beautiful birds have become fairly available at a very high price. This is due to some innovative Canadian aviculturists using Artificial Insemination (A.I.) With some birds brought over to Canada from Europe. The method was very successful and after several generations some are having success with them. (A.I. is fully discussed in the Appendix).

Like all tragopans, these birds spend most of the day up high on perches and become active only in the early morning and late evening. Since their activity is limited, most birds become too fat on the rich diet they receive. The smart game bird breeder would monitor their diets very carefully.

Description of Male

HEAD AND NECK:

Head and Neck, black, except the sides and tip of the crest and the sides of the neck.

Crest, black in the center with the sides and tip orange-red.

Neck Sides, Indian red, extending down to the body and on the neck front forming a second complete throat band beneath the black.

Bare Facial Skin, orange yellow, including a fold on the chin and throat.

Eyelids, violet purple.

Horns, Pale blue.

Lappet, orange with purple spots in the center, surrounded with cobalt blue, the margins with nine patches of pale greenish-grey on each side.

Iris, brown.

Bill, horny.

BODY:

Upper Body, spotted black, red and pale buff, with large buff ocellus, separated by black bands from red borders.

Breast and Abdomen, plain pale buff.

Flanks and Thighs, plain pale buff, marked with red and black.

WINGS:

Inner Secondaries, plain pale buff, marked with red and black.

Outer Secondaries, Black, mottled and vermiculated with whitish buff.

Primaries, dark brown, with slight buffy mottling.

TAIL:

Under Tail Coverts, plain pale buff, marked with red and black.

Rectrices, mottled brown and whitish buff, with broad black tips.

LEGS AND FEET:

Legs and Feet, pink to whitish.

FEMALE

HEAD AND NECK:

Forehead and Crown, black, with a pale buff shaft-stripe, and tipped with chestnut.

Face, Chin and Throat, white or pale buff, with black margins.

Orbital Skin, reddish-orange.

Iris, brown.

Bill, pinkish horn.

BODY:

Upper Body, mottled black and rufous brown, with whitish triangular markings.

Under Body, greyish brown, with black, and with large white markings.

WINGS:

Secondaries, black, with triangular, buffy indentations on the outer web broken by mottling.

Primaries, dark brown, with slight buffy mottling, on the outer margins.

TAIL:

Rectrices, mottled rufous, pale buff and black.

LEGS AND FEET:

Legs and Feet, pinkish horn. The general tone varies with the individual from greyish brown to a more rufous tone.

Blyth's Tragopans
(Tragopan blythi)   **PLATE F**

This species is not often kept in captivity. There are records of their having first been trapped and imported in limited numbers from the wild in the past. Delacour says the first were brought to the London Zoo in 1970 but only lived a short time. Another man imported them in 1982. Records show that all imported stock soon died out in captivity until fresh specimens again reached Europe. In 1933 Delacour got two pairs out of Calcutta to his pheasantry in France and began producing them in 1934 and every year thereafter until 1940. The German invasion wiped out Delacour's stock.

In the past few years Glenn Howe in Canada is producing young (Allen). He represents the best hope to keep the species going in captivity. He is a very successful breeder of all kinds of waterfowl and upland game birds, and is especially noted as a Tragopan propagator since he has raised large numbers of Satyr and Temminck's Tragopans and over 80 of the very rare Cabot's Tragopan. There is not a better person to entrust these rare Blyth's.

Glenn says Blyth's chicks are a joy to raise. They seem naturally tame and eat readily. They have no tendency toward cannibalism like some other tragopan chicks. He starts them on Purina Duck Startina containing 18% protein. He also feeds greens and mealworm sparingly.

Western Tragopans
(Tragopan melanocephalus)   **PLATE F**

The Western tragopan is as its name implies the most westerly member of the genus and is found in the western Himalayas between 8,000 and 12,000 feet. Owing to its restricted range it is also on the brink of extinction.

A few of this species were imported into Europe towards the 19th century and chicks were raised in a few cases. The birds soon died out and to my knowledge there is none in captivity in the western world today.

The Junglefowl

(Gallus)

J unglefowl are members of the Pheasant family although few people are aware of this fact. Perhaps, it is because they resemble the common chicken that confuses the mind. (Most people are not aware that the beautiful Peacocks are members of the Pheasant family). Most agree that the Red junglefowl is the ancestor of the domestic chicken. Because of this probably no other birdhas contributed more to man's welfare through the years as has the Junglefowl.

Fowls have traveled to every corner of the globe and primitive tribes on every continent have benefited from the meat and eggs through many years. It seems that fowl were domesticated before historic times. They were known in China before 1400 B.C. These birds can be documented through most of recorded history so that few dispute their ancestry. Domestic fowls were known around 2500 B.C. in Indus valley, whence shortly they reached Persia. They were in Crete and in Phoenicia in 1500 B.C.; they seemed to have reached Mesopotamia around 700 B.C., and Greece a few years later. From Egypt we know only of a few early records (1500 B.C.) and domestic birds do not seem to have been commonly raised before the first century B.C. It is possible that up to that time they were kept away from the people because of religious superstitions. The early European conquerors brought them to the Americas (Delacour).

Junglefowl are easy and some are difficult to raise depending on the species being propagated. No doubt there needs to be much work and research toward raising the Green junglefowl as it is probably the most difficult to raise in captivity.

In the wild state, junglefowl inhabit the warmer parts of Asia. They are also found on many islands of the Pacific, but man likely carried them there as no other birds of the pheasant group exist there.

DISTRIBUTION OF THE JUNGLEFOWL FAMILY
(Ceylon, India, Assam, Burma, Indo-China, Hainan, Malaysia)

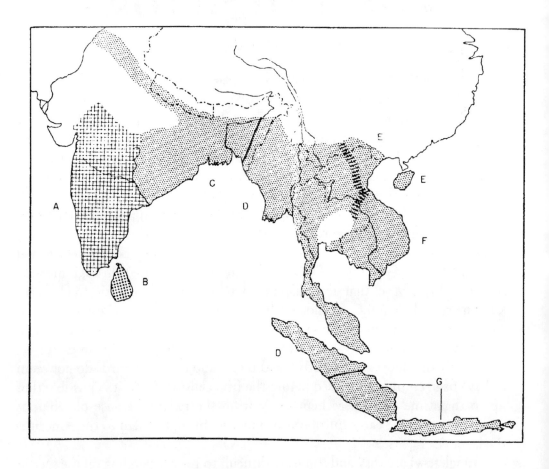

A. Gallus sonnerati;   *B. G. Layfayettei;*   *C. G. Gallus murghi;*   *D. G. G. Spadiceus;*
E. G. G. Jabouillei;   *F. G. G. Gallus;*   *G. G. G. Bankiva*
(Pheasants of the World, by Delacour)

Under each species I will discuss the care and breeding as each requires different handling. I hope this information will encourage the reader to get into these marvelous birds.

232 *Some Favorite Junglefowl*

Red Junglefowl

(Gallus gallus)

PLATE G

The Red junglefowl, Cochin-Chinese Red junglefowl, *(Gallus gallus gallus)*, has four subspecies as follows:

Gallus gallus spadiceus, Burmese Red junglefowl. Resident in southwest Yunnan, Burma, Thailand, Northern Laos, Malaya and Northern Sumatra.

Gallus gallus jabouillei, Tonkinese Red junglefowl. Resident in Tokin extreme southeast of Yunnan, Kwangsi and Hainan.

Gallus gallus murghi, Indian Red junglefowl. Resident in northern and northeast India, the lower ranges of the Himalayas, normally not above the foothills.

Gallus gallus bankiva, Javan Red junglefowl. Resident in the southern half of Sumatra, Java, and Bali.

The captive population of Red junglefowl may be made up of the common Indian *(murghi)* subspecies. The late J. B. Suthard who wrote in the book on *The Junglefowls and Spurfowl of the World* said the following about the Red junglefowl kept and bred by many people today:

"The red junglefowl with its four subspecies is found throughout India, Burma, Siam, Cochin China, Hainan, and Malaysia. It has spread by the natives to the Phillippines, Polynesia, and Micronesia and thence to other South Pacific islands. Even in the native habitat is difficult to obtain pure blooded birds, as it has been crossed and recrossed with domestic chickens."

Concerning getting pure stock Dr. Delacour suggests the following method of distinguishing the true from the crossed: *"It is easy to ascertain whether imported Red junglefowl are pure or not. In the cock the presence of a complete eclipse plumage in the summer and a shrill, short crow abruptly ended are exclusive to the genuine wild birds, while pure hens show neither comb nor lappets, both sexes hold their tail almost horizontal."*

"Breeding in captivity presents no particular problem, as the hens are good mothers, and it is not necessary to remove the cock from the breeding pen in the presence of the chicks."

Description

Following is a detailed description of the common Indian Red junglefowl *(G. g. Murghi)* (Baker, 1917):

Adult male: Crown of the head, nape and upper mantle, together with the sides of the neck, deep bright orange-red, changing to reddish gold or orange on the longest hackles, which are marked with black down their centres; upper back, below these long hackles, black glossed with Prussian blue or green; lower back deep maroon red, highly glossed and gradually changing into fiery orange on the long hackles of the rump; these latter are more or less centered with black, the centers, however, being concealed by the overlying feathers; upper tail-coverts and tail feathers black brilliantly glossed with green, blue-green or copper green; the blue generally dominant, on the coverts, and the gloss absent or light on the outermost tail feathers. Smallest wing coverts, and shoulder of the wing black, glossed like the back with blue or blue-green, or purple-blue; median wing coverts like the lower back; greater coverts black like the smallest; quills dark brown, in some specimens almost black; the primaries edged on the outer web with light cinnamon and the secondaries with the whole of their visible portions of this colour except the innermost which are of a glossy blue-green with only a part of the outer webs cinnamon. Under plumage, under wing-coverts and under tail-coverts deep brown or blackish, faintly glossed with green.

Colors of soft parts: Irides varying from reddish brown in the young bird, through red to bright orange red in old males. Comb generally a bright scarlet crimson, sometimes duller, ear lappets white, sometimes touched with pinkish on the lower posterior portions, skin of face, throat and upper neck red, bluish fleshy tint. Bill horny brown. The colour of the combs and wattle is much brighter during the breeding season than at other times, both in the male and the female.

Measurements: Wing 8 inches to 9.6 inches; tail anything between 12 inches and 15 inches; tarsus about 3 inches or more. Weight, according to Hume, 1 pound 12 ounces. Some larger males weigh over 2 pounds but reports say that most average just under 2 pounds.

Adult Female: Top of the head bluish brown, the feathers broadly edged with golden yellow. In most birds the forehead is more or less metallic crimson and this colour is produced backwards as supercilia above and behind the ear coverts whence they widen and meet on the foreneck in a broad gorget. In some specimens the red will be found to occupy nearly the whole of the fore crown and to deepen the yellow of the posterior crown to a deep orange. Feathers of the nape orange yellow, with blackish centers, changes to pale golden yellow on the longer hackles along the back. Tail blackish brown. Breast below the red gorget light Indian red with pale shafts, gradually becoming paler and duller on the lower breast, and shading into pale dull cinnamon on the belly, much vermiculated brown; under tail coverts black or blackish brown.

Colors of the soft parts: Iris brown or hazel; bill horny brown, gape and lower mandible fleshy; comb and orbital skin reddish crimson; wattles very rarely present and very small, like the comb but paler and more livid, legs generally dull brown. Undeveloped spurs are occasionally present.

Measurements: Wing 7 inches to 7.7 inches; tail from vent 5.5 inches to 6.5 inches; tarsus about 2.5 inches. Weight: 1 pound 2 ounces to 1 pound 10 ounces.

In behavior and voice this bird completely resembles the barnyard chickens that everyone is familiar with. Red junglefowl are very gregarious, gather in larger parties than the other species and keep together longer during the yearly cycle. They lay more eggs than the others, but fewer than the Greens. They are easy to breed in captivity and do well at liberty in large parks.

The Red junglefowl is a first class gamebird, wary, cunning and strong, and it is good eating. Some years ago several states had programs to release it into the wild for hunting purposes but abandoned the project as the hunters felt too much like they were shooting domestic chickens.

Each subspecies of the Red junglefowl is different in small respects. The author refers the reader to other accounts for a detailed description of the differences that to the untrained eye seem insignificant, but to the one who knows, are very real and distinguishing. I visited a breeder that had all of the subspecies. He pointed out the difference in size, shape, and coloration which I would not have noticed as a novice. If you do not know which subspecies to get, I recommend you visit a breeder that has kept the species separate and can point out the differences to you.

The young can be raised using a bantam hen with success. Also, artificial incubating and brooding is quite successful. Chicks need high protein to get them going right. Feed some greens and an occasional mealworm to complete their diet.

The beginning breeder of Junglefowl would do well to start with this species. If after a year or two of success he may want to go on and raise some of the more difficult species. Which species chosen is a matter of choice as each of them have some wonderful assets.

Ceylon Junglefowl
(Gallus lafayettei)

The Ceylon junglefowl is native to and found only in the island of Ceylon. This species is easily distinguished from the other species by its general reddish-orange color and by the large yellow spot on the red comb (Allen, 1964).

" *This bird is found in all parts of its native country which is uncultivated and where the jungle is of moderate growth. It is abundant in the low country where it makes the undergrowth its home, only coming out into the open to feed.*"

"*The Ceylon junglefowl is first heard at daybreak and for an hour or so after sunrise. They can be heard challenging each other with their clear call 'chick-George-Joyce.' The chances of seeing the bird are very good if one remains perfectly still.*"

"*The food in the wild state consists of grain, seeds, berries, various tender leaves, grasses and buds, and a very large proportion of termites and other insects. They are very industrious scratchers and obtain many seeds from among decaying leaves. (Weinman, 1958).*"

Description

Male: Comb (with very small dents) and two lappets crimson red, a yellow patch is on the comb especially during breeding season; naked face and throat red; crown rufous; a border of large purple feathers around the throat; neck hackles very long, bright rufous with a broad disintegrated orange yellow fringe; feathers of upper back and lesser wing-coverts similar but redder; broad feathers of lower back and rump and flank hackles purple-violet with a red border; rest of wings and tail metallic purplish similar to those of the upper back but redder; abdomen black. Iris yellow; bill horny red with pale tip; legs yellow.

The adult plumage is assumed the second year only and we have been told that first year males are incapable of breeding. There is not a real eclipse plumage change in this species, but the cocks molt slowly in the summer and their combs are reduced in size.

Female: Crown brown with minute black vermiculations; neck dark brown with pale buff shaft-lines and yellowish borders; mantle, back and upper tail-coverts rufous buff finely vermiculated with black; wings boldly barred black, pale buff, and rufous brown; tail rufous brown, barred and vermiculated with black; throat dull buffy brown; breast and sides of body rufous brown vermiculated with black and with wide whitish central patch and borders to the feathers; abdomen whitish. Iris dull yellow; bill horny brown.

The Ceylon junglefowl are found only on the island of Ceylon. LaFayette's or Ceylonese junglefowl do not differ greatly in habits from the Reds, except they keep more to the jungle, shun cultivation, and never gather in such big parties. In voice, they differ from the other species. Both sexes have a hard cackling.

G. M. Henry in *Avicultural Magazine* gives some interesting information about raising this bird in captivity. He says that they are not easy to raise at all. The young are very fragile. The cocks have a bad habit of eating the eggs so it is desirable to collect them several times during the day. The hen will lay about five eggs before she begins incubation. Some hens will not incubate thier eggs. Some breeders report that a good hen will lay up to forty eggs in each clutch. This only occurs if the eggs are removed each day to keep the hen laying.

We can raise the chicks using THE ASSEMBLY LINE METHOD described earlier in this book. The boxes will need to be larger, of course, than those used for smaller quail-like chicks. Many successful breeders have only used a bantam hen to hatch and raise these skittish birds. I do believe that success has been enjoyed from breeders who use artificial incubation and brooding methods.

We must handle the young chicks gently and we must try to get them to eat. They are sometimes reluctant to eat on their own and need a teacher to help them learn. The most difficult time in the life of the chick is getting started and getting through the feathering out process. They have a reputation of being delicate whether nor not it is justified is another question. Some breeders have no trouble with them while others have a difficult time raising Ceylons. Once feathered, the chick is rather hardy and can be put outside in the warm fresh air.

Ceylon junglefowl are primarily birds of dry regions. Major Weinman mentions that in captivity it is impossible to keep them from wading in their water dish. He insists that they probably would wade in a pond if one was available.

They appear to nest all year long in the wild and chicks are seen just about anytime in their native land except during the late winter months. In captivity, they lay their eggs and nest in the Spring. Some breeders have reported that yearling hens will lay eggs their first year.

Sonnerat's Junglefowl

(G. Gallus sonnerati)

Grey or Sonnerat's junglefowl are quitecommon in captivity. They are very popular because of their beautiful plumage. In the wilds Greys prefer to feed in cultivated or abandoned clearings that adjoin low thick jungle into which it can escape if need be. It is not gregarious like the Red junglefowl and is generally found in small flocks consisting of adults and young of the year. In the wild, it is reported not be pugnacious, which is odd, as it is well equipped with long, sharp spurs (Allen, 1982).

The breeding season may be February through May, but can extend throughout the year, depending on the weather pattern and the feed supply. The diet of the Greys in the wild consists of most anything that is edible. They take seasonal food, such as berries and fruits, abundantly. The cock remains with the hen in the wild, but is not reported to help in raising the young chicks.

These are beautiful birds. The male has a slightly dented comb, lappets, bare face, and throat red; neck hackles long, rounded at tips, black with grey fringes, two or three white subterminal and one deep yellow terminal horny, wax-like spangle; lanceolate feathers of under parts are black, with white shaft lines and pale grey borders, tinged with rusty red on flanks; back feathers tipped with rusty red and having large horny spots of yellow and white; tail flossy purplish black; wing-coverts black with white shafts and long, horny rusty yellow tips; rest of wing black. Iris yellow to orange; bill horny black, yellowish at tip and below; legs yellow to salmon-red. During the summer eclipse the cocks lose the long tail feathers and the neck hackles are replaced by short black feathers, while the comb becomes small and shriveled up.

The female has a crown brown with reddish shaft-lines; face pale brown; neck feathers with buff centers, black lines and brown frenges; mantle finely mottled light brown and black; lateral rectrices and primaries dull black; throat buffy white; breast feathers white with broad black or brown borders; flanks with broken brownish borders; abdomen pale buffy brown. Iris, bill and feet as the male.

Sonnerat's junglefowl are found as high up as 5,000 feet on mountain hills and slopes. The Greys have a special voice. The crow is a curious four-syllable, *kuck-kaya-kaya-kuck* and the call is a two syllable *kiurkun-kiurkun*. The hen has a brisk cackle. Wayre says this species appears to be monogamous in the wild and does not congregate in large flocks.

In captivity Allen says, the Sonnerat's present two problems: they are pugnacious and extremely noisy. Some individuals will be docile even to the point of shyness, but I find the robust birds noisy and aggressive. Sometimes a shield is necessary when entering the pen. The cock will attack feet and legs, and even fly at one's face. The crow is so loud that it would not be wise to raise them in a populated neighborhood. Again, there are individuals that are quieter, crowing only in the mornings and evenings. I do not know how these birds could possible stay alive in the wild if they make such noise as it would attract the predators day and night.

Green Junglefowl

(G. gallus varius)

Most agree that the Green junglefowl is by far the most beautiful and most delicate of the four species. They are the most tropical and thus require protection from frost during the winter months if kept in a cold climate. George Allen, Jr. kept these birds more than thirty years ago in Salt Lake City where he had success along with J. G. Southard. The stock kept back then was excellent and imported from the Malayan National Zoo. The Allen's phased out this species from their collection due to the severe winter's but enjoyed the experience with them.

Mr. Southard, who lived at Long Beach, California, had wonderful success with these birds so it is fitting that I draw upon his expertise with these birds. "This species is readily distinguished from the other junglefowl by its darker coloration. Its dentless vari-colored comb of green and purplish red, and its beautiful single throat wattle of red, yellow, and blue. In the sun its greenish bronze, yellow and black shine like metal. The hen too is darker than the other junglefowl species, with considerable green and black."

"This is a bird of low elevations, being found in desert-type rolling hills along the sea coast rather than in real jungle country. They are not gregarious, usually being found single or in small groups of adults with young of the year. Its diet in the wild is composed of termites, seashore invertebrates such as small shrimp, crabs, and snails. Its favorite fruit is that of the cactus that grows on the rocky ridges near the seashore."

"In captivity, this species lays five to seven eggs, white or buff white. The incubation period is twenty-one days, In an enclosure with adequate shelter, the hen may lay up to ten eggs before starting to incubate. Where sufficient brush is not provided in her pen the hen will scatter the eggs. With sufficient cover, the hen will hatch and rear her brood with the help of the cock. In an incubator, hatchibility seems better if put in to start incubation at once, although this is a bit of a nuisance having chicks hatch every day."

"On hatching, the chicks when dry should be put into a warm brooder. The chicks are reluctant to eat alone so they are helped by putting in a young chick to be a teacher. A small bantam breed works all right. The starting feed should be a fine mash, finely chopped lettuce, and boiled egg sieved through small wire. On the second or third day, the young can be tempted with small mealworms, and once they eat these, the feeding problem is solved. We should feed mealworms twice a day until the chicks are six weeks old. The feeding of the boiled egg should be limited to the first three days. In about three weeks millet can be added to the diet. Warm sunshine is helpful but do not let the brooder get too hot from the summer sun. I have stressed warmth as chilling is fatal to young Greens, and Ceylon too because we use the same methods with both species."

"Once completely feathered the Greens present no special problem. They are high protein eaters and are given as adults freshly ground beef along with the mealworms. They enjoy fruit such as oranges and anything else in season. Mealworms are especially important to chicks and adults."

"The Greens have a tendency to spring up and scalp themselves on the top of the pen so protection should be provided in the form of plastic netting or soft material. Young Greens show little tendency to fight among themselves until nearly fully grown. I have never seen a pugnacious adult. As a rule, they are timid and easily frightened. Some become as tame as hand-reared chickens and will eat out of your hand."

"The Green junglefowl is an uncertain breeder in captivity. Some hens will lay many fertile eggs, and other will not lay at all. Some cock birds never show any interest in the hens." These methods for raising the Green junglefowl were used many years ago and should work well today provided the breeder has strong bloodlines.

Part 5

SOME FAVORITE WILD TURKEYS

244 *Some Favorite Wild Turkeys*

Wild Turkeys

(Meleagris gallopavo)

Nearly everyone in America has heard of or has seen a turkey. Perhaps this is because of our traditional celebration of the Thanksgiving holiday. None will argue that the turkey is a tasty old bird. Millions of domesticated turkeys are raised by the turkey industry each year for the table. This domesticated and improved "meat bird" was bred and developed from the wild turkey.

What most people do not know about the turkey is that it is found only in the Western hemisphere in modern times as well as in the past. Not even a fossil of a turkey has ever been found anywhere else in the world (Williams, 1991). The only other living relative of the American wild turkey is the smaller and more colorful Ocellated turkey found in Southern Mexico.

American Indians introduced European immigrants to tomatoes, corn, beans, tobacco, and other vegetable crops. They also introduced the turkey in a domesticated form. It is interesting to note that the wild turkey of the Eastern United States has never been domesticated. It is not the scope of this book to get into the many different strains of the domesticated turkey but a better understanding of the wild turkey can be had if one is somewhat familiar with the domesticated turkey. The common bronze domesticated turkey still exhibits some of the beautiful shining colorings of the wild turkey. Also, the behavior of the domesticated turkey is very similar to the wild turkey.

My first experiences with the turkey was many years ago when I was in high school. My parents bought me five hens and one gobbler bronze turkeys to use as a Vocational Agriculture Project. My assignment was to raise young turkeys to maturity and of course keep adequate records to get a good grade. These birds had free range on about four acres of land and at night they roosted in the trees away from predators. In the Spring when laying season came around they "stole" their nests out in the woods and fields just like their wild cousins. It was no easy chore to follow a hen back to her nest as they are very wary birds. As I remember, they were beautiful birds, became quite tame and was very good layers and parents.

The wild turkey's head is a patriotic red, white and blue and the bird was highly revered by early Americans, it was not nominated for a place on the National Emblem of the United States as is widely believed. I have always believed that Benjamin Franklin nominated the bird but history proves me wrong. He actually preferred a scene of Moses parting the Red Sea and Pharaoh's chariots being engulfed in the flood. Franklin's support for the wild turkey and his unfavorable comments about the bald eagle were written in a letter to his daughter Sarah in 1784 after the bald eagle had already been selected as our national bird. Certainly, we who know the wild turkey would agree with Franklin in the matter.

A wild turkey gobbler.

WILD TURKEY
Present Distribution

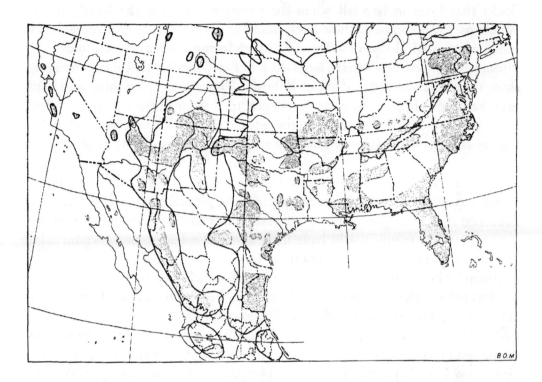

A study of past and present wild turkey census is very interesting as it shows them becoming extinct in many areas, thriving in others, and making a come back thanks to restocking programs. During the last 50 years the wild turkey has been reinstated back into its original range and wild populations exist in 11 states that formerly had no wild turkeys. They occur in 49 states and their number has been estimated to be more than three million. Now they are abundant enough for many states to have a hunting season each year to harvest thousands of surplus birds.

In the wild there are four types of wild turkey flocks: 1) family flocks, made up of brood hens with their young; 2) adult hen flocks, make up of hens that were not successful in raising poults; 3) adult gobbler flocks, comprised of gobblers that regrouped following the mating season, and 4) immature gobbler flocks that form in late fall when the young males leave the family flocks (Williams, 1991). Some of these flocks number over 20 birds but more stability is had when small flocks of a dozen or so are formed. Recently when driving through West Texas I spotted a large flock of Rio Grande wild turkeys foraging along the road and I counted about 18 birds. This was in the winter and I am sure that some of the birds were young poults. I stopped the car and watched them as they casually walked down the side of the road looking for food. This was on an Interstate highway but they apparently are used to the noise of the road.

Turkeys can become quite tame. I learned that they respond to "kindness" as much as any bird. If the keeper is gentle to the birds they tame down and are not afraid at all. Rough treatment will reverse this which indicates that they are not as dumb as many would have us believe. We had some Merriam wild turkeys in Montana and they became so tame I could walk into their pen and pet them. Their pen was open on the top as I had clipped their wings. It was hard to believe these were real wild turkeys. However, the wild turkey is a very high strung creature and is very nervous under certain circumstances. Clifford Glabe, who was trapping and relocating wild turkeys for Florida State Game and Freshwater Fish Commission relates how he closed the trap door on eighteen wild turkeys and immediately 14 of them fell dead. Autopsies showed ruptured blood vessels around the heart. Studies have shown that throughout their life this nervousness is prevalent. Perhaps this characteristic enables them to survive in the wild. I suppose some strains of wild turkey have been in captivity long enough to loose some of this nervousness.

Raising Wild Turkeys

Ideally, wild turkeys should be raised away from other types of birds. Peacocks mix with wild turkeys as they have the same types of constitution and disease resistance. Never, never put waterfowl near wild turkeys as there is a disease problem. Ground pens are necessary for breeding wild turkeys because of their size. The ground should not have been used in the past for other livestock especially swine. The breeding pens should be as large as possible to give the birds plenty of room to strut and not feel crowded.

Predator control is a must because of the flighty nature of wild turkeys. If scared, they will fly up and hurt or kill themselves as they hit the top of the pen. As always, I recommend the electric fence as a predator deterrent. I put one strand along the bottom of the fence about three inches above the ground. Another strand is placed at about six inches above the ground and a third is placed about five or six feet above the ground. This plan will deter the smaller animals such as skunks and rodents from digging under the fence while the higher wire will deter the climbers such as house cats and raccoons. As a final touch I always put a strand along the top outside rail about six inches high to keep cats from walking along the rail and also to keep hawks and owls from perching on the fence disturbing the birds. Always keep the grass poisoned out or trimmed along the bottom of the fence to avoid shorting out the circuit. I have used this method of predator control for over 40 years and it has never failed. I could tell you stories of terrible losses before I started using the electric fence charger.

Since the gobblers separate from the hens during the off-breeding season I separate the sexes during this time. This little trick really gets action as both the hens and gobblers are ready to breed when I put them together. Also, the competition of several gobblers strutting seems to stimulate breeding.

Eggs should be gathered every day during hot weather. Leave three eggs in the nest to encourage the hen to continue to lay a full clutch. Many have reported that wild turkey eggs are rather difficult to hatch in an incubator. To get around this set back, some breeders use broody chicken hens to do the work of incubation. Handle the eggs like any other egg by turning them each day while awaiting incubation. Keep the temperature around 55° F. while awaiting the start of incubation. The length of incubation is rather long for wild turkeys, 28 days at 99¼° F.

Wild turkey poults are very sensitive to chilling. They must be kept warm and dry especially the first two weeks. Sometimes they are slow to learn to eat so a teacher chick may be valuable. This is no problem when brooded by a bantam hen. If you use a brooder, use the same methods for pheasants except make things larger and taller to accommodate the larger bird. Care must be taken not to crowd the chicks as they are so big and they grow so fast. Feed a high protein starter feed and supplement the diet with some kind of animal protein such as mealworms. If you give this treat food by hand, the poults will become quite tame.

Cleanliness is very important in dealing with wild turkeys. They are susceptible to the common disease of Blackhead especially when they are young. I put a commercial product in the water to avoid this disease. See the **Game Bird Medication Guide** in Part Seven of this book for the name of several products that work. The drug "Bacitracin" works very well in dealing with stress related problems in wild turkeys. I use the brand name Solu-tracin 200 which is really a miracle drug.

The above information applies to any of the subspecies of the wild turkey. If you are going to get into some of the more rare subspecies, I would recommend that you practice raising the more common ones for a year or two before getting the valuable birds. As a matter of fact, some experience raising the domesticated turkey will do wonders in wild turkey management. Learn how to incubate the common eggs and raise the common poults so you can handle the wild turkeys in a more educated way. The methods are the same for any turkey except some measures should be made to control the nervous nature of the wild turkey mentioned earlier such as wing clipping and having plenty of good hiding places for the birds.

WILD TURKEY SUBSPECIES

Not all wild turkeys have the so-called normal coloration in their plumage. Mutations occur along with rare recessive genes which account for a few specimens that are white, roan, speckled, and other colors (Williams, 1991). Just because a wild turkey has a different color does not mean that he is a cross between a domesticated variety.

In distinguishing the subspecies of the wild turkey, the scientists considered such things as color, size, and geographical location. There are five subspecies of the American wild turkey recognized. The subspecies of southern Mexico which is said to be the progenitor of the modern domestic turkey became extinct before the Spaniards arrived. This subspecies was killed out by the Indians near the heavily populated areas around Mexico City (Leopold, 1959).

In North America and Canada the other five subspecies still are found in their original range and in newly stocked ranges. The Ocellated turkey is the only other living turkey species in the world and lives in Southern Mexico and Central America. I will discuss this bird later.

Eastern Wild Turkey
(Meleagris gallopavo silvestris)

The name *silvestris* is given to this subspecies which means "of the woodlands" to designate populations in the Eastern United States north of Florida. This is perhaps the best known subspecies because of the experiences of the early Pilgrims and the beginning of the Thanksgiving holiday. Thomas Morton (1637) one of the earliest writers, says:

> "Turkies there are, which divers times in great flocks have sallied by our doores; and then a gunne, being commonly in a redinesse, salutes them with such a courtesie, as makes them take a turne in the Cooke roome. They daunce by the doore so well."

The rump and tail margins are brown. The tips of the wing primary feathers have white and black bars that extend from the outer edge across each feather to the feather shaft. In this subspecies the white bars are as wide and prominent as the black. The secondary wing feathers also have prominent white bars and are edged in white, producing a whitish triangular area on each side of the back when the wings are closed.

Florida Wild Turkey
(Meleagris gallopavo osceola)

The name *osceola* designates populations of the Florida Peninsula as a distinct subspecies. The subspecies is names in honor of the 19th century Florida Seminole Indian leader.

The Florida wild turkey is much like the eastern subspecies except that more black and less white are seen in the primary and secondary wing feathers. The general tone is somewhat darker. The white wing feather bars are narrow, irregular and broken. When the wing is folded on the back, these feathers do not form a whitish triangular patch as in the eastern.

Birds and mammals that live in humid climates are darker colored than examples of the same species living in more arid climates (Williams, 1991). Feather wear is accelerated when they are damp. Nature prevents excessive wear by providing additional substance called *melanin* which makes feathers appear darker. Thus, the Florida subspecies is darker than any of the rest.

The brown markings on the outer edge of the tail and rump distinguish both the Eastern and Florida subspecies from the three western subspecies. Their feathers are tipped with a much lighter shade of tan, buff, and white. The tail margin is darkest in the Florida subspecies, next darkest in the eastern turkey, and progressively lighter in the Rio Grande, Merriams, and Goulds turkeys, in that order (Williams, 1991).

Rio Grande Wild Turkey
(Meleagris gallopavo intermedia)

When George B. Sennett (1879) first called attention to the characteristics in which the Rio Grande turkey differs from the other races of wild turkeys, he evidently thought it was an intermediate and should not be named, for he said, at that time: "All Lower Rio Grande specimens, therefore, must be held as the Mexican form— an alternative not to be desired." Later on, however, he (1892) described and named it *ellioti,* in honor of Dr. Daniel Elliot. But his earlier name, *intermedia,* must stand under the law of priority (Bent, 1932). This subspecies was discovered and named some time later than the other subspecies of the east.

The Rio Grande subspecies is distinguished from the eastern and Florida subspecies by having tail feathers and tail coverts tipped with light tan, rather than medium brown, and from the two other western subspecies by having a brownish tail margin that is darker than theirs (Williams, 1991).

Merriam's Wild Turkey
(Meleagris gallopavo merriami)

This is a bird of the ponderosa pine foothills of the Rocky Mountains. This subspecies was named in honor of zoologist C. Hart Merriam. It is a cold weather bird and has been successfully stocked much farther north of its natural range. The Merriams wild turkey is distinguished from the eastern, Florida, and Rio Grande subspecies by the nearly white feathers of its lower back and tail margin (Williams, 1991).

Gould's Wild Turkey
(Meleagris gallopavo mexicani)
This is also a bird of the high mountains. Named for the famous zoologist Gould who was the first to describe it. The Goulds is the largest wild turkey of the five subspecies. There is said to be a small population in the U.S. along parts of the U.S.—Mexico border but it is said to be abundant in Mexico.

Wild Turkeys

Beautiful Ocellated turkeys at Houpert and Lastere's Rare Bird Collection, France.

The Ocellated Turkey
(Agriocharis ocellata)

This beautiful bird is a native of the Yucatan Peninsula in Mexico, Honduras, Guatemala, and generally of Central America. It lives in subtropical lowland jungles through the summer and early fall, but about October 1 the birds begin visiting isolated cornfields to feed in early morning and afternoon (Leopold, 1972). As indicated by its name, its plumage is covered with metallic flashing ocelli like emeralds and diamonds which gave the species its vernacular name.

This bird is much smaller than any of the subspecies of the wild turkey and the skin of its head is partly bluish instead of being red as in the other wild turkeys. Ocellated round-ended tail feathers are very specific of the species. The reddish tail is tipped with pale cinnamon-brown, buffy, or light white. The mature males have the beard as in other turkeys.

Ocellated turkeys are polygamous in captivity as well as in the wild. The hen lays about a dozen eggs on the ground in a deep scrape. The eggs are cream colored with brown specks. The best temperature according to Lastere is 38.5° degrees C. (Lastere, 1986). Humidity should be around 50% and raised a few days before hatching to help break down the calcium in the egg shell.

These birds have become very rare in captivity in recent years. The stock became badly inbred through the years and no new blood was brought into the captive bloodlines. Years ago Mickey Olsen was very successful with these birds and raised many. Because of the shortage of good blood the price has gone to the roof with pairs being sold for as much as $4000 per pair. The shortage of good blood is only one of the problems encountered with these beautiful birds. The males are often lethargic and have no interest in breeding although the hens are in good breeding condition. It has been discovered that another gobbler or two strutting sometimes provokes or stimulates the Ocellated gobbler to get interested in setting up house. Some breeders have run wild turkeys in a pen next to the Ocellated turkeys to give stimulation to the males.

I hope to try these birds in the future. They not only offer the game bird breeder a challenge, but would give many hours of pleasure looking at their outstanding beauty.

Mountain Quail
(*Oreortyx pictus*).
Photo by Lincoln Allen.

PLATE A

Upper left, Mountain Quail *(Oreortyx pictus);* upper right, Mearns Quail *(Cyrtonyx montezumae).* These photographs taken at Rick Winkel's Game Bird Collection, West Bountiful, Utah.

All photographs on th page taken George A. Allen,

Bamboo Partridge *(Bambusicola thoracica).* Photographed at Tracy Aviary, Salt Lake City, Utah.

Philby's Rock Partridge *(Alectoris philbyi).* Photographed at Tracy Aviary.

PLATE B

Columbia Crested quail *(Colinus cristatus)*. Photographed by Lincoln Allen at Pat and Al Cuelho's Game Bird Collection.

Ferruginous Wood Partridge

(Caloperdix oculea)

by Richard Robjent

PLATE C

**Palawan Peacock Pheasant
(Polyplectron emphanum).
Photo by Lincoln Allen.**

**Roul Roul Partridge at the
San Diego Wild Animal Park.
Photo by Lincoln Allen.**

PLATE D

Strutting Yellow Golden Pheasants *(Chrysolophus pictus luteus).* Photographed by Lincoln Allen at Ron Brown's Pheasantry, Ontario, Canada.

Strutting Golden Pheasants *(Chrysolophus pictus).* Photographed by Lincoln Allen at Bob Rader's Pheasantry, Bean Station, Tennessee.

PLATE E

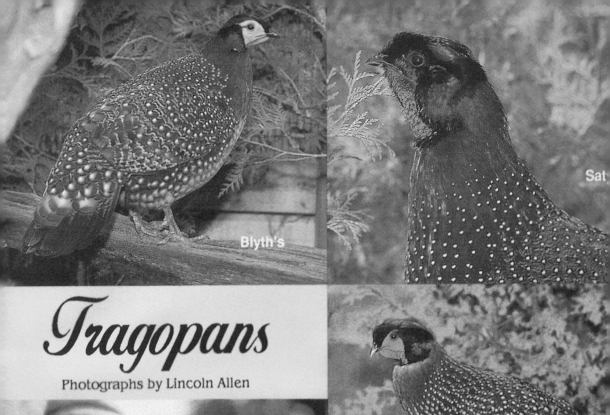

Blyth's

Sat[urn]

Tragopans

Photographs by Lincoln Allen

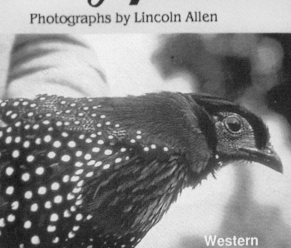

Western

Temminck's

Cabot's

Cabot's

PLATE F

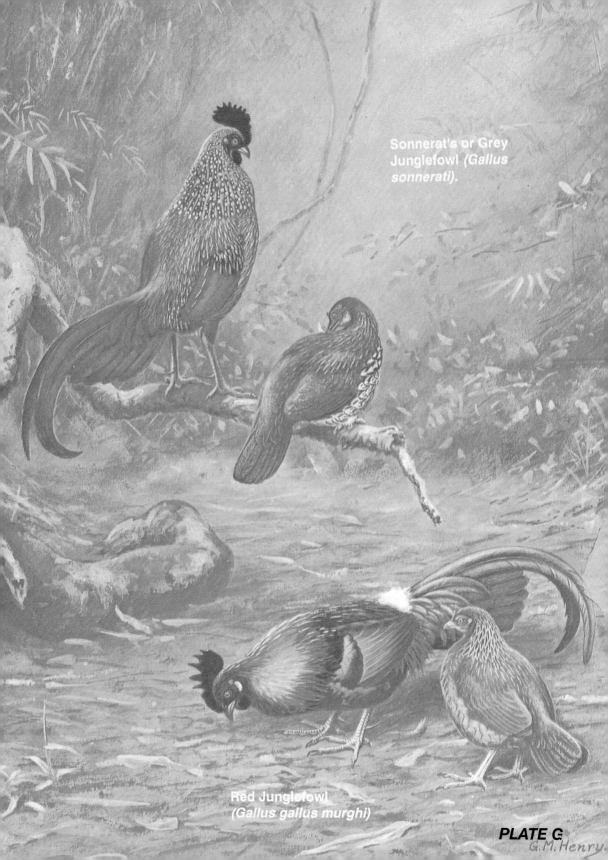

Sonnerat's or Grey
Junglefowl *(Gallus
sonnerati)*.

Red Junglefowl
(Gallus gallus murghi)

PLATE G

G.M.Henry

Vulturine Guineafowl
(Acryllium vulturinum).
Photo by Lincoln Allen.

Reeves Pheasant (Syrmaticus reevesi).
Photo by Lincoln Allen.

PLATE H

Part 6

SOME FAVORITE GUINEAFOWL

Guineafowl of the World

Helmeted

Illustrations
by
S. David McKelvey

White Breasted

Kenya Crested

Vulturine

Richenow's Helmeted

Guineafowl

(Numididae)

Since pre-Biblical times, Guineafowl have been the subject of early Africans who raised them for food. The name usually refers to the common guineafowl which undoubtedly came from the Helmeted subspecies. The fossilized remains of guineafowl approximating to the common variety have been found in Czechoslovakia. These have been dated from the upper Pleistocene Era, about 2,500,000 years ago. In that period elephants and lions were roaming as far north as England (Belshaw, 1984).

Guineafowl are not the most beautiful birds when it comes to their heads. The vulture family and the guineafowl family have much in common when it comes to "looks." However, if one can overlook the head, these are truly beautiful birds that are a joy to behold. One must look at the feathers closely to appreciate the delicate pattern and coloration. Although most are dark colored, they are most appreciated in direct light really to show their colors.

I had Domestic guineafowl when I was a youngster in High School. Mine were the solid white mutations that I raised from keets. They were so unusual and enjoyable that I have never really forgotten them. Later, on two other occasions we had some Domestic guineafowl and really enjoyed them. They are characters as they have terrific personalities.

The Species

Since the 18th century ornithologists have been trying to develop a classification system that would be accepted by the scientific community. They have done quite a good job after having to make several changes through the years. As new discoveries and distinctions were found it became necessary to reallocate some species. Guineafowl have been at the source of the confusion of these changes. The first classification of this family put them with *Phasianidae*. This changed after several years. The confusion comes when one goes back to the older sources and finds a completely different classification. Most ornithologists today recognize the guineafowl as belonging to a separate family called *Numididae*. This is probably as it should be. These are unique birds and have distinctions that make them deserving of a separate listing.

Today, thirty-eight natural species and subspecies are currently recognized. These are divided between four genera and seven species. Excluding the common Domestic guineafowl, in the United States, only three or four of these subspecies are kept by private breeders in any numbers while several more rare subspecies are kept by several zoos. This is a shame, as the more one knows these birds, the better they come across.

Guineafowl are noisy, personable, beautiful and often quite bizarre or weird looking, and this last especially add interest to keeping them (Allen, 1983). Originating from Africa, overall they cannot stand much cold. The exception to this is the common Domestic guineafowl that can stand below zero weather quite well. We kept them in Montana in an open shed and they did very well. I brought about 20 birds up from Texas and turned them loose in the barn. There was several inches of snow on the ground and the temperature got below zero at night. They took off and flew away as soon as I let them out. Up to the top of the nearest very large cottonwood tree they went and spent three days roosting up there on bare limbs. I know they got cold! When they came down and joined in with our other chickens they were just fine. Those game bird breeders that live in the colder climates must provide some heat in cold weather for all of the other subspecies. This has deterred many from getting into these interesting birds.

If you have heavy frost at night or for long periods of time you can put some type of heat lamp in one corner of the pen at night under the roost. The heat will rise and keep the bird's feet from freezing. Soon the birds will learn to get near the heat as they are very smart when it comes to survival. It is also a good idea to put about six inches of straw on the floor to help protect their feet. Some breeders put up temperary plactic sheeting around the shelter area during the winter to help hold in the heat during cold nights. This is good as it cuts down drafts which dissapate heat in an area rapidly.

Vulturine Guineafowl

(Acryllium vulturinum)

These birds come from Ethiopia, Somali Republic, Kenya, eastern Uganda, and north eastern Tanzania. Vulturine guineafowl like the desert areas with grasslands and patches of scrub and thorns. They roam in flocks of 70 or more birds with often just their heads visible above the tall grasses.

They are by far the most striking of the guineafowl subspecies. They are perhaps the largest of the species and are sometimes called the "Royal guineafowl" which is a commentary on the striking colors and most elegant carriage and shape. *"It is tall and has a long thin neck. The bare skin of the head and neck is greyish blue, the iris is crimson. A broad band of short velvet like chestnut feathers extends around the back of the cranium from ear to ear, producing an effect like a monk's tonsure. The feathers of lower neck and upper mantle extend into very long pointed hackles, black with stripes of white and cobalt blue. The upper parts of the body and abdomen are black, dotted with white spots. The breast has long bright cobalt blue patches on either side. Wings and tail are black with white stripes. The central tail retrices are long and pointed with the laterals much shorter. The edges of the outer secondaries are pale mauve and the white spots on the flanks are ringed with lilac. The legs and feet are grey brown. The male has a blunt spur on one or both legs and is often slightly larger, otherwise the sexes are alike"* (Belshaw, 1984).

Vulturine guineafowl are great runners and seldom fly except to roost in their favorite trees. The can survive long periods without water and absorb drops of dew from the green food that they consume. Perhaps, more than any of the other species, these birds get much of their needed moisture from their food that consists of not only green vegetable matter but many insects.

In captivity, these birds are prone to frost bite so need to be housed in frost free houses during cold weather. They are a desert bird and can stand short periods of cold weather but cannot take several days in succession of extreme cold. They should be out in full sunlight during the summer on well drained soil. Pens should be as large as possible as they are such large birds. David McKelvey at the San Antonio Zoo has success with planted pens measuring 20 by 10 by 8 feet with the back third covered for protection from direct rain and by 10 by 8 feet with the back third covered for protection from direct rain and sun.

In the wild, these birds are said to lay usually more than 12 eggs per clutch incubated by the hen in 24 days. Incubator temperature should be 99.5° F. with the wet bulb reading of 80° F. That is drier than required by most game bird species. In captivity, some hens never lay.

Chicks can be brooder reared. Feed the chicks like any other game bird chick. Start them out on a high protein starter and give them shredded lettuce and boiled egg to give them a good start. The ASSEMBLY LINE METHOD described earlier in this book works very well with any of the guineafowl species. Do not let the keets chill especially the first two weeks. They are very sensitive to cold when very young. Keep the keets as clean as possible until they build up disease immunity. Feed some type of live food such as mealworms. Vulturine guineafowl require more of this type of feed.

Vulturine guineafowl photographed at Mickey Ollson's Wildlife Zoo, Phoenix Arizona.

Kenya Crested Guineafowl

(Guttera pucherani pucherani)

The Kenya Crested guineafowl is by far the tamest of the species kept in captivity. David McKelvey reports that at the San Antonio Zoo where these birds are kept in a large walk-in pen they will untie shoelaces, jump on laps, and allow themselves to be stroked and picked up by the zoo visitors. This endears these birds to me as I love to have birds that interrelate to humans like this.

"The body plumage is uniformly grey/black and covered with medium sized bright blue spots. These are large and very distinct on the primary coverts. There are long distinct blue and white stripes along the primaries and secondaries, these are spaced on a black ground. It is without the common black collar of the Guttera edouardi group. The uniformly sized blue spots continue on the neck, tightly creased on the lower nape and slightly raised under the ears. The bare skin of the head and neck are a bright cobalt blue except for patches of scarlet around the eyes, behind the crest, on chin, throat and from of neck. The black crest is of medium length, thick, fine and slightly crinkled. It extends from the base of the upper mandible across the crown and onto the occiput. The outer edges of the flight feathers have a cream to pale coffee coloured edging. The spotting on the under plumage is finer and the overall impression of the plumage gives a bright blue effect. The eyes are a light red brown, legs and feet pale blue grey" (Belshaw, 1984).

Actually, these birds are quite attractive and can be kept comfortably in a mixed aviary. They are non-aggressive and will build their nest in a corner if good cover is provided. They can even be kept with other subspecies of guineafowl without any problems. They like mealworms and enjoy some grain to pick at during the day.

Kenya Crested guineafowl photographed at Bernard Roer's bird collection, Phoenix, Arizona by Lincoln Allen.

264 *Some Favorite Guineafowl*

Edward's Crested Guineafowl

(Guttera edourdi)

This is perhaps the most rare of the guineafowl in the United States. Some private breeders have these and so do some zoos. They are similar to the Kenya Crested but are distinctively different.

"The black crest feathers are short, dense and very tightly curled. The bare skin around the head and neck is very dark blue black. There is a distinguishing triangular patch of white around and under the ears, sometimes reaching back on the nape. The plumage is deep black with a hint of dark chestnut. This is uniformly covered with tiny bluish white spots which are surrounded by indistinct black circles. Around the lower neck there is a wide unspotted black collar which extends down unto the upper breast. The primaries and secondaries are strongly edged with white and the secondaries have longitudinal blue streaks. The eyes are deep red, beak is horn coloured with blue tinged at base. Legs and feet bluish grey" (Belshaw, 1984).

In the wild, these birds are found in Zambia, southern Malawi and Zambezi valley in Mozambique. There are eight subspecies which have minor distinctive differences. I am not sure which of these are in the collections in America.

Some of these specimens are reported to be quite belligerent in the aviary and should not be mixed with other species. This could be a characteristic of only certain of the subspecies, but it would be wise to watch them closely if you should get some.

The chicks resemble others of the group. They are barred on the head and back and the shading is lighter underneath. Handle them as the other species of guineafowl.

Edward's Crested guineafowl photographed at Bernard Roer's bird collection, Phoenix, Arizona by Lincoln Allen.

266   *Some Favorite Guineafowl*

Helmeted Guineafowl

(Numida galeata)

Several private breeders and zoos have in their collections subspecies of the Helmeted guineafowl. Most of the subspecies have been imported around the world and were used to develop the domesticated guineafowl. They are unique in their appearance mainly around the head region.

"Bare skin around the chin, throat, lower neck and along nape is brownish black, dark grey in front of the helmet. Pale bluish white on sides of head and cheeks and around eyes, ears and sides of upper neck. Medium sized umber colored helmet, usually with a backward curve. Rows of stiff dark filoplumes proceed up the nape. The large broad wattles on either side of the head are usually scarlet with a bluish white base but sometimes they are half bluish white and half scarlet or even just scarlet tipped. The fleshy membrane around the nostrils and down to the corner of the gape on either side is scarlet to deep red. The plumage is black, occasionally washed or streaked with dark chestnut brown and covered with large pearl white spots ringed with deep black outer circles. It has a wide slate grey collar washed with purple or pale lilac extending from the lower throat down over the upper breast and back around the mantle. The primaries are more barred than speckled. Legs and feet are grey brown. The hen is usually smaller but similar to the cock" (Belshaw, 1984).

The Helmeted can be sexed by casque size and shape as well as by voice. The hen calls a raspy *"buck wheat - buck wheat"* repeatedly, however, the cock bird never calls this double noted sequence. The male produces a strident *"Deet! Deet! Deet! Deet!"* sound. To be sure of the sex of this guineafowl, a laprascope in the hands of a competent veterinarian will best solve the riddle of sexing these birds. The DNA and feather sexing methods may be used if preferred by the breeder.

Common guineafowl (from *Lewis Wright's Poultry, 1905).*

Domestic Pearl Guineafowl

These direct decedents of the Helmeted guineafowl are raised by the millions each year all over the world. At one time guineas made up 7% of the poultry meat production of France. They have not attained that popularity yet in the United States. However, on thousands of small farms, one can find a flock of these birds running at large and producing lots of eggs and fine tasting meat. Some restaurants serve young guineas as a real delicacy.

Guineas consume large numbers of insects and will seldom scratch or bother gardens or flower beds. Once started, they can fend for themselves and will even kill small snakes. The most beneficial thing about them is they are a natural "alarm system" giving off loud raucous calls when anything out of the ordinary happens. I have had a small flock of guineas drive out of our driveway a stray herd of cattle that wandered one day. This was quite a thing to see if you can imagine several small birds herding seven big steers with loud noise and short attacks.

Since so many of these birds are produced, some very beautiful mutations have been developed by breeders. There are more than 15 different mutations available in the United States with several more available in other countries. These mutations include: Pearl Gray, White, Lavender, Royal Purple, Coral Blue, Buff Dundotte, Buff, Porcelain, Opaline, Slate, Brown, Powder Blue, Chocolate, Violet, Chamois, and Fauve. Variations of these include: Splashed, Pied, Silver Wing, and White Breasted.

Domestic guineas are a good beginning for the breeder who wants to get into the more rare guineafowl. They are enough like their wild kinfolk to give good practice in getting fertile eggs, hatching and rearing of the keets. I now have two dozen eggs in the incubator and all of them are fertile. This is good as it is September 28, very late in the laying season.

The chicks are easy to raise after they are about a week old. Very young chicks must be kept warm and not allowed out into the chilly morning or else they may get wet and chill. Warm and dry is what these little chicks like in the beginning.

Feed a high protein feed. We use game bird starter feed that has about 28% protein. Treat them much the same as you would treat any species of pheasant or quail. I have never known them to be cannibalistic or to pick feathers. Perhaps this is because we never had them in great numbers. The chicks can fly at about 10 days and if you have open top pens you should clip wings or if you want permanent non-flying pinion one of their wings. Some of the commercial breeders use brailles to keep the birds from flying out of their pens.

Part 7

KEEPING GAME BIRDS HEALTHY

Management For Good Health

The fact that disease organisms are everywhere in the living world is frightening. They are found in the air, in water, and attached to every living creature. Some carriers of disease include domestic poultry, other game birds and cage birds, wild birds, wild animals (including rodents), livestock, household pets, humans, earthworms, snails, slugs, arthropods including fleas, mites, ticks, lice, mosquitoes, sow bugs, crickets, and grasshoppers (Damerow, 1995).

The game bird breeder can assume that his birds are constantly exposed to these disease causing organisms and manage his birds to the best of his ability to keep their resistance as high as possible. Healthy birds are comparatively speaking disease resistant. Unhealthy birds will catch any one or any number of diseases as their natural ability to control disease is inhibited. One might say that a game bird is a reservoir of infection just waiting for the dam to break.

Predator control

Mice and rats are probably the most common predators that the game bird breeder must work hard at controlling. They not only eat many dollars worth of feed each year but they are common spreaders of disease. These two facts alone make all of us want to control them in earnest. You may not have rats in your area, but all of us have mice. The way to identify the droppings is quite simple. Mice droppings are small, dark brown to black, and rod-shaped. Rat droppings are large, various colors, and capsule-shaped. When you decide that you have one or both predators immediate actions should be taken.

Rodent bait is probably the easiest method of control. There are several types of poison baits on the market. Your state has licensed certain types that can be used legally on these pests. Some states are more strict than others in allowing the type of bait to be used. Basically there are two types of baits available. Those baits that require a single-dose and those that require multiple-doses. Baits that contain chemicals called *Brodifacoum*, or *Bromadiolon*, or *Bromethalin* (works on nervous system so is more dangerous to other pets and animals), or *Cholecalciferol* are single-dose rodenticides and kill after only one feeding. Baits that contain the chemical *Chlorphacinone*, or *Diphacinone*, or *Pival*, or *Warfarin* are multiple-dose poison and must be ingested over many days to be effective.

I remember when we lived in Montana the manager of a local feed dealer was overrun with rats in his feed mill. They put out a multi-dose bait containing Warfarin for several months but the problem got worse and worse until they did not have a single bag of stored feed into which the rats had not eaten. They were completely out of hand. They called in a professional rodent exterminator for consultation. They discovered that the rats were eating the bait with no problem. The problem was they were also eating a high protein dog food with vitamin K added big time. This vitamin was counteracting the Warfarin's ability to cause internal hemorrhaging and the rats were getting fat on the whole program. They switched the bait to a single-dose type and solved the problem. They fortify most of our game bird feed with vitamin K so breeders beware.

Traps can be used for rodent control. There are many mechanical devices on the market that claim to be very effective against these pests. I have found that the problem with traps is they must be constantly attended. If dead animals or live trapped animals are not removed on a regular basis, they quickly loose their effectiveness as the rodents are smart and soon figure things out. People that are somewhat queasy about dead things may prefer to use the bait where the animals die underground and disposal is usually not necessary.

Other types of rodents can be a problem. We have *millions* of ground squirrels and gophers that are taking over the world. We must expend lots of time and diligence to keep these under control.

Then there are the hawks and owls, not to mention the skunks, foxes, coyotes, and raccoons. These just love to dine on game birds. These predators can be controlled with the use of an electric fence charger. This really has done the trick for me in this matter. As always, be very careful when you are dealing with any poison or electricity as someone or something could get hurt through negligence.

Proper nutrition

Capable management is the key to the success of most any venture. Success proportionally increases with the more efficient operation. Keeping up with advances in the "field" is almost as important as learning enough to enter the "field." This is surely true with aviculture. Finding the sources is very difficult. Time, and even motivation is hard to come by these days. Some best time spent would be in learning how to manage the game farm. The following information will be helpful for the experienced aviculturist and the "green horn."

The feed used is your choice. If the birds could choose their own feed, they would probably be like the rest of us and take candy and cookies. I have found that using the free choice system, letting the birds choose their foods, does not work for my birds. The birds will choose the "goodies" and ignore the proper balanced ration before them. So great care must be used to get your birds on a proper balanced ration. The breeder should use the best feed that is available. One that they especially formulate for game birds is preferable. The best feed may cost a little more, but the results are well worth it.

Many breeders regularly blend home-grown grains with formulated game bird feeds to reduce the total feed cost. They fail to realize or consider the effect of this practice on production. In most all instances this practice of reducing feed cost results in the feeding of inferior quality feed.

Changes in the feed's composition usually result in a feed deficient in amino acids, energy, minerals, or vitamins. They may substitute some ingredients for others in a ration, but at a reduced level. Overall, no two ingredients can be interchanged on an equal basis without affecting the diet composition.

Some ingredients can be added, but only as a certain percentage of the ration before they produce undesirable effects. Among these ingredients are various fish meals, some meat meals, fats, molasses, and fermentation by-products. Other ingredients should not be added in any amounts to game bird diets.

Sorghum grain (milo) and corn can be used interchangeably at a maximum ration of 90 percent sorghum grain and 10 percent corn. Oats and barley are lower in energy than corn and sorghum grain. Usually, their price and lower energy contents restrict their use in laying rations. They can be used effectively in rearing rations where energy level is not as critical as in other rations.

Wheat can replace corn if the price is right. It has about 92 to 95 percent the feeding value of corn. Coarsely grind the wheat if possible, as it tends to cling to the birds' beaks due to its gelatinous characteristic.

Besides considering the energy and protein contents of the cereal grains, we must also look at the special characteristics of each grain. Examples are:

Particle size—Extremely finely ground, grain is dusty and unpalatable. Too large particle size may allow the birds to selectively consume excess grain at the expense of the other ingredients.

Tannic acid content—Bird resistant varieties of sorghum grain may contain considerable tannic acid.

Protein content—The protein (amino acids) in grain makes a significant contribution to the total amino acid concentration of the ration. Differences between grains in amino content must be considered when substituting cereal grains. The protein content of sorghum grain can vary widely. Several years ago, the Department of Grain Science at Kansas State University analyzed many samples of sorghum grain from different areas of Kansas and found their protein contents ranged from 4.5 to 11.5 percent. The book value is 8.9 percent.

Presence of toxic materials—Mycotoxin (toxins produced by molds) is a danger, particularly in corn. Be sure the feed you receive is from a mill with a good quality control program. Other potential contaminants are residues of heavy metal, fungicides, and pesticides.

You should realize by now that if changes are to be made in a ration it should be done by someone familiar with ration formulation. If one needs assistance, he can contact an Extension County Agent in his area (Smith, 1984).

Vitamins

One essential element in the bird diet is **vitamins**. Studies show the truth of this statement. So much is not known about the function of vitamins that a smart bird breeder would not take a chance on shorting this important element in the diet. A lack of proper vitamins has been shown to cause some specific disease symptoms.

Even with the balanced rations, giving supplemental vitamins and minerals is best. Ideally, these are best coming from natural sources. However, sometimes this is impossible, so vitamins and minerals should be added to the ration. The bird's own body manufactures some required vitamins.

When chemical additives (preventive medication) have been added to the ration, experts think that they hamper the body's natural ability to ward off disease. An example is vitamin K and C. They recommend that some type of supplemental vitamin be added to the birds' feed or water to make sure enough of these essential elements are available. When adding vitamins to the drinking water, keeping the mixture fresh is important. This is especially true in the warm summer months as the enriched mixture is a very good breeding ground for bacteria. You can administer vitamins by putting the powder on the feed. If you feed "treats" as I do, you can make the vitamins stick on the bird seed or mealworm by adding wheat germ oil and sprinkling the powdered vitamins on. It works!

Birds on wire (wire bottomed cages) are more prone to vitamin deficiencies than ground raised birds. The earth somehow provides a source for some vitamins that the birds need. I always give my caged birds a large dust box where they have an opportunity to dust and keep their feathers clean. While they are doing this, I know they are eating some dust that gives them some vitamins and trace mineral elements. I am always wondering what is the cleanest dirt to give them! Since I have seen them eat the dirt, I am hesitant to put any kind of insect dust in the dust boxes as I do not want them to eat it. Regardless, they seem to enjoy the diversion of dusting.

Stress affects the absorbing ability of game birds. They are prone to have vitamin deficiencies because of stress whether related to disease or environment. When your birds are stressed, give them an extra dose of vitamins in the water or feed. It may be the thing that keeps them from coming down with a disease.

When you give your birds worm medication, be sure to give them extra vitamins for a week or so as the medication inhibits the bird's body from proper absorbing of needed vitamins.

Medicated feeds

Many game bird producers wonder why game bird feed cannot be bought with the same medication in it as for poultry. The reason usually being the Bureau of Veterinary Medicine within the Federal Drug Administration (FDA) has not approved the drug for use in game bird feeds. The approval of drug usage takes many years and many dollars before a decision is made. The real problem is that the potential sale of any approved drug and feed is so limited that few are willing to make the investment fearing that they probably cannot recover it from anticipated sales. The market for game bird feeds is minute compared with the market for poultry feeds.

They have approved only two drugs at the time of this writing for use in game bird feed, **bacitracin** and **penicillin**. (I use Turkey Starter when it is available for all my game bird chicks because of the medication for Coccidiosis and Blackhead and the high protein content).

A concern of officials is the lingering "residue" which many drugs leave in the carcass of the birds. Commercial breeders that produce birds for the table are affected more than the hobbyist that has a few ornamentals in his back yard. This is an ongoing problem that every game bird producer should be aware of to be sure that he is not personally contaminated with residues or someone that uses his product is not contaminated. Be sure to follow the manufacturer's instructions for using any medicated feed products.

Using diagnostic Laboratories

There is available to the game bird breeder a valuable tool. Over America there are dozens of DIAGNOSTIC LABORATORIES that have facilities to do postmortems and grow cultures for disease identification. These Laboratories are efficient, established and maintained to help in disease control. The United States Department of Agriculture (USDA) has an interest in good quality diagnostic work and sponsors a Laboratory in every state for this purpose. The only **sure way** to know what disease your birds may have is to use the facility of one of these Laboratories. A qualified Laboratory. can only diagnose some diseases Every breeder has regretted waiting too late to get professional help.

Finding your diagnostic Laboratory

Every State University has a Laboratory that will do postmortems on dead and diseased birds. They will also conduct Laboratory cultures to decide exactly the cause of abnormality. In some states, there is a charge for this service to breeders of game birds. Any serious breeder should acquaint himself with the location of his State Laboratory.

In large metropolitan areas some private commercial Laboratories will do this service. Please, find one that is near you and knows the procedures before you have a disease outbreak.

(SEE THE LISTING OF THE STATE LABORATORIES IN THE APPENDIX).

Selecting and submitting specimens

Sometimes finding out the exact cause of the problem is impossible, for one reason or another, for the Laboratory. I have taken sick or dead birds in several times and no problem could be found. I know for a fact that they were sick as some were dead. Most of the time an obvious problem exists, and the Laboratory can isolate it and make recommendations about what medications to use. This is a much better approach than the "shot gun" method of medication where the breeder begins to use the various medications until he finds one that works. Meanwhile some valuable birds can be lost.

Select birds that represent the disease. Birds in various stages of the disease will help the Laboratory. Decomposed birds are of no value for NECROPSY (autopsy). If possible, get the birds to the Laboratory quickly. If that is not possible, then keep the birds cool. If it will be a few days before you can get them to a Laboratory, freeze the dead birds. Some Laboratories are not open for business over the weekend or on holidays, so this must be considered. Sometimes you can get a night or weekend telephone number to call if you have an emergency with your birds. It always helps to get to know the Laboratory personnel on a personal basis so as to get good personalized service. Make friends at the Laboratory and they will befriend you when in need.

Give the Laboratory as much information as possible about the birds. The Laboratory will want to know some things about your situation:

1) Name of breeder
2) Address
3) Phone number
4) Species
5) Sex of specimen
6) Age of specimen
7) Feed used
8) Vaccinations
9) When first seen
10) Number sick birds
11) Mortality (deaths)
12) Symptoms
13) Medications
14) How many birds on farm?
15) Any other problems
16) Any ideas about the problem?

Transporting specimens to the laboratory

Do not transport dead birds across state lines as state law may prohibit interstate transportation. If you must travel across state lines to your Laboratory, be sure to check with authorities to find out what permits or permission must be obtained.

The containers used to carry dead birds should be well ventilated and should be disposable. Do not bring birds or containers back to your farm. Most Laboratories will not let this be done even if requested. Send the birds to the Laboratory the fastest way. I have used the Package Express Service of the bus company that serves our area. I always call the Laboratory to give them the method of delivery, and often they will have someone pick the parcel up at the bus station. Thus, in a few hours, the Laboratory has the birds. Pack the dead birds in dry ice if available, as this inhibits decomposition.

When the pathologist can diagnose the cause without tests, a report can be had in a few hours. I always request that if there is a serious contagious disease that they phone me immediately. My Laboratory is always glad to do this. A formal report follows this phone call in a few days. Sometimes it takes two to seven days to run the culture growth tests, so be patient.

20 tips for keeping birds healthy

Many game bird breeders like to have suggestions or tips to go by which help them be a better breeder. Listed below are some tips that will give any astute game bird breeder some spring boards to use to develop a system of keeping their birds healthy. Some like to keep a check list to insure that they forget nothing.

1) Proper management is essential.
2) Never mix different age birds.
3) When caring for your birds, go from the youngest to the oldest.
4) Isolate immediately any sick bird.
5) Feed the best feed available.
6) Use vitamins.
7) Keep pens and water clean.
8) Use safe water.
9) Isolate after returning from bird shows for at least thirty days.
10) Vaccinate when appropriate.
11) Build pens for benefit of birds.
12) Safely destroy dead birds immediately.
13) Buy stock from reliable breeders, look at the stock before buying if possible.
14) Eggs brought in have least disease.
15) Clean between groups of birds.
16) Keep species separate.
17) Keep chicks away from incubators.
18) Discourage visitors to your farm.
19) Get an early diagnostic report.
20) Maintain good records.

I must mention the effect that the weather and the resulting stress affects the health of our birds. The weather where you live at times causes stress to your birds. No one lives in a perfect climate (even here in San Diego County), so we must take steps to insure that the heat of Summer does not harm our birds.

Thousands of chickens died in the middle states this year because of the terrible heat. Birds cannot sweat to dissipate body heat, they pant and hold their wings out from their body. Most of the time this works well but when the heat and humidity is high, this natural air-conditioning system does not work efficiently.

We can install fans for such emergencies. The tops and sides of the buildings can be hosed down with water during the heat of the day that helps when it is not too humid. Misting systems can be used which help the birds dissipate their body heat. Always have enough airflow to dry the birds out after the misting process. Do whatever you can think of to get the temperature down to a tolerable number during such stressful times. In very hot weather, birds do not eat as much and therefore if they are in a laying mode, egg production drops rapidly, and they become susceptible to outbreaks of disease because of their weakened condition. Most of our game birds are tough. They have to be to survive out in the wilds. However, we should try on our part to make them as comfortable as possible during high heat periods.

Very cold weather also causes stress for our birds. If you live in the colder climates, you are very aware at what can happen in very cold weather. Toes and feet freeze, feed consumption goes way down, and the birds are put under stress. Having said that, I am amazed at how tough game birds are and how adaptable they can be in very cold weather. Please, be sure that they have open drinking water during freezing weather. They need some shelter to get out of the cold wind and a place for feed pans out of the snow. You may discover, like me, that your birds will not use the provided shelters. If they do not, at least we can sleep at night and not worry about them if they make that choice. It took me many years to learn that my responsibility went just so far, after that it was not my problem. Again, do all you can to make them comfortable.

Vaccination

The world of preventive medicine has come a long way! The use of VACCINATION has put us into the space age of medicine. Several diseases that formerly threatened the poultry industry have been eradicated or controlled by proper vaccination. Because of the advance in research, the modern game bird breeder has tools at his disposal to prevent and control many contagious diseases.

When our birds are vaccinated, they simply are helped to build up an immunity to a certain disease group. To do this, we either use **live or dead virus** serum.

It should be emphasized that a qualified person should supervise any vaccination program. Your local veterinarian can give information and guidance to the need to vaccinate. Another good choice for getting help would be your state's Veterinarian School. State authorities must supervise some "live virus vaccines" to prevent outbreaks of the disease. Great care should be used in developing any vaccination program.

Some common diseases that have vaccines available are:

1) Newcastle,
2) Coccidiosis,
3) Infectious Bronchitis,
4) Fowl Pox,
5) Avian Encephalomyelitis,
6) Gumboro,
7) Marek's Disease.

Again, be sure and check with your state's authorities before using any type of vaccination. Your VETERINARIAN or COUNTY AGENT will be glad to get you in touch with the proper people in your location.

Understanding diseases

The game bird breeder should have a general understanding of diseases if he or she is to combat disease. There should be a grasp of some principles that govern the spread and control of diseases.

It is helpful for the game bird breeder to understand something of the causative agents of the common diseases that affect his birds. This important understanding will help to combat the problem of disease in a much more effective way.

Dr. Thomas Eleazer gives us a very understandable "review" of the major causes of diseases in game birds (Eleazer, Clemson University).

1. **Bacteria**—One celled microorganisms, multiply by simple division, and can be seen only through a microscope.
   Common Diseases: Salmonellosis (Pullorum, Typhoid, and Paratyphoid), Colibacillosis, (E. coli), Fowl Cholera, Erysipelas, Staphylococcosis, Mycoplasmosis, Ornithosis, Clostridium, infections, (Ulcerative & Necrotic Enteritis), Anatipestifer.
2. **Viruses**—Ultramicroscopic infectious agents capable of multiplying only about living cells. Regarded as both living organisms and complex proteins. Usually infect within the body cells.
   Common diseases: Newcastle Disease, Quail Bronchitis, Hemorrhagic Enteritis, Avian Pox, Corona Viral Enteritis.
3. **Fungi (Molds)**—Parasitic or saproytic plants that lack chlorophyll, roots, leaves or stems and reproduce by spores.
   Common diseases: Candidiasis (crop mold), Aspergillosis.
4. **Protozoa**—Single celled animals, mostly microscopic in size, some are mobile by way of flagella or cilia or by amoeboid movement, some are fixed (cannot move about).
   Common diseases: Coccidiosis, Histomoniasis (Blackhead), Trichomoniasis.
5. **Intestinal worms**—Worm-like parasites infecting the digestive tract.
   Common diseases: Roundworms, Capillary worms, Cecal worms, Tapeworms.
6. **Bio-Toxins**—Various poisonous substances produced by some microorganisms that cause certain diseases.
   Common disease: Botulism.
7. **Chemicals, drugs, miscellaneous and unknown.**
   Common diseases: Sulfonamide toxicity, insecticide poisonings, lead poisoning, cannibalism.
8. **Dietary deficiencies**—Game birds have different nutritional requirements than poultry both in quantity and quality of ingredients in the diet.
   Common diseases: Selenium deficiency, vitamin-mineral deficiencies, (Rickets, B complex vitamin, etc.), ingredient quality problems.

9. **Folks**—A bird in a pen or house cannot get out and fend for itself so they have to depend on people to provide life's necessities. All too often one or more of these necessities are lacking due either to deficiencies in a guidance program or oversight by the man-in-charge.
Common diseases: Feed and/or water deprivation, improper debeaking, vaccination, handling, ventilation, lighting.

10. **Combination**—Combinations of any of the above can cause problems or greater problems than either can cause alone.
Common diseases: Coccidiosis, stress, Ulcerative Enteritis organisms.

Direct causes of disease

1) Bacteria
2) Viruses
3) Protozoa
4) Parasites

5) Fungi
6) Nutritional deficiencies
7) Chemical poisons
8) Unknown causes

How diseases spread

Diseases spread in many ways. The plain truth is the fact that **disease agents are everywhere.** Why then, are not all of our birds sick or diseased? Well, there is a defense system in every living thing that wards off infections. If this defense system or mechanism is understood, the bird breeder can use it to help keep his birds free of disease. The term most often used to describe this defense is **immunity**. Birds can obtain immunity or resistance from several sources:

1) Birds can inherit it from the parent stock,
2) People can give it to the bird through artificial methods (vaccination),
3) Birds can have it from a mild case of the disease.

Common ways that diseases are spread

1. Contaminated grounds, pens, or old litter. It is common sense to keep the bird area clean.

2. Airborne organisms. Disease agents are everywhere and blow with the wind. Keeping dust down will help, but nothing can be done to completely do away with this problem. Raising birds in clinically pure conditions is much too expensive for the average bird breeder.

3. Wild birds and rodents. These pests not only carry diseases, but can be costly if they rob the feed pan.

4. Impure water. If you are unsure about this, have your water tested for purity.

5. Recovered stock that are "carriers." Careful attention needs to be given to recovered birds. When they are known to be carriers, they should not be mixed with other stock.

6. Newly acquired diseased stock. A good practice is to put new stock in a quarantine area for several days before putting with resident birds.

7. Egg transmission. Many bird breeders get hatching eggs.

When getting hatching eggs, fumigate the eggs before putting them into the incubator.

Ideas to prevent disease

These recommendations should be of help in preventing diseases (Haynes, 1983):

1. Do not add birds from another source to your flock.
2. If you must have additional birds, try to get eggs and hatch them yourself.
3. Keep breeders away from growing birds. Have a separate caretaker for the breeders if possible.
4. Normally, the younger the birds the more susceptible they are to most diseases. Therefore, starting birds on wire floors should provide an advantage.
5. Do not allow visitors on your farm without making certain they are wearing clothing and shoes that have not been near

other birds. If you must have visitors give them rubber boots and clean overalls.

6. Keep wild birds out of your pens.
7. Thoroughly clean and disinfect any equipment.
8. If you sell birds, do not allow the buyer to bring unclean crates, boxes or cages on your farm to pick up birds.

Here is a good place to mention the "general cleanliness" of your birds. Feeders and water founts should be cleaned at least once each day. My old Agriculture teacher used to tell us the drinking water should be clean enough that we would not mind drinking it. The bottom of the pens should be clean also. In old droppings one finds all sorts of disease causing germs. This is a good place for insects to breed and in turn spread many of the disease organisms that adversely affect our birds. Let your nose tell you id the place is clean. Strong urine odor or other obnoxious odors can tell a lot. If possible find the place where the smell is coming from and see just what is the cause. When a farm is clean, there is no odor. That does not mean there is no droppings under the pens at all; it means that everything is under control. Something we do to stop odor and flies is to put agricultural lime under our pens. If this is sprinkled periodically under the pens it stops all odors and flies.

Do not buy birds or eggs from a farm that is not clean. You are asking for problems if you do. This is where a visit to a potential supplier is really worth the time and expense.

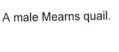

A male Mearns quail.

Keeping Game Birds Healthy 287

GAME BIRD MEDICATION GUIDE

Prepared by Veterinary Science Extension,
The Pennsylvania State University

CODE

SC	= Subcutaneous	d	= day
Wd	= Withdraw	w	= week
IM	= Intramuscular	mg	= milligrams
C	= Continuous	gm	= grams
T	= Treatment	pkt	= packet
t	= ton		

See Label   Concentration varies from brand to brand. Formulations change requiring adjustment of dosage.

The information given here is for educational purposes only. Reference to commercial products or trade names is made with the understanding that no discrimination is intended and no endorsement is implied. Only a limited number of drugs have FDA clearance for game birds and some of them have only "limited use." Until then the user assumes full responsibility for any medication administered to game birds. Therefore, it is wise for him, before using any drug, to check its safety, warnings, contra-indications, and slaughter withdrawal period. Most drugs mentioned do have clearance for use in domestic poultry and are known to be safe for game birds in listed dosages. Treatments and dosages also recommended for small flocks of domestic poultry.

Disease	Method	Treatment	Dosage
Arizona/ Paratyphoid	Injectable	1. Garasol	1 mg/chick (1 d) SC
		2. Spectam	5 mg/chick (1 d) SC
		3. LS 50	5 mg/chick (1 d) SC
	Feed	**1. Nitrofurans	150 gm/t/10-14 d
		2. Neomycin	140 gm/t/5-7 d
	Water	**1. Amifur (Swine)	16 oz/50 gal/5-7 d
		**2. NFZ	3-4 gm/gal/5-7 d
		3. Garasol (injectable)	4 cc/gal/5-7 d
		4. Neomycin	150 mg/gal 5-7 d (if available)
		5. LS 50	2 gm/gal/7-14 d
Clostridial Diseases— Botulism Ulcerative enteritis Necrotic enteritis Necrotic dermatitis	General	1. Clean feeders, change feed	
		2. Remove dead and sick birds (4x/d)-treat area of dead bird with aluminum sulfate to oxidize soil (botulism)	
		3. Remove decaying vegetation in pens	
		4. Dose sick birds with 10-20 cc water or epsom salts solution 1 tbsp/pt. Hold in sick pen—repeat (water only) 2x/d.	
	Feed	1. Mycostatin-20	50 gm/t/5-7 d; 20 gm/t C
		2. Sodium proprionate	1 lb/t C
	Water	1. Epsom salts	1 lb/5 gal/1 d
		2. Epsom salts solution	20 cc/sick bird. See above.
Coliform Infections (*E. coli*)	Injectable	1. Garasol	1 mg (0.2 ml)/Chick/1-4 d SC
		2. Spectam	5 mg (0.2 ml)/chick/1-4 d SC
		3. LS 50	5 mg/chick/1-4 d SC
	Feed	**1. Furox, NF 180	50-100 gm/t/3-5 d
		**2. Amifur, NFZ	1-2 lb/t/3-5 d
		3. Neomycin	140 gm/t/3-5 d (if available)
		4. Bacitracin	150-200 gm/t/5 d
		5. Albamix	200 gm (8 lb)/t/5 d
	Water	**1. Amifur (Swine)	16 oz/50 gal (2 tsp/gal)/3-5 d
		**2. NFZ (soluble)	3-4 gm/gal/3-5 d
		3. Garasol	4 cc (20 mg)/gal/3 d
		4. Neomycin	150 mg/gal/3-4 d
		5. LS 50	Pkt (50 gm)/25 gal/3 d

**Nitrofurans [furazolidone (NF 180, Furox); Nitrofurazone (NFZ, Amifur)] are toxic to chukar especially chicks under 14 days old.

Coryza,	Injectables	1. LS 50	15 mg/bird SC
Infectious		2. Streptomycin	25 mg/bird SC
Hemophilus		3. Gallimycin	25 mg (½ ml)/bird SC
gallinarums			
	Feed	1. Sulfathiazole	0.05% level/7-10 d
		2. Agribon	0.05% level/7-10 d
		3. Gallimycin	185 gm/t/7-10 d
		4. Albamix	200 gm (8 lb)/t/7 d
		5. Lincomycin	200 gm/t/7 d
		6. Tetracycline	200 gm/t/7-10 d
	Water	1. Sulfathiazole	1 lb/50 gal/5-7 d
		2. Streptomycin	1 gm/gal/5-7 d (if available)
		3. Agribon (12½%)	1 tbsp (½ oz) per gal/5-7 d
		4. Tetracycline	400 mg/gal/5-7 d
		5. Gallimycin	4 gm/gal/5-7 d (500 gm/128 gal)

Coccidiosis	Feed	1. Agribon	See Label/7-14 d
		2. Rofenaid	.0125%/14 d C
		3. SQ	.033%/7-14 d
		4. Amprol	.0125%/C
	Water	1. Ambrol 16 oz/50 (liquid)	1 oz/3 gal/3-5 d
		2. Agribon (12½%)	½ oz/gal/3-5 d
		3. ESB₃ (soluble)	1 tbsp/gal/3-5 d
		4. SQ, Sulmet	½ oz/gal/2-3 d

Enteritis,	Feed	1. Neomycin	140 gm/t/5-7 d
Nonspecific		2. Bacitracin	200 gm/t/5-7 d
(Enteric bacteria)		**3. Furox	100 gm/t/5-7 d
		**4. Amifur	3 lb/t/5-7 d
		5. Pen-Strep	180 gm (combo)/t/5-7 d
	Water	1. Neomycin	150 mg/gal/3-5 d
		**2. NFZ (soluble)	3-4 gm/gal/3-5 d
		3. Bacitracin	400 mg/gal/3-5 d
		4. Pen-Strep	2 gm (combo)/gal/3-5 d
		5. Streptomycin	1 gm/gal/3 d
		6. Neoterra	See Label (poultry)
		7. Aureomycin	See Label (poultry)

**Toxic to chukar under 14 days of age.
**Toxic to water fowl

Fowl Cholera* (Pasteurella spp)	Injectable	1. Spectam	5-10 mg/lb bodywt. SC
		2. Streptomycin	5 mg/lb bodywt. SC
	Feed	1. Agribon	See Label/7-14 d
		2. Albamix	200-350 gm/t/7-10 d
		3. SQ	.033% level/14 d
		4. Other Sulfas	See Label
		5. Aureomycin	200 gm/T/14 d
	Water	1. Agribon (12½%)	½ oz/gal/ 6 d
		2. SQ (on 3, off 2, on 2 d)	½ oz/gal .
		3. ESB$_3$ (soluble)	1 tbsp/gal/5 d
		4. Sulmet (12½%)	See SQ

Histomoniasis (Blackhead)			
	Feed	1. Carbosep	.025% T .0375% C
		2. Emtrymix	.08% T .02% C
		**3. Histostat	.01875%
		4. Ipropan	See Label for turkeys
	Water	2. Histocarb	1 oz/gal/5 d
		3. Histosep	1 tbsp/3 gal/7 d
		4. Ipropan	½ gm/gal (1 pkt/128 gal)/7 d

Marble Spleen Disease (Pulmonary Edema Disease)—Pheasants	Feed	1. Neo-Terramycin	150-200 gm/t/7 d
		**2. Nitrofurans	50-100 gm/t/7 d
		3. Mycostatin-20	100 gm/t/5 d
		4. Albamix	200 gm/t/5 d
	Water	1. Neo-Terramycin	1 tbsp/gal/4 d
		**2. Nitrofurans	1-2 gm/gal/5-7 d
		3. Bacitracin	400 mg/gal/5 d
		4. Streptomycin	1 gm/gal/5 d
		5. LS 50	1 gm/gal 3-5 d
		6. Garasol	4 cc/gal/3 d
		7. Tylan	200 mg/gal/7 d

*When Fowl Cholera becomes endemic, it can best be controlled by vaccination to prevent reoccurrence. Vaccines include bacterins which are inpected under the skin at the back of neck or the Clemson U. vaccine which is live attenuated culture given in the drinking water. Consult your avian pathologist before using either.

**Toxic to chukar under 14 days of age.
**Toxic to water fowl

Keeping Game Birds Healthy   291

Mycoplasma	Injectable	1. Tylan (25 mg/cc)	12.5 mg/lb. bodywt. IM/max. dose 1.5 cc
		2. Spectam Dose:	0.2 ml (5 mg)/chick; 1 ml/adult, SC
		3. Gallimycin	See Label
	Feed	1. Tylan	200 gm/t/5-7 d—50 gm/t C
		2. Gallimycin	185 gm/t/8 d
		3. Lincomycin	200 gm/t/7 d
	Water	1. Tylan	300 mg/gal 3-7 d
		2. Gallimycin	1 tsp/gal/3-7 d
		3. LS 50	1 gm/gal/7 d
		4. Terramycin (poultry)	1 tsp/gal/3-5 d
		5. Aureomycin	300 mg/gal/4-5 df

Mycosis and Mycotoxicosis	Feed	1. Empty feeders—refill with fresh feed. Mycostatin-20	50-100 gm/t/5-7 d
		2. Sodium propionate (mold inhibitor)	3 lb/t/5-7 d
		3. CuSO$_4$ (2x vitamins)	2 lb/t/7 d
		4. Myconox	3 lb/t/5 d
	Water	1. Myconox	See Label
		2. Res-Cu	1 pt/ 50 gal/5 d
		3. Iodine sanitizers	25 ppm/water/every other day

Necrotic enteritis (*clostridium perfringens* type C)		See Ulcerative enteritis	

Paratyphoid (Salmonella)	Injectable	1. Spectam	1-5 mg/chick at 1 d; 5 mg/chick to 4 w
	Feed	*1. Nitrofurans (NFZ, Furox, Amifur NF180)	100-200 gm/t/10-14 d
		2. Ogribon (12½%)	See Label
		3. ESB$_3$	See Label
	Water	*1. Nitrofurans (NFZ, Amifur, NF180 furox)	See Label
		2. Agribon (12½%)	1 tbsp/gal/6 d
		3. Neomycin	See Label
		4. Other sulfas	See Label
		5. LS 50	2 gm/gal/7-14 d

*Toxic to chukar under 14 days old.

Staphylococcosis	Feed	1. Gallimycin	185 gm/t/4 d
			Wd 48 hr. before slaughter
		2. Albamix	100 gm (4 lb)/t/4 d
			Wd 4 d before slaughter
		3. Penicillin	100 gm/t/5-7 d
		4. Lincomycin	200 gm/t/5-7 D
	Water	1. Gallimycin	1 tsp (4 gm)/gal/3 d
		2. Penicillin	1 gm/gal/3 d
		3. Albamycin	1 gm/gal/3 d
		4. Spectam	2 gm/gal/3 d
		5. LS 50	2 gm/gal/3 d

Streptococcosis		Same as Staphylococcosis

Stress	Feed	1. Pen-Strep	See Label
		2. Terramycin	100 gm/t/4 d
		3. Aureomycin	100 gm/t/4 d
		4. Vita-Electrolytes	1 pk/t/3-7 d
	Water	1. Pen-Strep	See Label
		2. Streptomycin	1 gm/gal/3 d
		3. Terramycin	400 mg/gal/3 d
		4. Aureomycin	400 mg/gal/3 d
		5. Gallimycin	1 tsp/gal/3 d
		6. Vitamin-Electrolytes	See Label

Ulcerative Enteritis (Quail Disease) (*clostridium colinum*)	Feed	1. Bacitracin	200 gm/t/7 d
		2. Streptomycin	180 gm/t/7 d
		3. Neomycin	140 gm/t/7 d
		4. Lincomix	2 gm/t C
	Water	1. Bacitracin	400 mg/gal/14 d
		2. Streptomycin	1 gm/gal 7 d
		3. Neomycin	200 mg/gal 5 d

Medicate simultaneously with two drugs (example: bacitracin and streptomycin), one in feed, other in water until mortality stops, then discontinue water medication but continue feed medication as preventative.

Toxicity (Drug)	Feed	1. Vitamin fortification/7 d	
	Water	1. Vitamin—A, C, K	See Label
		2. Vitamin—Multiple	See Label
		3. Vitamin electrolytes	See Label
		4. Electrolytes	See Label

Tricomoniasis		Same as for Histomoniasis

INTERNAL PARASITES

Ascaridia	Feed	1. Hygromycin 2. Worm-A-Floc 3. Piperazine 4. Wormal (Salsbury)	8-12 cm/t C See Label 0.1-0.4%/1 d Repeat at 30 d interval 1 lb/100 lb feed/350 adults (1dd)
	Water	1. Piperazine *2. Tramisol	See Label 1 gm/gal/1 d New drug

Capillaria (6 species) (crop-2, intestine-3, cecum-1)	Feed	1. Hygromix 2. Thibenzole	8-12 gm/t C 432 gm/t/14 d—30 day interval
	Water	1. Tramisol	1-2 gm/gal/1 d—Repeat monthly

Heterakis (Cecal Worm)	Feed	1. Hygromix 2. Worm-A-Floc 3. Phenothiazine (1 lb 30%/100 lb feed/350 head/1 d)	8-12 gm/t C See Label 0.5-1 gm/bird/1 d
	Water	1. Tramisol	1 gm/gal/1 d

Syngamus (Gapeworm)	Feed	**1. Thibenzole 2. Tramisol pellets (cattle) 3. Telmin (Mebendazole-Pitman Moore)—available only from veterinarians	432 gm/t/10-14 d 1 lb/20 lb feed/150 birds/2 d 400 gm/t/14 d
	Water	1. Tramisol	2 gm/gal/1 d repeat monthly

Total worm Control (all above worms)	Feed	1. Thibenzole · 2. Tramisol pellets (cattle) 3. Telmin (Pitman-Moore)	432 gm (4 pkt)/t/7 d/mo OR 216 gm (2 pkt)/t C 1 lb/20 lb feed/150 birds/2 d 400 gm/t/14 d
	Water	1. Tramisol	2 gm/gal/1 d repeat monthly

*Tramisol (soluble) in 3 size packets—52 cattle, 18 sheep, 13 swine, grams each (Dosage calculations:
1 gm/40 birds/treatment 1 day)
**Thibenzole—(sheep formula) 104 gms/packet

Diseases caused by bacteria

Bacteria are normally larger than viruses, but still microscopic (Beer, 1988). They are considered to be micro-organisms which must be seen with a microscope. Bacteria are said to be kin more to plants than animals and are often involved in the biological cycle of growth, death, decomposition, and fresh growth. Some attack living organisms and are responsible, in many instances, for death. Their effect can be rapid and dramatic.

Unlike viruses, bacteria can live and reproduce independently of other living cells. When they are mature, they begin the multiplying process through rapid division of themselves in just a few minutes. Fortunately, there are many drugs that can be used to combat bacteria. However, they can build resistance to drugs and no longer be affected by them.

Botulism

This is a disease problem that can be completely avoided. The birds become poisoned by the ingestion of decaying matter. The agent that causes the poison is **Clostridium botulinum**, a bacterium that causes deadly food poisoning. There are several types of this toxin, but types A and C normally affect fowl and type B affects man. The Vulture family is the only animal host known to man to be resistant to Botulism.

SYMPTOMS: Paralysis of first the legs and wings, and then the neck as the poison progresses. Neck feathers become loose in the follicle and can be easily pulled. Pheasants affected by Botulism remain alert, but paralyzed.

AUTOPSY FINDINGS: There are no lesions. Loose feathers on the neck and maggots in the crop (or decaying matter) are found.

Botulism must be differentiated from **Mycotoxicosis** that can also cause paralysis.

TREATMENT: Find and remove spoiled food or decaying matter. Flush the birds with Epsom salt in the water. An old home remedy for turkeys and ducks is to mix three drops of turpentine in a cup of water. Mix well and give two tablespoons to each bird. (The idea is to kill the maggots.) Birds with advanced stages can only be saved with an antitoxin that is difficult to find locally.

PREVENTION: Be sure no dead birds are left in the pens to decay and host maggots. Maggots can also live in damp, sour piles of spilled feed. Damp areas around drinking fountains can also host maggots. **Sanitation** is the key to prevention.

Pullorum

This infection is world wide in scope. This disease plagues virtually every country that has captive bird life. A rather common bacterium causes pullorum, **Salmonella pullorum**. They sometimes call it bacillary white diarrhea. There are more than 100 species and nearly 2,000 serotypes belonging to the genus *SALMONELLA*. Incubation for the disease is four to five days and the bacterium will live up to one year in a bird house. Once contracted, this disease spreads rapidly, usually from hen to egg to a chick and again to a chick through the incubator, brooder, and chick boxes. Mortality is very high in young chicks. Many die before any symptoms develop. Acute outbreaks are now rare in the U.S. because of the emphasis on eradication and control among commercial poultry producers.

SYMPTOMS: Death begins at five to seven days in infected chicks and peaks in another four to five days. Typical symptoms are droopiness, ruffled feathers, huddling, white diarrhea, and hard breathing. In adult birds there are no visible symptoms.

LESIONS: In chicks there may be pinpoint white nodules in the heart muscle, liver, lungs, and other organs. Yellow or cream-colored cecal cores or plugs may be present in the blind intestine not unlike Cecal Coccidiosis. **Sure diagnosis must come from Laboratory cultures.** The breeder needs to be aware that the same lesions may appear in several other diseases of birds such as **Typhoid, Cholera, Paratyphoid,** and **Staphylococcosis.**

TREATMENT: There is no effective cure to eradicate the disease from the flock. Recovered birds will always be "carriers" and should not be used for breeding stock. The only sure way to rid the disease from the farm is to eliminate all birds, disinfect, and clean up the premises extensively. Antibiotics in the "Sulfa" family will keep mortality down until Laboratory diagnosis can be made.

Omphalitis

This is also call this condition "**navel ill**" or "**mushy chick disease**." An inflammation of the navel involving improper healing characterizes it with bacterial infection.

OMPHALITIS is caused by poor incubator and hatchery sanitation, high humidity, and chilling or overheating. Navel closure is incomplete, allowing the entry of a variety of intestinal bacteria. Putting dirty eggs in the incubator may promote the condition, thus contaminating the area with bacteria that penetrates the egg shells that are poorly formed. Upon hatching, the chicks are contaminated.

The disease occurs during the first few days of life and seems to peak by the fifth to seventh day.

SYMPTOMS: Affected chicks appear drowsy or droopy with the down being fluffed up. Chicks huddle and have enlarged abdomens and lack body tone (mushy). A moist inflamed navel with diarrhea will be a telltale sign of this disease.

TREATMENT: There is none. Most of the affected chicks will die quickly even before they begin to eat and drink.

The only way to combat this condition is through **prevention**. The breeder should be careful to disinfect all equipment and establish a habit of regular **fumigation** of incubators, brooders, and eggs.

Ulcerative Enteritis

This is often call this problem "**quail disease**" which until controlled and understood was serious. Even today I hear of breeders having problems with this disease.

The scientific name for the spore forming rod bacteria is **Clostridium colinum**. The disease occurs when these bacteria build up to excessive numbers usually in soil or droppings.

This disease is a killer, especially among quail raised or maintained on the ground. It spreads through droppings, direct contact, and carrier birds. If not controlled, it will spread to all susceptible birds.

SYMPTOMS: All age quail get this disease. Birds can die with Enteritis while being in good flesh and have little or no symptoms or lesions. Other birds will appear listless, with ruffled feathers, white diarrhea, and have a "humped-up appearance."

A postmortem should reveal small whitish-grey ulcers in the intestine. To verify the disease a Laboratory should be used.

LESIONS: Lesions are characteristic in nature, but professional help needs to be secured for confirmation. The intestines have yellow-white perforates that have a typical eroded center. In the acute stage of the disease, the birds die of massive hemorrhages. Often the birds have **Coccidiosis and Enteritis simultaneously** and thus show blood in the droppings. **Coccidiosis, Salmonellae, Trichomoniasis,** and **Blackhead** all show similar symptoms and lesions, so care must be made in diagnosis.

TREATMENT: Bacitracin and Streptomycin are effective drugs. Good sanitary conditions can best accomplish prevention and by raising young birds on wire.

Infectious Coryza

Infectious Coryza is a specific respiratory disease that occurs more often in semi-mature or adult birds. It is often confused with **Endemic Fowl Cholera**. Infection may result in a slow spreading, chronic disease that affects only several birds at once or in a rapid spreading disease with most of the birds affected. The occurrence of infectious coryza is not widespread. However, the incidence appears to have increased in recent years in certain areas, where the infection has been introduced and has become endemic.

A bacterium causes the disease known as **Hemophilus gallinarum**. Transmission of the disease within the flock occurs by direct contact; airborne infective dust or droplets; and drinking water contaminated with infective nasal exudate. Symptoms usually develop in one to three days. Once a flock has been infected, each individual bird must be considered a "carrier."

SYMPTOMS AND LESIONS: The most characteristic symptoms of infectious coryza include: Severe swelling of the face around the eyes, nasal discharge, swollen sinuses, and water discharge from the eyes. Vision may also be affected. The disease results in a decrease in feed and water consumption and an increase in the number of cull birds.

DIAGNOSIS: Diagnosis can be confirmed only by isolation and identification of the causative organism. The organism, **Hemophilus gallinarum**, is extremely fastidious and often difficult to isolate. Birds should be submitted to a Diagnostic Laboratory early during the infection before complications make recovery of the organism even more difficult.

PREVENTION: Prevention is the only sound approach in controlling Infectious Coryza. Management programs that prevent contact between susceptible and infected birds can prevent it usually. If infection does occur, eliminate the total flock and thoroughly clean and disinfect the facilities and equipment.

TREATMENT: Several drugs can effectively treat this infection. Various antibiotics and sulfonamides are used. In the event sulfonamides are used, caution should be exercised in the administrations since lengthy treatments or high drug levels can result in toxicity, a drop in egg production and mortality. One should consult with diagnostic personnel concerning a recommended treatment. Treatment does not eliminate the infection in carrier birds, therefore, dispose of affected flocks when practical to eliminate them as a source of infection.

Diseases caused by viruses

Viruses cause diseases in animals such as the common cold and measles in a man, and foot-in-mouth in cattle. These minute organisms, usually far too small to be seen with the highest power of an ordinary microscope, can live and multiply only in other living cells. They can often survive for long periods outside the host, remaining capable of spreading infection (Beer, 1988).

There are no specific products available that can be used effectively to treat viral disease, they can treat or control only the secondary infections.

Laryngotracheitis

This is a highly contagious, infectious disease that occurs occasionally in most states. It affects poultry and pheasants. The causative **VIRUS** is spread from bird to bird, dead, infected birds, and man (clothing, shoes, containers, etc.).

SYMPTOMS: These are first noticed by watery eyes. Affected birds are inactive and have problems breathing. Coughing, sneezing, and shaking of the head to dislodge exudate plugs in the windpipe follow. They make a wheezing noise on inhalation. They call these birds "**callers**." Many birds die of **asphyxiation** (blockage of the trachea). No nervous symptoms as in Newcastle.

LESIONS: Gross lesions are confined to the respiratory tract. Blood clots or blood-tinged exudate is in the trachea. False membrane develops in the trachea. This mucus membrane wipes off without resistance or pressure, in contrast to POX LESIONS that are adhering and leave a raw, bleeding surface. This false membrane is diagnostic. A Laboratory antibody test must confirm diagnosis.

TREATMENT: When this disease occurs, it will probably infect the entire flock. Use Bacitracin to help the birds withstand secondary infections. Initiate severe quarantine procedures.

Newcastle

This is a contagious **viral infection** causing a respiratory nervous disorder. Newcastle disease was named from the British town of Newcastle-upon-Tyne, one of the first places it was studied. Newcastle is recognized to be in two forms: the mild strain (American) and the Exotic (foreign) strain. The former is not as serious as the latter, but both are fatal in young birds and cannot be cured.

The USDA has a stringent "**quarantine**" program for all birds entering the U.S. from most foreign countries. Despite this law, many birds are smuggled into the U.S. each year and some are infected with this disease. Do not buy a cheap bird from a stranger. This is a serious disease. All recovered birds become **carriers** and **shedders** of the virus and must be destroyed.

Visual symptoms include common respiratory problems of hard breathing, coughing, and hoarse chirping. The final stages will include paralysis, nervousness, and muscular tremor or spasms.

There is no treatment for Exotic Newcastle. When Laboratory confirmation is made, the state authorities will isolate the birds, and if the disease is present, destroy all birds according to law. The breeder will be compensated by the government for part of his loss.

Quail Bronchitis

This is a disease that can wipe out the commercial quail producer. The best way to approach Quail Bronchitis is to avoid it. Dr. Eleazer from Clemson University gives some good information about this disease.

An Avian Adenovirus in association with an adeno-associated virus causes this condition. Little is known about the disease in species other than Bobwhite quail.

HOW SPREAD: This is a highly contagious disease that easily spreads. Evidence shows that another avian species may carry the virus without showing signs of disease and be a source of infections for Bobwhite Quail.

PATHOGENESIS: This is an acute, highly contagious disease of the respiratory and intestinal tract. The disease usually starts in birds two to three weeks old and works back with subsequent hatches to where signs start at seven to ten days. Incubation period is three to seven days. Mortality can run from forty to 100% if not treated early.

TREATMENT AND CONTROL: Treatment with Tylosin helps frequently. Controls on multiple age farms are difficult without total depopulation and clean out to break the cycle.

In past years Quail Bronchitis has been a real problem to the large commercial producers. It has wiped out several operations completely. Since it is a viral disease, it spreads very rapidly through the flock. Wild birds and rodents and other carriers can take it to adjoining farms. Prompt diagnosis is essential! The breeder should have competent professional help in dealing with Quail Bronchitis as it is a very serious problem.

It is imperative that the breeder does not get stock exposed to this or any other disease. Be sure and check the record of the breeder before you buy any of his products.

Roup

This disease is very similar to Infectious Coryza. The two diseases are often confused. The disease is a specific respiratory infection caused by an organism similar to the one causing acute Fowl Cholera.

The disease is transmitted only by direct contact between susceptible and infected birds. Separation of the susceptible and carrier birds to prevent such contact will prevent the spread of the disease. Recovered birds may remain "carriers" indefinitely.

SYMPTOMS AND LESIONS: this chronic disease at once affects only some the birds. There is nasal discharge, inflammation of the eye and swelling of the sinus under the eye. The sinus becomes filled with a hard exudate that has a distinctive odor. Sometimes the lungs and air sacs are affected.

DIAGNOSIS: A trained Diagnostician can recognize this infection by the history, symptoms, and lesions. The isolation and identification of the causative organism can make a confirmed diagnosis only. This can sometimes be difficult because of the chronic nature of the infection and the presence of secondary and complicating bacterial organisms.

PREVENTION: Certain management practices can readily prevent this disease. Just separate the affected or carrier birds from the susceptible flock. Always try to introduce started or adult birds only from sources known to be free of the infection. Complete elimination of infected birds is a necessity and should be followed by thoroughly cleaning and disinfecting pens and equipment.

TREATMENT: Usually treatment is unsatisfactory. Various sulfonamides and antibiotics are used and lengthy treatments are necessary.

Avian pox

This is a slow spreading viral disease, characterized by skin and throat lesions. There are two forms__the dry and the wet. A VIRUS that affects all birds in some form causes Fowl Pox. Air or vector transmits this virus (mosquito most common) or by eating infected scabs.

SYMPTOMS: The wartlike lesions appear on the bare areas of the bird (head, legs, vent, etc.). In the wet form the lesions are found in the mouth and throat and form CANKERS. All birds will not be infected simultaneously, but a few will get the disease at a time. The wet form will often cause the birds to gasp for air due to the throat obstruction.

LESIONS: Typical lesions can easily be recognized. The scabs will fall off in about two weeks. A Laboratory can confirm the presence of the virus.

TREATMENT: When one case is diagnosed little can be done except to vaccinate the whole flock with Fowl Pox Vaccine. Be sure to vaccinate all birds on the farm. Treat the affected scabs with silver nitrate and give Bacitracin for about five days to prevent secondary infections.

PREVENTION: Control mosquitoes as much as possible. If you have had an outbreak, vaccinate all birds on your farm and encourage your neighbors with birds to do the same. You will generally get cooperation as the serum is very economical.

Coronaviral Enteritis (CE)

This is a newly discovered disease affecting mainly quail. Walking from pen to pen spreads the virus to farm equipment including dirty shipping crates and other common methods of disease spread. The corona virus seems to occur only in the intestinal tract and has been difficult to study because reproducing the corona virus in the Laboratory is difficult.

SYMPTOMS: As the birds get older they show signs of nervous flightiness, chirp, seek heat, and loose weight. Birds that recover are immune, but are permanent carriers of the virus and shed the corona virus in their droppings for life. A Diagnostic Laboratory must confirm this disease.

TREATMENT: Depopulate the farm and thoroughly clean the premises.

Marble Spleen

This is a rare disease affecting mainly captive-raised pheasants. However, a form of this disease affects other birds such as grouse and quail. The other forms of the virus are very specific and some cannot be cultured in chick embryos. It is on the increase and thus needs mentioning. **A virus causes this malady** and recovered birds are **immune for life**. There is an experimental vaccine being developed.

The disease invariably kills good condition birds suddenly. The spleen is enlarged and mottled simulating marble patterning. This is where the disease gets its name.

SYMPTOMS: Birds usually die suddenly, are well fleshed and apparently in good health. Get professional help in diagnosing the problem immediately. Only a competent Laboratory can detect this virus through cultures.

LESIONS: Swollen and marbled spleen, hemorrhage of the lungs, and enlarged liver plus the absence of other disease will suggest Marbled Spleen Disease.

TREATMENT: Give Bacitracin to ward off secondary infections while the disease runs its course. Mortality ranges from five to 15%.

The course of the outbreak is usually short and repeats in the same flock are unusual. Breeding from the survivors seems to produce progeny that are immune from some forms of this disease.

Breeders of large numbers of pheasants should by all means contact the authorities in your state to see if there have been any outbreaks. If there has, you may want to consider using the vaccine if it is available.

Diseases caused by protozoa

The protozoa are said to be the smallest and most primitive members of the animal kingdom. They consist of a single cell and some are large enough to be seen by the naked eye. They do not need light to survive as do plants. Having no skin, they dry out, and are subject to sunlight and disinfectants, however, some can encyst forming a very tough outer coat to get them through difficulties. They can remain in this form for long periods. They say that protozoan diseases are the most important microbial problem when raising game birds.

Blackhead
(Histomoniasis)

Most upland game birds are susceptible to this common disease. Blackhead is caused by an organism named **Histomonas meleagridis**. This organism is fragile outside the host and can survive only for a short time unless encased in the Cecal worm egg. If the breeder could rid his birds completely of Cecal worms there would be no need to worry about Blackhead.

Probably the most common carrier is the common earthworm. Earthworms can contain as many as 200 Cecal worm eggs that in turn contain the Blackhead organism and the cycle goes on and on.

SYMPTOMS: Birds infected have increased thirst. Droppings may appear yellowish.

TREATMENT AND CONTROL: The control of Cecal worms is essential. Eggs may be transferred on shoes or equipment. Many commercial feed mills add a preventive drug at a very low dosage to their feeds. If using this medicated feed and an outbreak occurs, it is usually not as severe. The breeder should not depend upon the medicated feed altogether for prevention, but should maintain an active preventive program stressing cleanliness.

Regarding a soil disinfectant, we use a simple lime (calcium oxide) and sulfur treatment. It is effective against most microorganisms and fungi, and the sulfur is effective against mites and lice. The lime stops odors and prevents the breeding of flies. Some soils tend to become sour when wet and lime will stop this. The method of application is simple. After raking any debris and feathers from the aviary, spread eight pounds of lime and four pounds of sulfur (soil sulfur) per 100 square feet of pen space. Spread evenly by light raking and turn the soil with a shovel. Rake smooth and dust about two pounds of lime and two pounds of sulfur on the surface and rake to distribute these into the surface. Such a treatment should be effective for six months. Extra application of lime between treatments under the water drippers or other type waterers is desirable to keep snails and slugs from breeding.

Several drugs are effective. See Game Bird Medication Guide for listings. Use the same directions for quail, chukars, and pheasants recommended for chickens.

Coccidiosis

This disease is a very common one found in captive-raised birds. Birds raised on the ground are very susceptible while birds raised on wire rarely get the disease. The causative agent, a **Protozoa,** is found in several forms. The coccidia that invades avian species does not affect other animals. There are some nine species of coccidia that affect birds, some are more serious than others. A fowl can be infected with more than one species at a time. The life cycles of the coccidia last seven to nine days that includes eight stages. The best control is to break into the life cycle with drugs and good sanitation thus avoiding multiplying of the organisms. Young birds are more susceptible than adults. Recovered birds have a resistance to the particular strain they recovered from, but can get the other strains.

SYMPTOMS: Weakness, ruffled feathers, hunched posture, and droppings that may be bloody are signs of this disease. Affected birds are inactive and become less interested in feed and water as the disease progresses.

LESIONS: Intestine and ceca may have bloody contents. There may be ballooning of the intestine with foul smelling contents. The outside wall of the intestine may be speckled in color.

DIAGNOSIS: The presence of oocyst will confirm the disease.

TREATMENT: There are several good medications available for this disease. It is a good idea to have medication on hand for treatment and control. Check with your feed store.

PREVENTION: Prevention can best control coccidiosis or letting the birds get a mild form thus building up immunity to the disease. The recognized ways of control are: 1) Mild case to build immunity, 2) Feed coccidiostat from first day to fourteen weeks. Then treat outbreaks, 3) Feed high levels of Vitamins A and K, 4) Treat any outbreaks as they occur.

Hexamitiasis

This is another **Protozoan** caused disease. It affects ducks, quail, partridge, and pheasants along with domestic turkeys. This is a recognized disease problem in commercial game bird operations. Chickens are not affected, but can be carriers to game birds, thus pointing out the importance of not mixing poultry with game birds. Greater losses occur in young chicks three to eight weeks old with a resistance developing by ten to twelve weeks of age. Adults seem to have a resistance.

SYMPTOMS: Affected birds' show chilling, ruffled feathers, watery diarrhea, and usually continue to eat, but lose weight. Birds will often huddle together close to the heat source and chirp constantly. They may be in pain or under great stress. Convulsions often occur shortly before death. Many survivors become stunted.

LESIONS: Birds become dehydrated and emaciated. The intestine may lose its tone and have watery and foamy contents. Microscopic examination of the intestinal contents will confirm the disease.

TRANSMISSION: The disease spreads from bird to bird and through infected droppings and through contaminated feed and water. They do not know the source of infections. Recovered birds remain carriers. Any exposed birds should be disposed of.

TREATMENT: Blackhead (Histomoniasis) medications are effective with this disease. Aureomycin at a level of 200 grams per ton of feed is of some benefit. Any medication will be limited in effect if healthy birds are exposed to carriers.

Trichomoniasis

This is a serious disease of young birds. It occurs in two forms: one affects the upper and one the lower digestive tract. A Protozoan organism causes it. The disease is spread through bad sanitation, free flying birds, rodents, or contaminated feed and water.

SYMPTOMS: **Upper form**: A depression, empty crop, stretching of the neck, swallowing, and a fetid odor. There is a greenish mouth fluid. **Lower form**: Birds have a yellow-watery diarrhea, lose weight, and die in two to three days. Appearance is similar to that of birds affected with Histomoniasis.

LESIONS: **Upper form**: Usually confined to the mouth, esophagus and crop. Necrotic patches and cheesy exude in the upper tract show up. LOWER FORM: Confined to lower intestine tract. Cecal lesions are same as in Histomoniasis.

DIAGNOSIS: Direct microscopy during the autopsy can identify the Protozoan Organisms. The presence of the protozoa does not necessarily mean it is a problem.

TREATMENT: Copper sulfate is effective in treating this disease. Move birds to sanitary surroundings if possible. Histomoniastatic drugs are all very effective and should be used when available rather than copper sulfate because they are safer. Water administration is the fastest route of medication.

Diseases caused by fungi

Fungi or molds vary in size from the large fungi seen on decaying trees through to the greenish growth on old bread. Fungi are very important in nature as they help break down and recycle dead animal and plant materials. Some are valuable producers of antibiotics and other chemicals. A few species can attack animal tissues and cause diseases. While only three or four species are commonly found causing disease in game birds, others may affect health indirectly by contaminating and degrading their food. There are only a few effective drugs for the treatment of the fungal diseases in game birds. The drugs in use are strong and have side effects. Some of the drugs must be put directly into the lung tissue by use of a tube. One can understand that this would be very stressful to any game bird.

ASPERGILLOSIS

This is a disease that is respiratory in nature and infects all age birds. It is also known as **BROODER PNEUMONIA**. Aspergillosis is the well-known killer of grouse that seem to lack an immunity to the fungus organisms. Some believe this is due to a quirk of nature. This disease is found in the wild among prairie grouse and is recognized as a killer of birds in captivity.

There is a **VACCINATION** procedure now being developed and tested against Aspergillosis. The vaccine works on all animal life. They have not licensed it yet by the government and is still in the experimental use only. We all hope that the release of this new vaccine will eradicate this dreaded disease which affects the more susceptible and rare birds raised in captivity.

Fortunately, the disease is not a highly contagious malady. Two birds raised side by side may get it or not. One may be healthy and the other die with the disease. There is a natural immunity in some birds so they do not contract Aspergillosis.

SYMPTOMS: In the **acute form**, there is gasping, loss of appetite, fluffed feathers, and paralysis or convulsions. The **chronic forms** of symptoms include loss of appetite, gasping, emaciation, and death. The vigor of the bird will determine the length of the disease.

LESIONS: Hard cores or nodules will be found in the respiratory tract, air sacs, and lungs. The nodules will vary in size from pinpoint to about the size of a pea. They will usually be yellow and soft or powdery. There may be signs of fungal growth in the body cavity and on the internal organs, especially in the lungs and air sacs. Culture growths in a Laboratory can make confirmation.

Although Aspergillosis is the most serious mold caused disease, three others affect game birds. They are Mycotoxicosis, Fusarium, and Candida.

The **prevention and treatment** of all mold diseases include the use of drugs and good preventive measures. Effective drugs control the growth and development of the molds. Copper Sulfate, Calcium Propionate and simple chlorox are useful drugs. For the average game bird breeder, water treatment with chlorox will be inexpensive, yet effective. Making sure that there are no decaying piles of litter, dead leaves or the like around the farm can greatly reduce the chances of your birds getting these diseases. A wind break of moldy hay or straw can be the cause of an outbreak. These are the breeding grounds for the organism and soon they will be spreading millions of spores into the air. Breathing in these spores in large numbers can cause the disease.

CHLOROX WATER TREATMENT: To make a stock solution, mix **one and one-half** (1½) ounce chlorox to a gallon of water. From this stock solution mix one ounce to each gallon of drinking water and give to the birds continuously (Poultry Health Handbook).

Diseases caused by parasitic worms

Many worms live inside animals as parasites causing little or no trouble, but others induce very serious disease. Sometimes these parasites weaken the host so that other much more serious diseases can occur. If your birds must go through some stressful times, be aware of the possibility of trouble if they are infected with worms. Some parasitic worms can cause death without showing any symptoms. The birds look healthy enough but die quite suddenly as the worms have been silently doing their work.

The goal of a successful treatment is to break the life-cycle of the worm and thus reduce its numbers. In some forms, their life-cycle is quite complex and varied so a variety of treatments must be used. A cycle can be broken or prevented by using a combination of treatments.

Gapeworms

This worm lives in the trachea (windpipe) of birds and causes the disease known as the "gapes" due to the gasping of the infected bird. Many infected birds die due to the lack of oxygen. Gapeworms are primarily a problem in young birds raised on the ground. Tilling the soil helps control this parasite.

These worms develop a tolerance to a drug in about two years. The breeder should vary his treatment drugs to avoid this built up resistance. Penn State suggests using two grams of Tramisol per gallon of drinking water for one day, repeat monthly. Another drug will have to be used in about two years to avoid resistance.

A "home" exam for the presence of worms can be made using a simple microscope. The procedure is simple and can be done by most anyone who takes the trouble to learn a few simple lab techniques.

The illustration below (Beer, 1988) will help explain the procedure to break the life-cycle of the gapeworm.

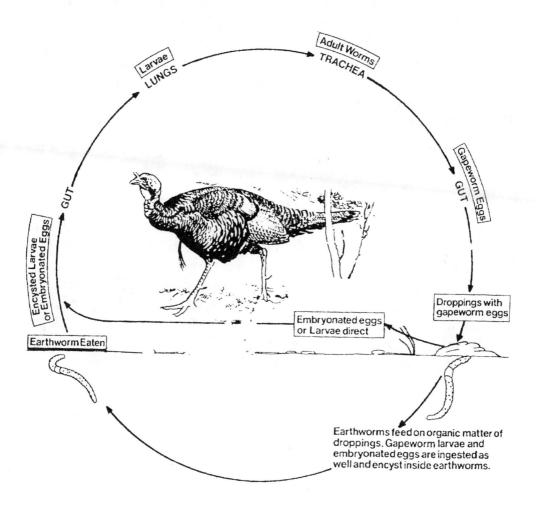

Earthworms feed on organic matter of droppings. Gapeworm larvae and embryonated eggs are ingested as well and encyst inside earthworms.

Capillaria

This is by far the most serious parasite problem. The breeder can be unaware of the problem until his birds begin to die. Several breeders have lost all their birds before they discovered the cause. These breeders were keeping their birds on the ground.

The worms are small and threadlike in nature, and can be found during an autopsy in the crop lining and intestine areas. In crop infestations there is an excessive amount of mucous substance, the crop is void of feed and the wall is thickened. In intestinal infections there is acute inflammation.

To control this worm, the breeder should be very careful because the drugs that must be used are very toxic. There is effective drug treatment available using the product called TRAMISOL (generic name, Levamisole). Dosages suggested by Pennsylvania State University Veterinary Science Extension are one to two grams per gallon of drinking water for one day. Repeat monthly for continued control.

Cecal worms

This worm is found in the "cecum" or blind gut of the host bird. The adult is about ⅜ to a 1¼ inch long and causes little damage to the host. The real damage comes because the Cecal worm plays a role in the spread of BLACKHEAD DISEASE. The worm serves as a breeding host for the causative protozoa that reproduce in the ceca and then are passed in the droppings to the ground where they develop into the infective larval stage.

Several products on the market may control Cecal worms. Tramisol is effective in the same dosage as suggested for Capillaria.

Tapeworms

These are flat, segmented worms that are sometimes found in birds. Insects and dirty droppings by other birds spread them thus infecting the flock. A good general wormer will control these worms.

Roundworms

This is the most common of all parasitic worms that infects all forms of animal life. It is found most everywhere in every animal and needs to be controlled by the bird breeder. The best way to control the Roundworm is to establish a regular system of medication and to keep the pen area clean. This keeps the parasite from building up its numbers to a dangerous level.

The life cycle is such that medication can kill only the adults. This makes it necessary to treat the birds again in ten to fifteen days thus ridding the host of the newly hatched young before they reach maturity to produce more eggs.

A very successful wormer that is put out by several companies is called **Piperazine**. It is effective and safe up to ten times the recommended dose. Follow the directions carefully. See the Game Bird Medication Guide for other specific treatments.

There are some new drugs available for the poultry industry that are much easier to administer to the birds. Check with your feed store and read all of the label to be sure the drug suits your particular needs.

To help the birds in their recovery from the stress of "worming," it is a good idea to give a high concentrate of Vitamin A for five to seven days.

Diseases caused by parasitic insects

Most of these parasites are found on the skin or among the feathers of their hosts. The lice, fleas and flies; the ticks; and the mites make up the three groups found on game birds (Beer, 1988). Often the game bird breeder fails to recognize and/or to treat his birds for these parasites. More cases than not, they do not cause any visible trouble and thus go unnoticed. The real danger is the spreading of serious diseases by these insects. Therefore, the breeder should try to control and eradicate them from his farm.

Flies and mosquitoes can be dangerous if not controlled. Fortunately, they can be controled them with a little expense and effort. Use caution when using insecticides around your birds. All are safe if used by the manufacturer's instructions.

Lice

These insects are the most common and widespread external parasites of ornamental game birds. Lousiness of birds can be diagnosed by finding on the birds wingless, flattened, brownish-yellow, quickly-moving insects. Lice spend their entire life cycle on the body of the bird. They attach eggs, often in clusters, to the feathers. The entire life cycle takes about two or three weeks for completion. One pair of lice may produce 120,000 descendants within a period of a few months. Their normal life span is several months, but away from the birds they can remain alive only five or six days. Regular dusting of the birds and house areas with an insecticide powder can control lice. Sometimes it takes several applications before the vermin are controlled as young are constantly hatching out until the life cycle is interrupted.

There are a number of good commercial louse powders on the market. Check with your feed store to see what has been approved by your state.

Mites

Most mites of birds use blood for food. Therefore, anemia is an almost common symptom with this problem. As might be expected, mites can easily transmit many bacterial and viral infections because they are bloodsucking insects. When hosts are available, they may not only produce anemia, by that seriously lowering production and otherwise infecting the birds, but they may actually kill the birds through the extraction of blood. This is particularly true of young chicks and growing stock. Control of red mites is best done at regular intervals. Dusting of the birds and house or pen areas is wise.

Some different mite's one may encounter are Red mites, Northern Round mites, Chigger mites, and Scaly Leg mites.

To control the Scaly Leg mite there needs to be special treatment methods adopted. Once a bird gets the parasite, getting rid of it is very difficult and painful. A special salve from a mixture of Vaseline, sulfur powder, turpentine or Campho-phenique will control this problem. Put the mixture on the affected legs after soaking in warm water and soap to remove the scales. The mites live under the scales and cause them to deform. Put the mixture on the bird's legs twice a day for about a week— that should do the trick.

Ticks

This pest is not common and is rarely found on game birds in most areas. They are blood suckers and are a serious menace to the host bird. Once established in an area, they are difficult to control. This pest can live up to two years without feeding.

Ticks carry serious diseases that affect humans. Therefore every effort should be made to control them. Watch your pet dogs and cats carefully and keep ticks off of them.

Diseases caused by faulty diet

The lack of certain vitamins and minerals causes some common diseases. Since vitamins and minerals are necessary for the bird to have normal, healthy body functions, their lack would obviously cause alterations. Prevention best handles these diseases. The breeder that sees to it that his birds get all the necessary nutrients, will never experience these disease problems with his birds. Sometimes, due to no fault of the breeder, a lack of vitamins and minerals causes his birds to get sick. Old feed that has lost its vitamin supplement potency can cause problems to the breeder. Formulate and mix feed that is improperly balanced with vitamins while the breeder is unaware. It is wise for the breeder to be aware of the problems that some more common vitamin deficiency situations cause.

Nutritional Roup

A deficiency in Vitamin A causes Nutritional Roup. Vitamin A is required for normal growth and tissue repair. It is the body's first line of defense against invading disease. When it is insufficient, it adversely affects the bird's resistance against disease.

SYMPTOMS: Young birds are stunted if there is a lack of Vitamin A being in the diet. Affected chicks become droopy and have ruffled feathers. In more advanced cases, nasal discharge, swelling eyes, and pustules form in the mouth and esophagus with a sticky exudate. Vitamin A deficiency in certain species of upland game birds is more serious than others.

DIAGNOSIS: The symptoms and lesions with the absence of infections will show Vitamin A deficiency.

TREATMENT: The condition can be reversed if treated before serious kidney damage. Correction of Vitamin A deficiency can be accomplished by using Vitamin A powder in the feed or water supply in high dosage for three to five days. Natural sources of Vitamin A are yellow corn, grasses, fish oils and legumes.

Vitamin A supplementation is good therapy for various infections, including disease stress such as Coccidiosis, molds, worms and other disorders.

Rickets

The term "**Rickets**" applies to the condition of young birds and a condition of adult birds. In either age group the condition is caused by an imbalance of sufficient calcium, Vitamin D3, or phosphorus. The result is deformed bone structure, especially in the leg bones of young birds. Adults will often show the same conditions and have additional skeletal body problems.

The key word is "imbalance" of these elements. Each is dependent on the other to provide absorption and use of the other. Deficiency of calcium and Vitamin D3 result in insufficient hardening of the bone. When calcium is lacking or cannot be absorbed from the feed, the same results occur. To get the calcium to be absorbed properly by the system is the role of Vitamin D3. A lack of the element, phosphorus, causes the same results.

SYMPTOMS: Rickets is most often found in young birds less than six weeks old. It is during this fast growing period that the deficiency usually occurs. The leg bones become soft and springy and birds may become paralyzed. Sometimes the leg joints tend to be enlarged.

CAUSES: This condition results from faulty medication practices, feeding error, or moldy feed. Certain molds and their toxins interfere with Vitamin D3 absorption, thus throwing the balance off. Calcium retards the absorption of some antibiotics. To make matters more complex, too much calcium or phosphorus in the feed can cause imbalance and cause Rickets. This is one disease that can be completely avoided with extra effort and care.

DIAGNOSIS: When the symptoms appear, it is usually Rickets. However, the conditions sometimes appear with other diseases. Infectious Bursal Disease can give the symptoms of Rickets and must be confirmed by a Laboratory test. Again, the use of a vitamin and mineral supplement will help avoid this problem. The disease cannot be reversed, but can easily be avoided.

Curled toe paralysis

True Curled Toe Paralysis **does not occur at hatching time**. This is a condition that all who hatch ornamental game birds have encountered. The exact cause is still a mystery! Some say it is oxygen getting into the lungs of the chick before it completely hatches out of the egg. The oxygen **"sets"** the toes in the curled position. This may be true of newly hatched chicks.

This paralysis can come on the chick at any age, but mostly occurs in the developmental stage of growth. However, I have heard of it happening to mature birds. Studies have shown that a lack of Vitamin B2 or Vitamin G (riboflavin) in the diet does cause this problem.

SYMPTOMS: The toes will curl medially toward the other foot. If this condition comes upon the bird after the first week it is surely caused by a lack of vitamins. They have shown that chicks reared under infrared lights have this problem more often than those having other colored lighting. The addition of riboflavin cannot prevent the condition when infrared lights are used. If the breeder has this problem, the first thing is to change the heating system away from infrared lights.

TREATMENT: True Curled Toe Paralysis responds to the addition of Vitamin B2 or G in the diet. Studies at the Game Bird Preservation Center in Salt Lake City show that this condition can be reversed in young cranes by the addition of high concentrate vitamin powder called Vionate. This treatment should also work for other species that have this problem.

Perosis
(Slipped Tendon)

A severe lack of MANGANESE in the diet causes this condition. Do not relate it to "sprattle leg" in newly hatched chicks. Sometimes this can be a problem in incubation also. Chicks less than a day old can have special treatment and become normal. Get some soft string and make a little harness that goes between the legs at the ankles. Make this harness just the right length to correct the problem. Leave it on for about three days and the legs should have "set" in a normal position. Two people are needed for this tying of the legs. Do not get the string too tight or the blood circulation will be hindered and the chick will loose a foot or toe. This will work with any game bird.

A condition found in a waterfowl (especially geese) of too much protein in the diet should not be confused with this problem.

SYMPTOMS: Enlargement of the hocks causing the slippage of the Achilles tendon that in turn makes the legs be thrown out at an angle to the body is the only symptom.

TREATMENT: Once the birds have true Perosis no treatment is successful. Usually three to five days of heavy vitamin supplement will prevent the other birds from getting the condition. This is a preventable condition. A proper nutrition and vitamin supplement will prevent Perosis.

Miscellaneous diseases

There are many unknown diseases in game birds. The research has not gone into this problem to solve all of the disorders one may encounter. However, they have researched the major diseases to give the modern game bird breeder a good idea of what his birds may encounter.

Birds suffer from the same ailments as any other animal. I have had Mearns quail and other birds just die in my hand to discover that they had what we commonly know as a "heart attack" when their blood vessels ruptured. This is more common in some species than others. Sudden death happens often when catching birds. Another reason for sudden death is severe change such as weather or attack by predators. We can never fully explain all of the deaths.

Birds have cancer. I had some grouse years ago that had Leukemia (which is cancer of the blood cells) and they all died. Growths that could be called cancer are sometimes found on our birds.

A very common problem is what the experts sometimes call "wasting syndrome." This is where for unknown reasons the bird just wastes away and finally dies in very poor condition. The pigeon people call this "going light" and they have tonics and vitamin mixtures that they give to combat it. No cause can be found in the Laboratory as the birds have no microbial, parasitic, or nutritional problems. The truth is many problems can cause this to happen to a bird.

When an "unknown" disease problem affects one of my birds, I usually cull it in case it is contagious. I had rather sacrifice one a bird to keep the many healthy. If it is a very expensive bird, or there are sentimental attachments, I isolate it immediately and try to figure out what the trouble is. However, usually, it is best to cull when the abnormality is discovered. I justify this in my thinking that it is better for the bird not to endure the suffering and painful death.

Problems resulting from faulty management

Management is not perfect when it comes to our upland game birds. Too often problems arise when attempts are made to cut corners or save costs or time. The correct management of our birds is vital to avoid disease and other problems. While good management does much to prevent the establishment of disease organisms, well-managed birds generally have a more acceptable well-being.

Here the old saying, "An ounce of prevention is worth a pound of cure" applies. Good management will often avoid what faulty management will encourage. For example, Aspergillosis is difficult to cure, but not using moldy materials can prevent it nor providing the conditions for the fungi to grow. Prevention makes sense in the long-run and our birds will enjoy a longer and healthier life along with our enjoyment being greatly enhanced.

Chilling is an important cause of young chick's death. Droughts, abnormally low or high temperature in the brooder house can cause this problem. Most of the time chilling occurs when the breeder is away from home or in the middle of the night and the breeder is unaware of the problem. For example, never give day old chicks cold water for their first drink. They will die because of chilling. Always give them warm water for the first day or two. After they get started, this is not an important matter.

Starve out is a problem in chicks of some species of upland game birds. If the chick in the wild is fed directly from the parents bill, they more than likely will have trouble learning how to eat. This is true with many species and the breeder must try to teach these chicks to eat. I have found that several Mearns chicks in every hatch will not learn to eat no matter what I do. Other breeders have discovered this to be true also.

Impaction can be a problem with upland game birds. The introduction of any new feed should be made gradually so the chick or birds will not completely fill their crop with the new feed. Grit should be introduced gradually to small chicks so they will not get impacted. Greens and other treats should be fed sparsely so as not to get the birds crops too full.

Years ago I had a pet Blue grouse that would come to me to get green grass that I would pull for him. I just pulled clumps of grass up by the roots and put it in his pen. After he suddenly died, I took him to get posted and was distraught to find out that my kindness had killed him. He ate the grass roots and could not digest the cellulose and thus the roots impacted his crop. He could not get food to go through his digestion system.

Part 8

APPENDIXES

Contents 321

Chinese Ringneck pheasants.

How to Raise Mealworms

Some breeders feed mealworms to their birds. These can be grown on the farm. Mealworms are the larvae of a beetle (Terebrio) which lives in grain based foods. They are high in protein and most all birds love them. It is very satisfying and some money can be saved if the breeder raises his own mealworms.

If you have ever seen a mealworm before it has molted, you can see why some breeders shy away from them. The worms are brown and jointed which makes them closely resemble a quail, pheasant, or partridge toe. Some say that feeding mealworms causes toe picking in young chicks. This may be true. However, if handled correctly, small immature mealworms are a *"real boon"* to the breeder who raises very rare upland game birds that are difficult to get to learn to eat. Mealworms that have just molted are whitish and smooth and can be fed without any danger of starting the habit of toe picking.

Mealworms are not maggots. It should be noted that mealworms are entirely different and pose no threat of giving *"botulism"* to the birds. They are clean and will not endanger the lives of the birds.

Mealworms can be cultivated in most any container at least 5 gallons in size. We have good success in 10 to 15 gallon containers. There must be a method of keeping the beetles and the worms in the container as they want to migrate during their cycle to find new and greener pastures. A box can be built of wood by any handyman. A wash tub can be used if a tight top is put on it. If a closed container is used there should be a ventilation vent covered with screen wire to keep the moisture down by proper air circulation. The box can be made to any size and any type of material may be used. The mealworms are not choosy where they set up their domestic chores. Whatever style and size of box you choose, be sure that it is well-vented or you will have problems with excess moisture even in dry climates. In wetter climates more ventilation must be provided.

I have talked to several breeders that get as much enjoyment from raising mealworms as I do. Their methods vary from mine but they have success. The size of the container, the type and amount of feed and moisture are the things that each breeder does differently in his or her mealworm production.

The late J. G. Suthard of California has designed a very usable box for growing mealworms (Suthard, 1953). His plans have proved successful and should work well for you.

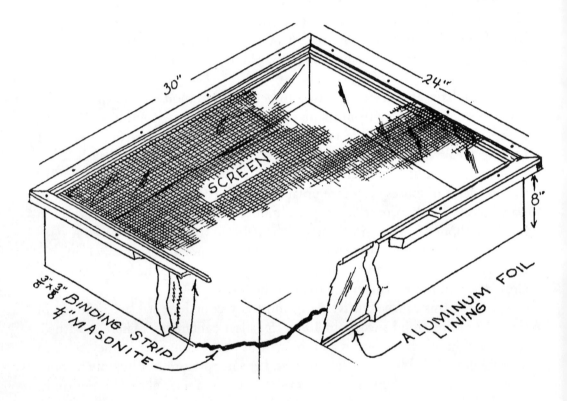

Fill the container about ⅔ full with *"wheat bran"* which can be bought at any feed store. We put crumpled up newspapers in the bottom of the box to keep the bran loose in the container. Simply crumple up wads of newspaper and pour the bran on top of them. We mix two cups of flour and a package of dry yeast to the medium. On top of the bran put halves of apple or potatoes to give the needed moisture to the growing colony. Cover this up with two or three layers of burlap sacks and all is ready. Begin with mealworms from another colony or with beetles. Check to be sure the apples or potatoes do not mold too badly. The worms will make tunnels in the potatoes and apples where they lay their tiny eggs. If you discard a rotten potato you may be throwing out eggs.

If the Mealworm *"culture"* develops well, it must constantly be given new food. We use the feed dust from the bottom of the bird feeders for our mealworms. This would normally be wasted but the mealworms thrive on the high protein content of the feed. Any kind of vegetable can also be used for food. One summer we put in halves of large squash and the mealworms really gave us a good crop in a month or two.

If conditions are just right, the potatoes will become rotten and small maggot-like worms will appear. Do not worry about this as they will go away and do not harm. The mealworm culture will support all kinds of little microscopic life. We looked at it through a microscope and was horrified to see all of the tiny lice and other little varmints.

Periodically, you will need to change the culture by discarding the old bran medium and starting over. Be sure to leave some of the old beetles, food, and mealworms in the new culture to get it off to a good start.

When mealworms are needed, it is a simple matter to lift carefully the layers of burlap and harvest what you need for a feeding. Never disturb the lower bran layers as it will upset the culture. Periodically add more bran as it is eaten by the culture.

A trick that we learned which gave us a supply of worms the entire year was to install light bulb heaters in the base of the mealworm container. Heat apparently is necessary for reproduction and this extra heat during the winter months triggered the culture to keep up the good work all year.

Another trick is to freeze the excess worms. We put a hand full in an air tight plastic bag and drop it in the freezer. When you are ready to feed them, just thaw them out and they are ready to go. Of course, they do not have the *"natural wiggle"* of live worms, but most birds seem to care less.

Mealworm Life Cycle

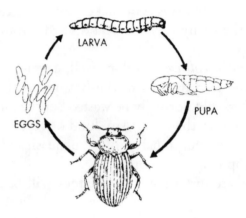

Mealworms are easy and fun to raise. To cultivate the mealworm it is necessary to understand its life cycle. The mealworm is a larvae and is a part of the lifecycle of the beetle. When fully grown the mealworm pupates, and the adult beetle emerges from the pupal case. At first the beetle is pale brown, but becomes coal black at maturity. The beetle then will lay eggs in about seven to ten days which will hatch in a few weeks if environmental conditions are suitable. The small mealworms grow fast until they go into the pupal state. The whole life cycle takes five to six months. This lengthy cycle is a drawback to raising mealworms. Planning will enable one to have a bumper crop when needed.

Give raising mealworms a try!

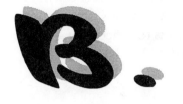

B. *Artificial Insemination*

(A.I.)

Artificial Insemination has been used in the poultry industry for many years to accomplish their selective breeding goals. It has only been in the past few years that the game bird breeder has taken advantage of this method of getting rare birds to breed.

Why would a breeder of upland game birds want to use A.I.? The major reason is when their best or rare birds fail to reproduce. Several factors contribute to this: 1) Shyness that they get from their potential mate or the fact that they have not adjusted to their environment. Wild caught birds fit well into this category. 2) Physical limitation that would include frost bitten toes and feet or another impairment. 3) Social incompatibility or lack of interest. Many interesting conditions including health and general well-being can cause this. 4) Unsatisfactory nutrition is another factor. 5) The age of breeders causes failure to breed. 6) Management conditions may not be satisfactory for reproduction (Skinner and Arrington, Agriculture Bulletin). Breeders of purebred Sebright bantams recommend A.I. because of the failure of the rooster to reach the hen (Holland, 1994). This is true anytime that the legs are short or long, or the body is very broad, as in the Cornish chicken. Birds with loose feathers sometimes have difficulty breeding and could benefit from A. I.

Artificial insemination is an art rather than a precise science. Once one understands the basics, anyone with interest and patience can use it successfully. You should gather these few simple tools before you begin the actual procedure. You will need glass eye cups if you plan to gather semen in large quantities as with larger birds. A medicine dropper and a 1 cc plastic syringe which will be disposed of after each use. Finally, a glass rod will be all the equipment needed provided you have an assistant. Success depends on the patience and skill of the inseminator. A good plan is to practice on common poultry before the actual work with the game bird.

The male used for the procedure:

1. Must be mature, healthy and physically normal.
2. Must be sexually active. This is especially important in birds that have a limited season such as game birds. Light stimulation may be used to control the season in some species.
3. Must be tame, or at least not terrified when restrained or handled.
4. Should be free from external parasites. Some parasites irritate the vent area, making male organ exposure difficult and painful to the bird.
5. Should be kept apart from, but preferably in sight of females.
6. Should not be subjected to extreme temperatures or allowed to become overheated.

The female used for the procedure:

1. Must be in production, or she may be injured.
2. Must not have a hard shell egg in the lower part of her oviduct, so the sperm can move easily to the area where it unites with the ova (Skinner and Arrington).

Points to remember:

1. Stimulate males and collect the semen immediately after catching. Holding a male, even a tame one, for only a few minutes may interfere with collection.
2. Successful semen collection usually results from an experienced operator and an experienced subject.
3. First attempts at "working" inexperienced males often produce unsatisfactory results. Some males pass feces or urates as they discharge semen. Try to collect only the semen; contaminated semen usually produces poor results. Withhold water and feed four to six hours before collection to lessen chances for contamination.
4. How much semen discharged varies from bird to bird. Each species produces a different volume and quality semen. A chicken rooster discharges .2 ml. to .35 ml. A turkey gobbler discharges .15 to 1.25

ml. While a Pearl guneafowl discharges only .05 to .15 ml. of semen. The concentration of spermatozoa in billions per milliliter is 5.0 for chickens, 9.0 for turkeys and 6.0 to 9.0 for guineafowl. High density of the sperm should be considered.

5. Individual males vary considerably in time needed to replenish their semen supply. Normally, you can collect semen every two to four days without harming the birds.

6. Use the semen as soon as possible. Wait no longer than 20 to 30 minutes to fertilize the hens. Keep the semen below the body temperature of the male that produced it.

7. How often insemination is needed for satisfactory results varies somewhat between species and females. It is best to inseminate more often at the onset of production, but once eggs have been fertilized, once each week should be enough to maintain a satisfactory level. Turkeys remain fertile longer than some other species.

8. Fertile eggs can normally be obtained 48 to 96 hours after insemination and up to three weeks afterwards. The percentage of fertile eggs from a particular hen will vary.

Whether or not you choose to use this method of propagation with your problem birds, will depend on your personal wishes. If you would like to try it, here is how you do it.

Select your breeding stock early and begin to handle them each day and accustom them to a wire cage. Be sure the cage allows you to catch the birds with your hands as gently as possible.

The procedure (male):

Experts have developed several ways to hold males for semen collection. Techniques may require one or two persons. Two persons working together simplifies the needed equipment and is easier on the bird. Hold the male with his head toward the operator and with the keel lying in the palm of the left hand. Secure the right leg between the first and second fingers. To make larger birds more comfortable, hold the left leg between the second and third fingers. Stroke the back from midpoint toward the tail with the right hand, massaging the abdomen from below with the fingers of the left hand. After several vigorous strokes, transfer the right hand from the back to a position where the thumb and forefinger can apply pressure to either side of the vent. Simultaneously, apply pressure to the abdomen with the fingers of the left hand. This normally extends the copulatory organ and causes a flow of semen. A slight milking action may increase semen flow. An assistant should catch the semen in an eye cup or other small smooth-edged vessel. A medicine dropper can be used also to collect the semen.

The procedure (female):

When handling and exposing the female, remember the hen is delicate and must be treated gently. Hold and stimulate her in much the same way as the male. As the operator applies pressure after the preliminary stroking and massage, the vent averts and an orifice appears on the left side. It may be a round rosette or a cleft or skin overfold. An assistant should place the semen ¼ to 1 inch deep into this opening with a 1 cc syringe or a medicine dropper.

When making individual matings—one male with one female—use the entire semen collection. Various studies show, however, that good results can be achieved with as little as .05 cc of semen per insemination.

Relax pressure on the female's body soon as possible after insemination so the oviduct can return to its normal position, drawing the semen inward.

 # State Diagnostic Pathological Laboratories

The average upland game bird breeder does not know where to go for help when he has disease problems. The following listings of State Diagnostic and Pathological Laboratories will be invaluable in getting immediate help posting sick and dead birds.

The services provided are usually free to qualified turkey and chicken growers. Some state laboratories charge a fee to do the service for game bird breeders. This fee is usually not a large one and well worth paying. The same services from private Veterinarian office will be much higher. Sometimes it is impossible to find one of these that is qualified to do the pathological tests necessary.

Follow the instructions when you submit a bird for postmortem. Each laboratory will have their own particular procedures that must be followed. Requesting any written instructions they may have is helpful from the start so you can know just what they require. This will help you and them find a satisfactory answer as quickly as possible. Some laboratories provide shipping containers that meet their specifications. You should have one on hand to use.

A telephone call to the laboratory before you have trouble will be helpful. Get acquainted with them and let them know you are pleased that their service is available should you ever need it.

ALABAMA
Alabama Veterinary Diagnostic Laboratory, 495 AL 203, Elba, AL 36323, 205-897-6340
Charles S. Roberts Veterinary Diagnostic Laboratory, PO Box 2209, Auburn, AL 36831-2209, 205-844-4987

ALASKA
Alaska State Federal Laboratory, 500 South Alaska Street, Palmer, AK 99645, 907-745-3236

ARIZONA
Veterinary Diagnostic Laboratory, University of Arizona, 2831 North Freeway, Tucson, AZ 85705, 602-621-2356

ARKANSAS
Arkansas Livestock and Poultry Commission Diagnostic Laboratory, PO Box 5497, Little Rock, AR 72215, 501-225-5650
Arkansas Livestock and Poultry Commission Diagnostic Laboratory, 3559 N Thompson, Springdale, AR 72764, 501-751-4869

CALIFORNIA
California Veterinary Diagnostic Laboratory System, University of California, PO Box 1770, Davis, CA 95617, 916-752-8700

Fresno Branch Laboratory, 2789 South Orange Avenue, Fresno, CA 93725, 209-498-7740
San Bernardino Branch Laboratory, 105 West Central Avenue, San Bernardino, CA 92408, 909-383-4287

San Diego County Veterinary Laboratory, 555 Overland Avenue, Building 4, San Diego, CA 92123, 619-694-2838
Tulare Branch Laboratory, 18830 Road 112, Tulare, CA 93274, 209-688-7543
Turlock Branch Laboratory, PO Box 1522, Turlock, CA 95381, 209-634-5837

COLORADO
Animal Disease Diagnostic Laboratory, Colorado State University Research Center, Rocky Ford, CO 81067, 719-254-6382
Veterinary Diagnostic Laboratory, Colorado State University, Fort Collins, CO 80523, 303-491-1281
Western Slope Animal Diagnostic Laboratory, 425-29 Road, Grand Junction, CO 81501, 303-243-0673

CONNECTICUT
Department of Pathobiology, Box U-89 61 North Eagleville Road, University of Connecticut, Storrs, CT 06269-3089, 203-486-3736

DELAWARE
Poultry and Animal Health Section, State Department of Agriculture, PO Drawer D, 2320 S Dupont Highway, Dover, DE 19901, 302-739-4811

FLORIDA
Bureau of Diagnostic Laboratories, Dade County Branch, PO Box 1031, 1414 Highway 52 W, Dade City, FL 33525, 904-521-1458
Bureau of Diagnostic Laboratories, 8701 Northwest 58th Street, Miami, FL 33178, 305-592-3059
Live Oak Diagnostic Laboratory, PO Box O, Live Oak, FL 32060, 904-362-1216

GEORGIA
Georgia Poultry Laboratory, 175 Airport Circle, Douglas Airport, Douglas, GA 31533, 912-384-3719
Georgia Poultry Laboratory, PO Box 20, Oakwood, GA 30566, 404-535-5996

HAWAII
Veterinary Laboratory Branch, Hawaii Department of Agriculture, 99-941 Halawa Valley Street, Aiea, HI 96701, 808-483-7100

IDAHO
Idaho Bureau of Animal Health Laboratories, PO Box 7249, 2230 Old Penitentiary Road, Boise, ID 83707, 208-334-3111

ILLINOIS
Animal Disease Laboratory, 9732 Shattuc Road, Centralia, IL 62801, 618-532-6701
Animal Disease Laboratory, 2100 South Lake Storey Road, Galesburg, IL 61402, 309-344-2451

INDIANA
Animal Disease Diagnostic Laboratory, Purdue University, 1175 ADDL, West Lafayette, IN 47907-1175, 317-494-7440
Animal Disease Diagnostic Laboratory, SIPAC, 11367 East Purdue Farm Road, Dubois, IN 47527, 812-678-3401

IOWA
Veterinary Diagnostic Laboratory, Iowa State University, Ames, IA 50011, 515-294-1950

KANSAS
Veterinary Diagnostic Laboratory, College of Veterinary Medicine, Veterinary Medical Center, Manhattan, KS 66506, 913-532-5650

KENTUCKY
Livestock Disease Diagnostic Center, 1429 Newtown Pike, Lexington, KY 40511, 606-253-0571
Murray State University, Breathitt Veterinary Center, PO Box 2000, 715 North Drive, Hopkinsville, KY 42240, 502-886-3959

LOUISIANA
Central Louisiana Livestock Diagnostic
Laboratory, 217 Middleton Drive,
Lecompte, LA 71346, 318-473-6500
Louisiana Veterinary Medical Diagnostic
Laboratory, LSU School of Veterinary
Medicine, 1909 South Stadium Drive,
Baton Rouge, LA 70803, 504-346-3193

MAINE
Pathology Diagnostic and Research
Laboratory, Hitchner Hall, University
of Maine, Orono, ME 04473,
207-581-2774

MARYLAND
Animal Health Department Laboratory,
PO Box 376, Oakland, MD 21550,
301-334-2185
Animal Health Laboratory, Maryland
Department of Agriculture, Route 1
Box 145, Centreville, MD 21617,
301-758-0846
Animal Health Laboratory, Maryland
Department of Agriculture, PO Box
1234, Frederick, MD 21701,
301-663-9528
Animal Health Laboratory, Maryland
Department of Agriculture, PO Box J,
Salisbury, MD 21802, 301-543-6610
Animal Health Laboratory-Central,
3740 Metzerott Road, College Park,
MD 20740, 301-935-6074

MASSACHUSETTS
Tufts University School of Veterinary
Medicine, 200 Westboro Road, North
Grafton, MA 01536, 508-839-5302

MICHIGAN
Animal Health Diagnostic Laboratory,
PO Box 30076, Lansing, MI 48909,
517-353-1683

MINNESOTA
Minnesota Veterinary Diagnostic
Laboratories, 1333 Gortoner Avenue,
College of Veterinary Medicine,
University of Minnesota, St. Paul, MN
55108, 612-625-8787

MISSISSIPPI
Mississippi Veterinary Diagnostic
Laboratory, PO Box 4389, Jackson,
MS 39216, 601-354-6091

MISSOURI
Veterinary Diagnostic Laboratory,
Missouri Department of Agriculture,
PO Box 2510, Springfield, MO 65801,
417-895-6861
Veterinary Medical Diagnostic Labora-
tory, College of Veterinary Medicine,
PO Box 6023, University of Missouri,
Columbia, MO 65205, 314-882-6811

MONTANA
Veterinary Diagnostic Laboratory
Division, Montana Department of
Livestock, PO Box 997, Bozeman,
MT 59771, 406-994-4885

NEBRASKA
Diagnostic Laboratory, Department of
Veterinary Science, University of
Nebraska, Lincoln, NE 68583,
402-472-1434

Veterinary Science Laboratory, University of Nebraska, West Central Research and Extension Center, North Platte, NE 69101, 308-532-3611

NEVADA
Animal Disease Laboratory, Nevada Department of Agriculture, PO Box 11100, Reno, NV 89510, 702-789-0185

NEW HAMPSHIRE
Veterinary Diagnostic Laboratory, University of New Hampshire, 319 Kendall Hall, Durham, NH 03824, *603-862-2726*

NEW JERSEY
New Jersey Animal Health Diagnostic Laboratory, John Fitch Plaza CN 330, Trenton, NJ 08625, 609-292-3965

NEW MEXICO
Veterinary Diagnostic Services, 700 Camino de Salud Northeast, Albuquerque, NM 87106, 505-841-2576

NEW YORK
Cornell University Duck Research Laboratory, Box 217, Old Country Road, Eastport, NY 11941, *516-325-0600*
Department of Avian and Aquatic Animal Medicine,College of Veterinary Medicine, Cornell University, *Ithaca, NY 14853, 607-253-3365*
Regional Veterinary Laboratory, 88 Prince Street, Kingston, NY 12401, 914-331-3415

NORTH CAROLINA
Rollins Animal Disease Diagnostic Laboratory, PO Box 12223 Cameron Village Station, 2101 Blue Ridge Road, Raleigh, NC 27605, 919-733-3986

NORTH DAKOTA
North Dakota Veterinary Diagnostic Laboratory, North Dakota State University, Fargo, ND 58105, 701-237-8307

OHIO
Animal Disease Diagnostic Laboratory, Ohio Department of Agriculture, 8995 East Main Street, Reynoldsburg, OH 43068, 614-866-6361

OKLAHOMA
Oklahoma Animal Disease Diagnostic Laboratory, College of Veterinary Medicine, Oklahoma State University, Stillwater, OK 74078, 405-744-6623

OREGON
Oregon State Department of Agriculture, Animal Health Laboratory, 635 Capitol Street Northeast, Salem, OR 97310, 503-378-4710
Oregon State University Poultry Science Dept., Dryden Hall, Corvallis, OR 97331, 503-737-2301
Veterinary Diagnostic Laboratory, Oregon State University, PO Box 429, Corvallis, OR 97339, 503-737-3261

PENNSYLVANIA

Bureau of Veterinary Laboratory Services, PO Box 367, Summerdale, PA 17093, 717-787-8808

Laboratory of Avian Medicine and Pathology, New Bolton Center, Kennett Square, PA 19348, 215-444-5800

Animal Diagnostic Laboratory, Veterinary Science Department, Pennsylvania State University, University Park, PA 16802, 814-863-0837

PUERTO RICO

Puerto Rico Animal Diagnostic Laboratory, PO Box 490, Dorado, PR 00646, 809-796-1650

RHODE ISLAND

Diagnostic Laboratory, Department of Animal and Veterinary Science, University of Rhode Island, Kingston, RI 02881, 401-792-2487

SOUTH CAROLINA

Clemson Animal Diagnostic Laboratory, PO Box 102406, Columbia, SC 29224, 803-788-2260

SOUTH DAKOTA

Animal Disease Research and Diagnostic Laboratory, South Dakota State University, 105 Veterinary Science, PO Box 2175, Brookings, SD 57007, 605-688-5171

TENNESSEE

C.E. Kord Animal Disease Laboratory, Ellington Agriculture Center, Porter Building, PO Box 40627 Melrose Station, Nashville, TN 37204, 615-360-0125

TEXAS

PBMDL Poultry Laboratory, PO Box 187, Center, TX 75935, 409-598-4451

Poultry Disease Laboratory, Department of Veterinary Microbiology, College of Veterinary Medicine, Texas A and M University, College Station, TX 77843, 409-845-5941

Poultry Disease Laboratory, Texas Veterinary Medical Diagnostic Laboratory System, PO Box 84, Gonzales, TX 78629, 210-672-2834

UTAH

Utah State University-Provo Veterinary Laboratory, Utah Agricultural Experimental Station, 2031 South State, Provo, UT 84606, 801-373-6383

State-Federal Cooperative Laboratory and State Chemist Office, Department of Agriculture, 350 North Redwood Road, Salt Lake City, UT 84116, 801-538-7128

Veterinary Diagnostic Laboratory, Utah State University, Logan, UT 84322-5600, 801-750-1895

VIRGINIA

Division of Animal Health, Regulatory
Laboratory, 116 Reservoir Street,
Harrisonburg, VA 22801,
703-434-3897

Division of Animal Health, Regulatory
Laboratory, Route 460 PO Box 290,
Ivor, VA 23866, 804-859-6221

Division of Animal Health, Regulatory
Laboratory, 1 North 14th Street,
Richmond, VA 23219, 804-786-2446

Division of Animal Health, Regulatory
Laboratory, 234 West Shirley Avenue,
Warrenton, VA 22186 703-347-6385

Virginia Dept. of Agriculture & Consumer Services, 196 Cassel Road,
Wytheville, VA 24382, 703-228-5501

Veterinary Teaching Hospital, VA-MD
Regional College of Veterinary
Medicine, Virginia Polytechnic
Institute and State University,
Blacksburg, VA 24061, 703-231-4621

Virginia Department of Agriculture and
Consumer Services, Division of
Animal Health Regulatory Laboratory, Bureau of Laboratory Services,
4832 Tyreanna, Lynchburg, VA 24504,
804-947-6731

WASHINGTON

Poultry Diagnostic Laboratory, Washington State University, 7612 Pioneer
Way East, Puyallup, WA 98371,
206-840-4536

Washington Animal Disease Diagnostic
Laboratory, PO Box 2037 College
Station, Washington State University,
Pullman, WA 99165, 509-335-9696

WEST VIRGINIA

State-Federal Laboratory, West Virginia
Department of Agriculture, Capitol
Building, Charleston, WV 25305,
304-348-3418

WISCONSIN

Wisconsin Animal Health Laboratory -
Barron, 1521 East Guy Avenue,
Barron, WI 54812, 715-537-3151

Wisconsin Animal Health Laboratory,
6101 Mineral Point Road, Madison,
WI 53705, 608-266-2465

WYOMING

Wyoming State Veterinary Laboratory,
1174 Snowy Range Road, Laramie,
WY 82070, 307-742-6638

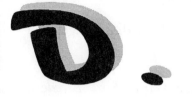 **SOURCES**

Abbott, Ursula K. 1983. *"Incubating and Hatching Game Bird Eggs,"* Game Bird Breeders, Aviculturists, Zoologists and Conservationists' Gazette, 32(6-7): 10-12.

Ali, Salim, and S. Dillon Ripley. 1980. *Handbook of The Birds of India and Pakistan*, London: Oxford University Press, 8-9.

Ibid. *"Himalayan Snowcock,"* 13-6.

Ibid. *"Black-breasted Quail or Rain Quail,"* 41-42.

Ibid. *"Common Hill Partridge,"* 57.

Allen, Jr., George A. 1958. "Seesee Partridge, "*Game Bird Breeders, Aviculturists, Zoologists and Conservationists' Gazette*, 7(12): 58-9.

Allen, III., George A., 1983., *"Guineafowl"*. Game Bird Breeders, Aviculturists, Zoologists and Conservationists' Gazette, 8-9.

Ibid. 1969. "Tragopans", "*Game Bird Breeders, Aviculturists, Zoologists and Conservationists' Gazette*, 3(18): 37-39.

_____. 1962. *"Ringneck Pheasant,"Game Bird Breeders, Aviculturists, Zoolo-gists and Conservationists' Gazette*, 11(11): 14.

_____. 1971. *"Roulroul Partridge,"Game Bird Breeders, Aviculturists, Zoolo-gists and Conservationists' Gazette*, 20(6): 12-4.

_____. 1984. *"Red Legged Partridge,"Game Bird Breeders, Aviculturists, Zoolo-gists and Conservationists' Gazette*, 33(6-7): 11-13.

_____. 1969. *Pheasant Standards*, Salt Lake City: American Game Bird Breeders' Cooperative Federation, 81.

Ibid. *"Jumbo Ringneck,"* 105.

_____. 1988. *Pheasant Standards*, Salt Lake City: American Game Bird Breeders' Cooperative Federation, 2nd Edition, 70-73.

Belshaw, R.H. Hastings. 1984. *Guinea Fowl of The World*, Liss, Hampshire, Nimrod Book Services, 3, 23, 29-30, 33.

Ibid. 106-7.

Bent, Arthur Cleveland. 1932. *Life Histories of North American Gallinaceous Birds*, New York: Dover Publications, Inc. 36-37.

Ibid. 342.

Beer, J. V., 1988. *Diseases of Gamebirds and Wildfowl*, Fordingbridge: The Game Conservancy, 318.

Ibid. 26,31, 44.

Billie, Francis, Jr. 1984. *"Roulroul Partridge,"Game Bird Breeders, Aviculturists, Zoologists and Conservationists' Gazette*, 33(2-3): 14-15.

_____. 1985. *"Ferruginous Wood Partridge,"Game Bird Breeders, Aviculturists, Zoologists and Conservationists' Gazette*, 34(4): 27-8.

Blake, Emmet R. 1977. *Manual of Neotropical Birds*, Vol. 1, Chicago: University of Chicago Press, 245-52.

Bump, Gardner. 1974. *"The Hungarian Partridge, "Game Bird Breeders, Aviculturists, Zoologists and Conservationists' Gazette*, 32(8): 20-22.

_____. 1971. *"The Coturnix or Old World Quail,"Game Bird Breeders, Avicul-turists, Zoologists and Conservationists' Gazette*, 20(7): 13-6.

Cain, J. R., and B. C. Wormeli. 1973. *"Japanese Quail (Coturnix) Care and Management,"Game Bird Breeders, Aviculturists, Zoologists and Conservationists' Gazette*, 22(2): 27-36.

Carlson, Eric. 1953. *"The Practice of Using Artificial Lights on Pheasants,"Game Bird Breeders, Aviculturists, Zoologists and Conservationists' Gazette*, 2(2): 9-10.

Clemson University. 1978. *Raising Bobwhite Quail*, 20-22.

Crosley, Angela. 1959. *"Button Quail,"* Game Bird Breeders, Aviculturists, Zoologists and Conservationists' Gazette, 8(2): 56, 70.

Damerow, Gail. 1995. *The Chicken Health Handbook*, Pownal: Storey Communications, Inc., 5.

Dement'ev, G. P., and N. A. Gladkov. 1952. *Birds of the Soviet Union*, Jerusalem: Israel Program for Scientific Translations, 145-159.

Ibid. *"Himalayan Snowcock,"*207-8.

Eleazer, Thomas H., (Memo Sheet) *"Causes of Diseases in Game Birds,"* Livestock-Poultry Health Division, Clemson University.

Flemming, Robert L. Sr., Robert L. Flemming, Jr., and Lain Singh. Bangdel. 1979. *Birds of Nepal*, Kathmandu: Avaloc Publishers, 70.

Ibid. *"Partridges, Quail and Pheasants,"*66.

Forbush, Edward H. 1917. *Birds of America,* Garden City: Garden City Books, Part 2, 8.

Gazette Editors. 1978. *"Bird Corn Bread," Game Bird Breeders, Aviculturists, Zoologists and Conservationists' Gazette,* 27(9): 9-10.

_____. 1976. *"Commercial Game Bird Breeding," Game Bird Breeders, Aviculturists, Zoologists and Conservationists' Gazette,* 25(9): 17-21.

_____. 1960. *"How Can Soil Be Treated To Prevent Disease?" Game Bird Breeders, Aviculturists, Zoologists and Conservationists' Gazette,* 9(10): 50.

Gerrits, H. A. 1974. *PHEASANTS - Including their Care in the Aviary,* London: Blandford Press, 39-43.

Ibid. *"The Silver Pheasant,"*65.

Gladish, Gilbert H. 1956. *A Hatching Guide,* Higginsville: Gilbert H. Gladish Publisher, 4.

_____. 1955. *"The Incubator and the Egg," Game Bird Breeders, Aviculturists, Zoologists and Conservationists' Gazette,* 4(4): 14-5.

Hardy, Harry J. 1977. *"Automatic Watering System," Game Bird Breeders, Aviculturists, Zoologists and Conservationists' Gazette,* 26(1): 10-11.

Hayes, Leland B. 1982. *Basic Quail Propagation,* Redmond: Leland B. Hayes, 7-9.

_____. 1982. *A Basic Guide to The Health and Common Diseases of Game Birds,* Redmond: Leland B. Hayes, 32.

Haynes, Robert. 1983. *Quail Quill,* #18, Cooperative Extension Service, Mississippi State University, "Very Important to Isolate Flocks,"2.

Hoffman, D.M. 1974. *"Raising Gray (Hungarian) Partridge," Game Bird Breeders, Aviculturists, Zoologists and Conservationists' Gazette,* 23(2): 30-34.

Holland, Bill, 1994. *Golden and Silver Sebright Bantams,* American Bantam Association, 8-9.

Holmgren, Samuel T. 1972, *"Tragopans," Game Bird Breeders, Aviculturists, Zoologists and Conservationists' Gazette,* 21(12): 27-34.

Johnsgard, Paul A. 1975. *North American Game Birds Of Upland And Shoreline,* Lincoln: University of Nebraska Press, 81-6.

_____. 1973. *Grouse and Quails of North America*, Lincoln: University of Nebraska, 343-44.

Ibid. *"Bobwhite Quail,"*408-10.

Ibid. *"California Quail,"*391-2.

Ibid. *"Gambel Quail,"*376-7.

Ibid. *"Harlequin Quail* (Mearns),"461-2.

Ibid. *"Benson Quail,"*370-1.

Ibid. *"Scaled Quail,"*356-7.

Keifer, Lee. *"Proceedings,"*Game Bird Production and Management of Shooting Preserves Conference, 1977.

Klan, Steve W. 1984. *"Red Legged Partridge,"Game Bird Breeders, Aviculturists, Zoologists and Conservationists' Gazette*, 33(6-7): 11-13.

Krueger, W. F. 1977. *"Maximizing Hatchability in Game Bird Operations,"Game Bird Breeders, Aviculturists, Zoologists and Conservationists' Gazette*, 26(2): 31,41-2.

Leopold, A. Starker. 1959. *Wildlife of Mexico*, Berkeley: Univ. of California Press, 247.

Ibid. *"Mearns Quail,"*258.

Ibid. *"Barred Quail,"*242.

Ibid. *"Black-throated Bobwhites,"*251.

Ibid. *"Douglas Quail,"*240.

Ibid. 278.

Leopold, A. Starker. 1977. *The California Quail*, Berkeley: University of California Press, 3.

Ibid. *"Sociality in the California Quail,"*69.

Masson, W. V., and Robert U. Mace. 1974. *Upland Game Birds*, Oregon Wildlife Bulletin No. 5, 19.

McKilvey, S. David, *"The Guineafowl"*, *Game Bird Breeders, Aviculturists, Zoologists and Conservationists' Gazette*, 6-8.

Orr, Robert. 1979. *"Mountain Quail,"Game Bird Breeders, Aviculturists, Zoologists and Conservationists' Gazette*, 28(8): 6-8.

_____. 1984. *"Raising Mountain Quail,"Game Bird Breeders, Aviculturists, Zoologists and Conservationists' Gazette*, 33(1): 26-7.

Pennsylvania State University. College of Agriculture, *Poultry Health Handbook,* 2nd Edition, N.D., 151.

Phillips, Charles. *"Sexing Day Old Pheasants,"* Owner, Mahantongo Game Farm, Pillow, PA (from a Speech).

Robbins, G.E.S. 1984. *Partridges, Their Breeding and Management,* Suffolk: Boydell Press, 35-6.

Ibid. *"Crested Wood Partridge,"* 72-73.

Ibid. *"Bamboo Partridge,"* 60-62.

Ibid. *"Barbary Partridge,"* 40-41.

Ibid. *"Common Hill Partridge,"* 45-7.

Ibid. *"Madagascar Partridge,"* 65.

Robbins, G.E.S. 1981. Quail, Their Breeding And Management, Suffolk: World Pheasant Association, 47-8.

Rutgers, A. 1968. *The Handbook of Foreign Birds in Colour,* Vol. 2, London: Blandford Press, 125-126.

Ibid. *"Rain Quail,"* 124-5.

Ibid. *"Chinese Painted Quail,"* 123-4.

Skinner, John L. And Arrington, Louis C. *Artificial Insemination of Poultry,* Madison: North Central Regional Publication Extension Services No. 216, 1-5.

Smith, Tom. *Quail Quill,* #23, Cooperative Extension Service, Mississippi State University, Sept. 1984. *"Litter And Manure Management,"* 4-6.

Ibid. #4, Oct. 1981. *"A New Way to Determine Drug Dosages,"* 2-3.

Ibid. #7, Feb. 1982. *"Vitamin Facts,"* 2.

Ibid. #10, May. 1982. *"Market Your Gamebirds,"* 5.

Ibid. #19, Jan. 1984. "Caution, Don't Ruin Your Feed," 4-5.

_____. 1983. *"Game Bird Nutrition,"* Gazette, 32(10-11): 15-6.

Spaulding, Edward S. 1949. The Quails, New York: The Macmillan Company, 102.

Strange, Frank E. 1958. *"Bamboo Partridge,"* Game Bird Breeders, Aviculturists, Zoologists and Conservationists' Gazette, 7(6): 35, 58.

Stromberg, Janet 1975. *A Guide to Better Hatching,* Fort Dodge: Stromberg Publishing Company, 28.

Suthard, J. G. and George Allen, Jr., 1964 *The Junglefowl, Spurfowl & Peafowl of the World*, Salt Lake City: Allen Publishing Co. Inc. 9-32.

Ibid. 1953. *"How To Construct An Escape Proof Mealworm Box,"Game Bird Breeders, Aviculturists, Zoologists and Conservationists' Gazette*, 2(3): 9.

Todd, Frank. 1971. *"More on Raising Roulroul Partridge,"Game Bird Breeders, Aviculturists, Zoologists and Conservationists' Gazette*, 20(10-11): 28.

Tybie, Robert. 1975. *"Mountain Quail,"Game Bird Breeders, Aviculturists, Zoologists and Conservationists' Gazette*, 24(10-11): 11,13.

Wayre, Philip. 1969. A *Guide to the Pheasants of the World*, London: Hamlyn Publishing Group Limited, 109-10, 44-53.

Weeks, Joe. 1986. *"The Douglas-Benson Quail,"Game Bird Breeders, Aviculturists, Zoologists and Conservationists' Gazette*, 35(3): 11-2.

White, J. C. 1957. *"Quail and Partridge of the New World,"Game Bird Breeders, Aviculturists, Zoologists and Conservationists' Gazette*, 6(12): 12,58.

Williams, Jr., Lovett E., 1991. *Wild Turkey Country*, Minocqua: Northword Press, Inc., 23.

Ibid. 53.

Ibid. 23-31.

Wilson, W. O. 1972. *"Cannibalism in Game Birds,"Game Bird Breeders, Aviculturists, Zoologists and Conservationists' Gazette*, 21(2): 15-6.

Woodard, A. E. 1977. *"Cannibalism: Its Causes and Control,"Game Bird Breeders, Aviculturists, Zoologists and Conservationists' Gazette*, 26(4): 9-10.

_____.1984. *"Photoperiod & Egg Production in Game Birds,"Game Bird Breeders, Aviculturists, Zoologists and Conservationists' Gazette*, 33(12): 16-18.

Woodard, A. E., H. Abplanalp, W.O. Wilson, and P.Vohra. 1973. *Japanese Quail Husbandry in The Laboratory*, Davis: University of California, 1.

Woodard, A. E. and Morzenti Alida. 1975. *"Effect of Turning and Age of Egg on Hatchability in the Pheasant, Chukar, and Japanese Quail,"Poultry Science*, 54:1708-11.

 **Index**

 # *Where to Buy*

We highly recommend that everyone remotely interested in birds subscribe to this informative and imaginative magazine. We just could not get along without the *Gazette* magazine.

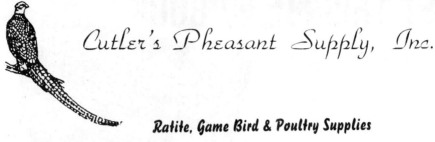

Sunrise Aviaries
QUAIL * DOVES * FINCHES

We are located in Orinda, near San Francisco, in California.

We are one of the largest breeders of Button Quail in the state, also specializing in Finches, Doves, and Canaries.

Our Finches include most of the Australian varieties; Goulds, Owls, Shafttails, ect., with a growing selection form around the world.

We do offer wholesale prices on Button Quail and some finches when quantities are available.

We will Ship

Please call or write for a price list of all birds. When writing, enclose a self addressed stamped envelope for a prompt reply.

Sunrise Aviaries
Tim and Chris Fowler
50 Oakwood Rd.
Orinda, Ca 94563

Phone or Fax: 510-254-7113

Join WPA-USA Today!

Help Insure the Future of the World's
Endangered Pheasants and Other Galliformes

Your membership in the International World Pheasant Association will support:
- Captive Breeding Programs of Endangered Species
  - WPA NEWS - A Quarterly International Publication
    - Ongoing Habitat Surveys, Protection and Conservation - Public Education
      - Data Bank and Information Center - Reintroduction Programs
        - The Publishing of Research, Articles and Books

As a WPA-USA member you will receive:
- WPA NEWS - A quarterly publication
  - The Journal - An International Scientific Publication (member status only)
    - Invitations to International Symposia
      - Discounts on books written by noted authors concerning Galliformes
        - Status Reports on Field Studies and Other Projects WPA-USA
          is Currently Supporting

Please register me as a member of WPA-USA. (Check desired status)
  ☐ MEMBER - $50.00 annual membership
  ☐ ASSOCIATE MEMBER - $40.00 annual membership

Name _____ Telephone _____

Address _____

City _____ State _____ Zip _____

WPA-USA, Ronald Sumner, President, 1800 S. Canyon Pk. Cir., Ste. 402, Edmond OK 73013-6634

All checks should be made payable in to WPA-USA.   All contributions are tax-deductible.

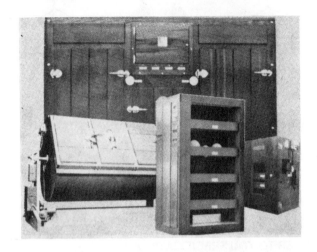